HOSPITALITY AND ISLAM

MONA SIDDIQUI

HOSPITALITY AND ISLAM

Welcoming in God's Name

YALE UNIVERSITY PRESS
NEW HAVEN AND LONDON

For information about this and other Yale University Press publications please contact:
U.S. Office: sales.press@yale.edu   yalebooks.com
Europe Office: sales@yaleup.co.uk   www.yalebooks.co.uk

Typeset in Adobe Caslon by IDSUK (DataConnection) Ltd
Printed in Great Britain by TJ International Ltd, Padstow, Cornwall

Library of Congress Control Number 2015949250

ISBN 978-0-300-21186-3

A catalogue record for this book is available from the British Library.

10 9 8 7 6 5 4 3 2 1

To Farhaj, Suhaib, Zuhayr and Fayz

Contents

Acknowledgments

I would like to thank Edinburgh University's Divinity School for giving me a period of research leave in 2014 to write this book. My thanks also go to Malcolm Gerratt at Yale University Press for his enthusiasm and encouragement throughout; he has been a gentle but encouraging presence from start to finish. This book has been inspired by the many friends and colleagues who have been part of my personal and academic journey and whose companionship has helped me reflect more deeply on the nature of hospitality; I am grateful to them all. Finally, my thanks to my husband and my sons who are present in all my works.

A Note on Presentation

I have kept the transliteration of Arabic names and terms to a relevant minimum, but where used in the main body of the text, these words have been fully vocalized. When quoting from other sources or citing the titles of Arabic (occasionally Persian) names and books, I have kept the original published transliteration and thus, many will not be standardized to full diacritic marks. Regarding scriptural translations, I have used online translations of the Bible, primarily the New Revised Standard Version via Biblegateway.com. The Qur'ān translations mainly follow Yusuf Ali via quran.com. In both cases, slight modifications have been made for ease of reading where necessary. This includes replacing Allah with God in many passages.

Introduction

When I first began thinking about writing this book, I often wondered why I had not given much thought to the concept of hospitality until now. I appreciate that the concept has no universal definition, is multi-layered and evokes a variety of theological and philosophical perspectives. But as I reflected on this, I would try to retrieve those moments in my life when I felt the power of real and structured hospitality had touched my own life and transformed the way I thought about others, even humbled me in my own prejudices and views. I could think of many experiences but I also realized that hospitality is fundamental to the spiritual life. It is not only acts we do, things we give, but more importantly a state of mind. A generosity of spirit lies at the core of human hospitality, making hospitality the virtue which defines humanity itself. Many have iterated this in different ways, but it is also worth pondering what are the emotional and personal drivers for those who write on hospitality? We may all be hospitable in different ways, but what brings us to think of religious or secular hospitality as an act and an attitude which stands to both humble and ennoble us and our society? I would also contend that today we struggle to find the affirmation of hospitality to guests or strangers as a distinct narrative in the public space but that actually this struggle has a long history.

Historically speaking, arguably the most famous Enlightenment philosopher Immanuel Kant saw hospitality as the defining element bringing people of different cultures together in a political context. For Kant, hospitality is a 'natural right' possessed of all humans 'by virtue of their rights to communal possession of the earth's surface'. He distinguished the right of hospitality which is a natural right belonging to each of us from the right of a guest who can make a claim only for a certain time.[1] A fervent critic of the Enlightenment, Alasdair MacIntyre also sees hospitality as a universal practice, central to the proper functioning of society:

> It is important to the functioning of communities that among the roles that play a part in their shared lives there should be that of 'the stranger', someone from outside the community who has happened to arrive amongst us and to whom we owe hospitality, just because she or he is a stranger.[2]

Aside from the scholarly impulse, and a greater presence of hospitality writings in Christian theology, this particular theme has been rather neglected in systematic writings in Islamic tradition. Its presence has been felt rather in the vast resources in Islamic thought and piety which speak of charity, neighbourliness and giving as a divine command. Hospitality in its modern usages is implied in an array of philosophical, mystical and *adab* literature. Both the major sects of Islam, Sunnī and Shīʿī, have their own narratives around hospitality, and while there is much overlap, this book looks primarily at the corpus of writings within Sunnī Islam.

Thus, if I look at some of the defining moments of hospitality in my own life, what they share is the element of surprise and humility; surprise at the gesture and humility in its consequences. When I was an undergraduate in the 1980s studying French and Arabic, I went to Cairo for the first time as part of my year abroad. After arriving at my pre-arranged accommodation in a relatively poor suburb of the city, I had to wait outside for a while as keys and rooms were being sorted out. I stood there with my new suitcase and new expectations and looked around anxious and curious at the dust, animals and poverty around me. A young woman with a small child was watching me as she squatted near the doorstep of my flat. She stared at me for a while and after some time I saw her get up, find a large piece of cardboard, dust it clean and place it on the doorstep. She patted on it, beckoning to me to sit down and take the weight off my feet. I smiled at her nervously, knowing that she had made a special effort for a new guest in the neighbourhood. I was neither friend nor enemy, but a stranger to whom she had reached out. I was unknown to this neighbourhood and they were unknown to me. Later on as I was getting settled in the flat, two young children came up and spoke to me in the local Arabic dialect. I couldn't understand what they were saying and became slightly impatient at their repeated visits and knocking on the door. That evening I discovered that they had been sent by their mother, the same woman, to ask if I needed anything as I was a guest in their midst; I felt ashamed and ungracious.

I remember this story with great fondness as I begin this book because it was my first experience of a particular kind of hospitality as a young, inexperienced woman alone in a new country and culture. It was a small gesture, but it spoke volumes about being a stranger, a guest and my own faith, and how I saw others and how others saw me. It was a practical and very visual, even simple act of welcome. It has stayed with me because often it is these very acts of kindness, these personal stories which we continue to remember in our lives, even when we have left behind a particular life well into the past. They provide us with reassurance about society even as we live daily with all kinds of hopes and fears.

This happened well before I was aware of my own journey into academia and the kind of theological and ethical debates which would bring me to write this book. There is a vast body of literature on hospitality in the western tradition. This comes from a religious angle or the philosophical and political debates on identity by the giants of the west on these subjects, namely Jacques Derrida and Emmanuel Lévinas. Derrida reminds us that hospitality begins first and foremost in language: 'We only ever speak one language—and, since it returns to the other, it exists asymmetrically, always for the *other*, from the other, kept by the other. Coming from the other, remaining with the other, and returning to the other.'[3] For both Lévinas and Derrida, hospitality with all its challenges and nuances must be seen as part of the human condition, a human virtue, where hospitality must precede hostility. Following Lévinas and Derrida, hospitality is often defined in two, distinct ways. First, it is defined in terms of the privacy of one's home and of welcoming others into one's home, or into one's being. Lévinas found his inspiration in Jewish ideals of brotherhood and fraternity and turned them toward a much more intimate level of being welcomed first in one's own home, even in the feeling of home and welcoming.[4] Studies of hospitality from this perspective often target the questions of subject- and identity-formation through welcoming others and being welcomed. Second, hospitality is explored in association with the cultural and the public by being an issue of public space and in the context of how a self-identified sociality welcomes strangers, immigrants, and refugees into one's country or territory. The latter is gaining a momentum as globalization, increased migrancy and refugees emerging from multiple conflicts and wars have forced many to think about what it means to welcome someone as stranger or guest. For Derrida, hospitality is ethics, and ethics is hospitality, 'culture itself and not simply one ethic amongst others'. It is about crossing boundaries, including between self and other, private and public.[5] For Derrida, hospitality stands for culture, deconstruction, and a radical alternative to current European politics and treatment of its 'others': ethnic minorities, immigrants, refugees, visitors. While inspired by Lévinas's writings on welcoming and by Abrahamic traditions of Jewish and Christian 'stories of hospitality', Derrida calls for more than tolerance in extending hospitality to others. Offering hospitality is not only about being in power but about taking risks and becoming vulnerable. This is especially the case with issues that pertain to an increasingly globalized and interconnected world but where strictly enforced territorial borders raise the question as to whether there exists a right to hospitality and what this might look like. Edward Said's words carry a particular potency today as multiple conflicts and wars are leading to new waves of migration in which many die, trying to flee. For Said, 'The greatest single fact of the past three decades has been, I believe, the vast human migration attendant upon war, colonialism and decolonization, economic and political revolution, and such devastating occurrences as famine, ethnic cleansing, and great power machinations.' For Said, the sad experience of 'contemporary exiles, émigrés, refugees, and expatriates has still to find its chroniclers'.[6]

In the case of hospitality connected to the sovereign, territorial nation-state, there are ethical questions linked to unconditional hospitality or borderless hospitality which calls for an unqualified welcoming of the 'other' who has been neither invited nor expected. As Thomas Claviez asks, 'Can a place possibly be imagined where unconditionality, which both Lévinas and Derrida helped to us think, can play a role – let alone be exercised – or does such an idea of hospitality represent a genuine utopia: a *u-topos*, a nonplace, in which by definition, nothing, can "take place"?'[7] Roxanne Doty argues that we can point to concrete practices of hospitality without conditions. She states that 'While Derrida refers to unconditional hospitality as an impossibility, a promise, a "to come", he also speaks of the possibility of the impossible. This phrase is only contradictory if we restrict our thinking and our imaginations regarding possibilities and impossibilities and close our minds to what Derrida is attempting to get at. Unconditional hospitality is in fact impossible if we look for it in the realms of policy, law, and sovereign state edicts.'[8] Expanding on the idea of the human rights aspect of mobility and free movement of people, Doty argues that to make the impossible possible, it is necessary to look beyond governmental realms and accepted course of action; only then can we have unconditional hospitality.

For many philosophers, the main issue was the tension between the moral person and the legal person. As a moral person, the individual has absolute value, and this value is unconditional because he is an end in himself. As a legal person, there is no absolute value, because membership of a legal community is conditional. The legal community is based on the notion of exclusivity setting out its criteria for membership. As Paul Cobben argues, the universality of the moral community and the locality of the legal community can only be reconciled within the world republic. Here 'there would be no legal community that could exclude any one person because only one legal community would exist which contains all possible persons. This hospitality can be expressed as "hospitality without boundaries", because every person would be unconditionally welcome all over the world and therefore, would be recognised as a moral person.' Yet, it is also apparent that a world without boundaries is not necessarily workable or desirable.[9]

However, this book is not a deconstruction of the writings and speeches of Derrida or Lévinas in relation to hospitality. I have refrained from turning my thoughts into a political or sociological critique, because it is the theological underpinnings of this concept which interest me. Contemporary critiques which share similar concerns can be both secular and religious. I have looked largely at religious writings using both pre-modern and more contemporary sources to formulate my arguments. However, I am aware that when commentators speak of our current public spaces, the stranger/foreigner and issues related to immigration today, they are implying a loss of hospitality, replaced by other sentiments of togetherness and pondering the effects of latent and explicit xenophobia. There is a concern here which has been encapsulated in the comment put forward by Jürgen Moltmann, 'We are always inclined to perceive

God, the Absolute, only in whatever is like ourselves. What is alien to us makes us uncertain. That is why we love what is like ourselves and are afraid of what is strange.' This perspective may be slightly more nuanced in certain areas of the world living with diversity, but at its heart, this statement still resonates within many societies.[10]

I use this word in a way most of us relate to today, i.e. largely within the host/guest or host/stranger domain. As is often said, the stranger–hospitality relationship has an ambivalent history and depth and can be understood in a range of ethical, religious and political ways. The ancient Greeks had their particular concept of hospitality contained in the word *xenia*. In the Latinate forms, *hospes* denotes host, guest, or stranger and *hostis* can suggest stranger as friend or foe. The stranger was seen as a problem in Classical Antiquity and in the biblical Near East and thus occupied a large niche in legal works. But the ancient Greeks also had an elaborate network of relations based on hospitality. Reciprocity was encouraged as crucial to the Homeric culture, and Zeus himself, as the god of strangers, Zeus Xenios, watched over these relationships. As Leon Kass writes, here, hospitality rested on piety amongst other things, because 'Zeus is protector of strangers, suppliants and beggars, and guards all proper relations between host and guest'. It was Zeus Xenios, according to some accounts, who sent Menelaus, Agamemnon and the Achaian host against Troy so as to avenge the violation of guest-friendship – in this case, a violation of host by guest and in matter of wife-stealing, not food:

> Given the powers of Greek gods to assume any shape or form, hospitality towards strangers could make prudence the better part

of piety: the stranger, one you may have never seen before and in fact may never see again, might in fact be a god. The Homeric poems are filled with examples of gods and goddesses appearing in the guise of beggars and suppliants. More often than not it is only those who treat them kindly who are able to penetrate their disguises.[11]

In the Hebraic universe, on the other hand, hospitality is a response to a rapidly changing and dangerous cultural climate. Hospitality is a mode of honouring, especially the stranger, 'for you yourself were once strangers in a strange land'. In comparing the two kinds of hospitality, Sandor Goodhart writes that we must keep both attitudes alive:

Greek-based hospitality is developed on the body, place, and the distinctions between the inside and the outside, in short, the abode. Food, athletic contest, tale-telling, music to soothe the soul within, is primary in the Greek conception. Outside is a hostile environment; inside is warmth and welcome. From the contest of the heath we move to the contest of the hearth. Nor is it a matter of choosing one over the other. Within both the Greek and the Hebrew conceptions remain two versions of hospitality.[12]

Christopher Yates gives an overview of why we have returned to the problem of hospitality:

Recent and contemporary scholars of philosophy and religion have returned to the problem of hospitality in a range of ways, perhaps most notably through phenomenologies of the stranger, the other, the foreigner, and the guest, and often with an alertness to the ethical dimensions intrinsic to the status of the refugee, the scope of alterity, and the experience of embodiment. The result is a trajectory of reflection well aware that its subject matter consists in an event that interrogates those who study it.[13]

Hospitality is a word pregnant with meaning, and as Yates says, 'the linguistic and etymological background to the thematic terrain of hospitality is one of the principal ways in which scholars of the matter reveal how its existential or phenomenological occurrence is already freighted with a provocative hermeneutic weight'.[14] At its simplest level, it is regarded as a virtue in all three monotheistic religions and has been a central feature of Islamic cultures with precedents rooted in both Byzantine and Sasanian traditions. A powerful motif in all three religions is the scriptural figure of Abraham, the father of the Semites. It is Abraham who responds as a host to three visitors, feeding them and giving them shelter, unaware that they were angels in guise.[15] By this act, Abraham inspired a theology of hospitality often echoed in Jewish, Christian and Islamic literature and used as a framework for interreligious dialogue.

Despite such references, in Islamic thought the concept of stranger, with an unknown identity, seems relatively less problematic and discussions on hospitality focus largely on the host/guest relationship and host/traveller rather than that of host/stranger. Islam holds hospitality as a virtue that lies at the very basis of the Islamic ethical system, a concept rooted in the pre-Islamic Bedouin virtues of welcome and generosity in the harsh desert environment. The concept can be found in the Arabic root *ḍayāfa*. The Prophet is reported to have said, 'There is no good in the one who is not hospitable.' Indeed, hosting the guest or welcoming the stranger is a central event in the world's great wisdom traditions. Many state that the stranger embodies the presence of God and brings blessings in multiple ways. Furthermore, ideas of reciprocity, unconditionality in the act of hospitality, are central to current religious and ethical thinking. In recent years this has also been reflected through a rise in scholarly works looking at interreligious hospitality where hospitality is a central motif in a theological 'reaching out' to other religions. While some remain cautious, even cynical, about the goals of interreligious encounters, others have welcomed this growing practice as a spiritual exercise where dialogue and hospitality are mutually dependent. And then there are those who have felt their faith to be transformed by their experience of another religion and the lived realities of another faith. They point out the limitations of the word alone, that talking and dialogue are not enough, that hospitality must go beyond logos and be practised at the 'level of being.' For example, Fr Pierre-François de Béthune writes that hospitality must go beyond communication and towards communion:

> Hospitality involves permitting another to enter one's house, or oneself entering the house of another. Communication is then made through gestures that are less explicit than words but also less ambiguous. To give lodging to a stranger, to offer him food and drink – these are gestures which speak plainly of one's respect

for him. Hospitality, then, belongs to the domain of ethos; it is an existential experience which goes beyond logos.[16]

It should be said, however, that this book is not about interreligious hospitality or even the histories of hospitality shared by Judaism, Christianity and Islam. Thus, it is not a comparative study of how the theme and act of hospitality is a unifying force between the three religions or about some of the historical tensions concerning the religions. Furthermore, there are now multiple works which explore shared narratives and shared histories through reading one's own scriptures and reaching out to the scriptures of other religions. Rather, in this book I look at the Qur'ān and other areas of Islamic thought to trace signs and words of hospitality which are both actions and exhortations to establishing more generous and giving relationships. Giving in itself, however, does not create more embracing relationships, but it does demand that our moral life should come to the fore when we think of others. These others often include people with whom we have no emotional connection but to whom we are connected through our common humanity. The aim is first to trace how concepts of hospitality are mentioned in the Qur'ān initially as divine commands, something human beings should do to and for each other. Hospitality is first and foremost a duty towards others, and a way of living in which we are constantly reminded of human diversity. There are overlapping discourses on food as a blessing to be shared with others and food as a means of enjoying the company of others. There are the multiple commandments to give charity and shelter, to feed others, to look after widows, neighbours, travellers and orphans. We must give and be generous because this is how God

12

is and God's giving knows no limits. Hospitality is not necessarily premised on pleasure, and yet pleasure enhances the experience of doing hospitality. Within Ṣūfī literature, giving is also associated with poverty, renunciation, self-denial, because the desired relationship with God leaves no room for any other desire. Worldly possessions or relationships lose meaning as the mystic longs only for a particular intimacy, to be the guest of God.

In the writings of Muslim scholars, such general exhortations were further tuned to setting certain limits. Human generosity and magnanimity reflect God's nature, but in the actual practice of welcoming and receiving guests, there are also limits to hospitality, limits and obligations on both the host and the guest. This is because hospitality is real, not an ideal. It is joyous but also time-consuming. It can be both physically and emotionally demanding. There are very few accounts of 'doing hospitality', with perhaps the most famous being Ghazālī's short treatise analysed in this book. However, the pre-modern literature encompassing hospitality is concerned with food, characteristics of generosity, and general manners and etiquette. The manner of doing hospitality often overlaps with pleasure and sociability, but while there are fluid boundaries, hospitality can lead to pleasure, though pleasure alone is not the intended purpose.

Perhaps the theme most associated with hospitality is food and eating. Life may be more than food and eating, but there is no life without food and eating. Thus the theological and philosophical significance of what we eat and who we eat with connect the ordinary life with the higher life. A consequence and objective of coming together, pleasure is always there, implicit and explicit, and pleasure derived from food can be cultivated like art. The philosopher Julian Baggini speaks of the experience of fine dining and good food, and while he advises against eating expensive food too regularly, against the extraordinary becoming the ordinary, he writes

> I do think then, that a life without good food would be at least as impoverished as life without good art, and that culinary arts should indeed take its place alongside the other arts. But its value lies more in its daily practice than in the exceptional achievements of its finest practitioners. It is an art of the everyday, and all the better for that.[17]

But pleasure on its own does not transform the individual or society. The goal of hospitality as an act and as an attitude to life is far more radical; it demands a transformation of the self towards goodness and grace, to how God wants us to be with one another. Even so, it is difficult to measure how Muslim societies think of hospitality as a theological imperative and how they relate their own attitudes to the pre-modern scholars who wrote about giving and receiving. We can arrive at some understanding of how states and societies in the medieval world conceptualized caring for travellers and wanderers through the existence of public inns and hostels. But despite the proliferation of such institutions, this does not give us an in-depth picture of how the ordinary individual thought of the practice of hospitality as a divine imperative. Yet we have our intellectual and devotional writings which offer us some insight that the pious of most religious traditions elevated being hospitable and doing hospitality, with all its challenges, to a sublime act.

My own interest in hospitality as a theological discourse stems to some extent from readings of Christian reflections on hospitality. While I am aware that I could have also explored Jewish literature and religious thought in terms of its association and relevance for Islamic thought, this work is not a comparison between all three monotheisms, nor an account of how one religion has been received by another. It is less this kind of dialogue, rather more my engagement with Christian theology which has influenced my thinking and ethical approach on the topic of hospitality.

Much of the contemporary literature in the west offers both theoretical writings on hospitality as a structure and the actual doing of hospitality written by Christian theologians and practitioners. So hospitality is both structure and practice, and yet both disciplines can seem worlds apart. For most people, hospitality still centres largely on inviting family, friends and guests into our homes or befriending those who are strangers to us. Alongside this, is the more radical insistence that true religiosity lies in renewing our hospitality to strangers, the marginalized and those who, for a variety of reasons, are vulnerable or even suspect in society. Thus alongside structure and practice, hospitality is also a mindset, an attitude of simply being with others irrespective of whether they are strangers or friends. The polyvalent meanings of stranger in urban spaces today also demand that we think carefully how the stranger today is no longer the wayfarer of ancient scripture. Whereas the wayfarer or traveller was one with whom we would have a chance encounter, the one who might ask for food, water or shelter, the stranger today is often one who lives quite near us, with whom we share physical space in our more cosmopolitan societies. Our social interaction in our urban public spaces is really shared space with other strangers. The urban intervention here is to deliberately create environments where people can become accustomed to living with difference. The urban is the assembly of infrastructures, technologies, built forms all of which mean that 'stranger relations are supposed to filter through this "urban unconscious" rather than through habits of interpersonal contact in public space'. While we should be aware of what Zygmun Bauman contends as liquid modernity to describe our age, this book is not making any political comments nor is it sociological survey. It is true that the continuous uprooting of people, displacement through globalization or conflict, voluntary migrancy and technologies where human contact has been replaced by machines, have all contributed to more unsettled communities. Here, collective cultures are breaking down, but the reaction is either a yearning for strong ties and defined communities or an appreciation for exteriority, where mobility and multiple ties are valued.[18]

Hospitality compels us to say something about who we socialize with and who we allow to enter into our lives. But for many Christians, hospitality is about seeing the face of Christ in every stranger and living God's triune grace-filled kingdom on this earth. This should call for a radical rethinking of our lives and the lives of others whom we invite to share in the ecclesial life. Many lament that our contemporary cultures have distorted hospitality, reducing it to mere sentimentality where hospitality has lost its power. As Henri Nouwen notes, hospitality can at first bring to mind, 'soft sweet kindness, tea parties, bland conversation and a general atmosphere of cosiness'.[19] But hospitality is not a domestic, sentimental affair, a watered-down piety. When honoured and exercised as a divine imperative, it is about knowing that reaching out to others is an act of worship, thus challenging, humbling and spiritually transformative. According to Nouwen, who was writing more than thirty years ago, 'If there is any concept worth restoring to its original depth, and evocative potential, it is the concept of hospitality.'[20]

I have benefited greatly from appreciating both the similarities and differences in Christian and Islamic thinking. The writings of the Church Fathers on poverty have parallels with Muslim mysticism as to how prayer and poverty are so closely aligned in the way we think about God and our reliance on God. The mystic wants only to be the guest of God. And while God is the ultimate host in the afterlife, there are intriguing similarities and differences in how both faiths conceptualize the heavenly banquet.

When it comes to gender relations, it seems more and more apparent that the paradigms between western and Muslim feminists have shifted over the decades. Western feminists use a variety of cultural and psychoanalytical frameworks to explore gender dynamics and the language of otherness, whereas in the Muslim world the issues continue to be largely centred on the language of rights and justice. The end results may be quite similar, in that on both sides women continue to plea for a greater generosity and hospitality in this most fundamental relationship. Yet even in these discourses, we can see how reference to scriptural texts by both sides often yields dramatically different results. The personal and social relationships between men and women challenge our understanding of what constitutes the divine ideal.

This book is not a work on food and drink, but it does incorporate some literary works by those for whom eating and guest hospitality was a civilizing force. While the book is not meant to be a systematic, comparative discourse on hospitality in Christianity and Islam or an East/West polarity, its arguments have been strengthened and broadened by this more textured approach. I live as a Muslim in the west and work in a thriving divinity school. My social and intellectual interactions with my colleagues and others have influenced the way I continue to think about interreligious encounters. For me, the theology of any religious tradition benefits intellectually from situating it in a larger milieu; this is a challenging process for some, but I see it as a gift. Reading and watching how people of different religious faiths speak of this most human of activities has taken me deeper into my own faith, and challenged my complacency. I have not, however, concentrated on speaking of 'otherness' or alterity in this book; many theologians and philosophers in recent decades have done this in great depth. My interest lies more in the way the Muslim intellectual tradition has spoken of hospitality as a concept and as an act. To this I have added my own reflections on Christian hospitality, seeing both similarities and contrasts in structure and language.

This book is a humble contribution to the seemingly unexplored discourse on hospitality in the field of Islamic Studies, particularly Sunnī Islam. It concludes with my personal thoughts on how we risk becoming complacent about human giving in all its forms. I believe strongly that 'doing hospitality' is not simply about making physical room for others in our homes, but is essentially an attitude to life. We need to make room for others in our hearts and minds, and with our words; a lightness of touch and good humour towards those we meet helps bring this about. Hospitality includes notions of forgiveness as well as reaching out to others, and we need occasionally to be more hospitable and kinder to ourselves rather than damage our souls over the harm we may have done to others. But at the very basis of hospitality is compassion, a compassion which shakes our complacency and leads us to think about more generous ways of being with one another. Compassion creates empathy, solidarity, and has the power to reduce personal and social conflicts. And often it is this compassion towards others which first sows the seeds of surprising friendships – the most challenging but rewarding experiences of our lives.

CHAPTER 1

Scriptural Reflections on Hospitality

While the construct 'Abrahamic religions' is as ubiquitous as it is contested in the study of monotheism, its ecumenical significance has a long history. Despite theological and historical difficulties around this concept, one of its attractions is that it is often interpreted as ahistorical where Abraham is the common forefather to all three religions. The invocation of Abraham as prophet or patriarch serves on many levels, but it is mainly in the area of hospitality as a lived virtue amongst the people of the Near East where we find the most references to Abraham in interreligious writings. In this context, perhaps the most famous name is that of Louis Massignon (1883–1962), the great but controversial Catholic scholar of Islam who developed the Muslim claim to Abraham for the Catholic Church. He was one of the first people to see theological commonality between the three religions in the person of Abraham. He argued that the one who believes 'in the equality of origin of the three Abrahamic religions, Israel, Christ and Islam, knows that they each refer to the same "God of Truth"'.[1]

One of the most significant stories relating to Abraham is that of Abraham receiving the 'honoured guests' in his tent, guests who were angels in disguise. This is often used as an image of unity and common ground between Judaism, Christianity and Islam on the theme of hospitality. Some would claim that the fundamental moral practice of hospitality which welcomes the stranger is the essence of the three monotheistic religions. Notwithstanding the issues of how to define a stranger, the biblical (Genesis 18: 1–10) and Qur'ānic (Q51:24–30) versions are by and large interpreted as positive stories of welcoming and offering space and shelter to the stranger or the wayfarer/traveller. The stranger or the traveller thus becomes a guest, and welcoming the guest into one's home means not simply inviting someone into our most personal space, but inviting that person with humility, grace and generosity. This may not be easy but it is a duty and all three religions have emphasized multiple ways of being hospitable. Hospitality is a sacred duty in most religions, where the commandment and encouragement to do this is often accompanied by the etiquettes of actually doing hospitality.

It is difficult to think of two scriptural passages which have been used as much as Genesis 18:1–10 and Q51:24–30 to speak of the unifying figure of Abraham as the father of the Semites and the figure par excellence of hospitality. While the Qur'ānic version appears in both *sūras* Hūd and Hijr, this particular passage has been used more by Jewish and Christian writers than by Muslims. The Islamic tradition does not speak of theories of hospitality through the use of such motifs. If there is any narrative at all on hospitality, it must be teased out from the Qur'ānic and Islamic literature which deals with the imperative to give from one's wealth, to give charity, to exercise generosity and to treat those who are vulnerable with compassion. Here, generosity and hospitality are seen as synonymous virtues. Profligacy should be avoided, but welcoming guests, and reaching out with one's wealth and being to a whole variety of people, are seen as fundamental imperatives of the faith.

In the Qur'ān, Abraham is the 'leader/model for mankind' (Q2:124), as well as the one who submitted to God and was named the friend of God (*Khalīl Allah*). When Abraham was chosen by God, he was a man with neither homeland nor family. Yet God chose him to be a blessing for all land and all nations. In his response to an interreligious conversation on Abraham, Mahmoud Ayoub writes of Abraham the prophet and patriarch as the one in whom 'we share a father in both the physical sense and the metaphysical, or spiritual, sense. Abraham is said to be the physical father of Arabs and Jews and, by extension, the moral and spiritual father of all Christians and Muslims as well.'[2]

Abraham has become the prototype of hospitality especially in interreligious encounters. It is worth quoting the relevant section of both sections of both scriptures

> The Lord appeared to Abraham by the oaks of Mamre, as he sat at the entrance of his tent in the heat of the day. He looked up and saw three men standing near him. When he saw them, he ran from the tent entrance to meet them, and bowed down to the ground. He said, 'My lord, if I find favour with you, do not pass by your servant. Let a little water be brought, and wash your feet,

and rest yourselves under the tree. Let me bring a little bread, that you may refresh yourselves, and after that you may pass on – since you have come to your servant.' So they said, 'Do as you have said.' And Abraham hastened into the tent to Sarah, and said, 'Make ready quickly three measures of choice flour, knead it, and make cakes.' Abraham ran to the herd, and took a calf, tender and good, and gave it to the servant, who hastened to prepare it. Then he took curds and milk and the calf that he had prepared, and set it before them; and he stood by them under the tree while they ate. They said to him, 'Where is your wife Sarah?' And he said, 'There, in the tent.' Then one said, 'I will surely return to you in due season, and your wife Sarah shall have a son.' And Sarah was listening at the tent entrance behind him (Genesis 18:1–10).

Has there reached you the story of the honoured guests of Abraham? When they entered upon him and said, '[We greet you with] peace.' He answered, '[And upon you] peace, [you are] a people unknown.'[3] Then he went to his family and came with a fat [roasted] calf and placed it near them; he said, 'Will you not eat?' And he felt fear of them. They said, 'Fear not', and gave him good tidings of a learned boy. And his wife approached with a cry [of alarm] and struck her face and said, '[I am] a barren old woman!' They said, 'Thus has said your Lord; indeed, He is the Wise, the Knowing' (Q51:24–30).

Much has already been said about these verses as examples of mutual hospitality between guest and stranger. Although there are differences in the two narratives and more detail of the practicalities of Abraham's hospitality in the biblical version, there is quite a similarity in the moral message of the two versions. In Genesis 18, God himself appears first, the theophany occurs in broad daylight. This is followed by the appearance of the three men, but there is no mention of angels. However, in the priestly sermon of Hebrews 13, there is a clear looking back to the Genesis text in the mention of angels and the implication of extending love towards either strangers or Christian brothers or travellers: 'Do not neglect to show hospitality to strangers, for by doing that some have entertained angels without knowing (Hebrews 13:2). In the Qur'ān, the 'honoured guests' are unusual and they do not eat, engendering a certain fear within Abraham. The Qur'ān does not state that God appeared himself. On this particular biblical interpretation, that God himself appears to Abraham but Abraham sees to his guests first, Marianne Moyaert writes that Abraham acts as if it is normal to leave God waiting. The value of hospitality to the stranger overrides the concerns of God himself. God can wait because 'greater is hospitality than welcoming the Divine presence. The story also teaches us that hospitality takes precedence over the spiritual enjoyment of an intimate encounter with God.'[4] Despite the differences between the biblical and Qur'ānic stories, both versions speak of an Abraham willing, even rushing to show hospitality to the three men whom the Qur'ān calls 'unusual people' (*munkar*). The three guests reward their host's hospitality by giving Abraham and Sarah the news of a son. Yet, it is Abraham's devoted attention to his guests which has captured the exegetical imagination in the Jewish and Christian tradition and in recent years absorbed the Qur'ānic verses into this dialogue. It has been the focus for much comment on host/guest and host/stranger relations, the interdependence of hospitable relationships, and the moral and religious obligations on both sides to be a gracious host and, in return, a gracious guest. With Abraham revered as the patriarch of the monotheistic religions, this story has been understood by many as a story of selflessness and openness in welcoming strangers and guests. In welcoming strangers to our homes with concern and care, not simply tolerance, we do not know how their presence might become a blessing for our own home.

According to Ibn Kathīr, these men were angels in the guise of handsome men; they were Gibrīl, Mīkhā'īl and Isrāfīl. It is only when their hands did not reach out for the food that Abraham becomes alarmed, even afraid as to why they weren't eating, but he is reassured by the angels themselves. Ibn Kathīr states that the biblical interpretation where the angels ate the three rolls, fat, and drank the milk, is not correct. This is because angels have no need for food.[5]

The reference to angels in the guise of beautiful men in the Qur'ānic version is consistent with a persistent theme in the Islamic narratives on angels. It is well known that their primary purpose is to worship God around his throne, but certain angels have specific responsibilities. They make or request earthly appearance to convey messages from God. Their visits can bring about awe and fear to mortals, including prophets who are made more holy by their visit. The following tradition from the death narratives reflects their ambiguity:

While Abraham (peace be upon him) was in his house one day, suddenly a man of beautiful appearance came into his presence, and [Abraham] said: 'Servant of God, who admitted you into my house?' He said: 'Its Lord admitted me into it.' He said: 'Its Lord is the most right [to do] that.' 'Who are you?' He said: 'The Angel of Death.' He said, 'Things have been described to me about you [that I cannot see in you]'. [Abraham] said: 'Turn around.' And so he turned around, and there were eyes at the front and eyes at the back and every one of his hairs were like people standing on end. So Abraham begged God for protection against that and said, 'Return to your first form.' He said: 'Abraham, when God sends me to someone He wants to meet, He sends me in the form which you saw first.'[6]

Angels visit and surround people and places for various reasons. The presence of angels articulates sacredness on a person as well as a place. In his work on angels in Islam, Stephen Burge states that the Islamic tradition has constructed a loose hierarchy of sacredness. Here, 'The Ka'ba, being the most sacred, has the most angels visiting it, the most frequent performances of ritual associated with it, the longest mythological history. At the opposite end of the spectrum, the space around a believer performing the ritual prayers can include a great number of angels, but only for a limited period and with no mythological history.'[7]

In this story, the angels assume their role of acting and speaking for God who is absent from the narrative. In the Christian tradition, John Chrysostom interprets Genesis 18 in his forty-first homily on Genesis. He emphasizes the degree to which Abraham is personally engaged in the extension of hospitality, stating that Abraham was 'unwilling to entrust to anyone else in the household the task of attending to guests', even though he had three hundred and eighteen servants, and was an old man himself. Chrysostom portrays Abraham as anticipating the need for hospitality. For instance, Abraham was intentionally sitting outside of his tent in the heat of the day, as opposed to resting inside the shade of his tent. He did this precisely because he wanted to see and help all visitors who passed by his tent. In fact, it is, in part, because Abraham was already so hospitable that the Lord rewarded Abraham with a visit in the first place.[8] Augustine, on the other hand, is more interested in the appearance of God, for it is God himself who visits Abraham. The three men who appeared were all equal in status, and for Augustine this was proof for a Trinitarian view of God.[9]

This description of hospitality has been compared to that of Genesis 14:18, in which Melchizedek, King of Salem and priest of the Most High, comes forth with bread and wine to greet and bless Abraham returning from battle against the four kings. In Christian theology, Melchizedek, a priest-king, is regarded as a saviour, an inspiration for the founder of that faith. In his comparison between Abraham's hospitality and Melchizedek's offering of bread and wine, Jeffrey Cohen writes that 'The fact that he served bread and wine, which later became part of the basic ritual of Christianity (albeit reinterpreted), suggests that the offering of a gift to Abraham was intended more as a religious ritual, symbolic food, than a meal to be relished.' According to Cohen, Melchizedek's primary purpose in coming out to meet Abraham was to bless a fellow worshipper of the One God; the offer of bread and wine was made as a token of religious fellowship, not as a demonstration of hospitality. This gesture of Melchizedek must be construed as an act of sacerdotal symbolism where he was essentially conferring upon Abraham a spiritual status equal to his own through the power of the symbolic food. Abraham's acceptance should be construed as humility and a recognition of spirituality in Melchizedek. But Cohen's defence of Abraham's rightfully deserved status as the more hospitable host nevertheless concludes that both men reacted to the stranger and the situation in the way they saw fit, 'Abraham as a hospitable host, and Melchizedek as a conscientious priest'.[10]

Abraham's story is also the story of Sarah and Hagar, and Abraham is not the only one to be visited by an angel. According to Bukhāri, when Sarah became jealous of Hagar, Abraham took both Hagar and Ishmael to Mecca and left them there with a basket of dates and a skin of water. He then turned to leave, at which point Hagar asked him, 'Abraham, where are you going, leaving us in a valley in which there are no people and no things?' She repeated this, but he did not look back at her. Then she asked him, 'Did God order you to do this?' He said, 'Yes.' She said, 'Then he will not allow us to remain weak.' Hagar continued to nurse Ishmael, but when the water dried up, Hagar went to look for help, climbing the hills of Safa and Marwa, going back and forth between the two hills, each time stopping in the valley to check on Ishmael. She heard a voice, and although she saw no one, she called out for help. When she did this, the angel was at the post of Zamzam and he dug the ground with his heel or his wing, until the water appeared. She drank from it and gave some to Ishmael, and the angel said, 'Do not be afraid of being weak. Here is the House of God. This boy and his father will build it. God does not allow his household to be weak.'[11] The angel provides water, the most essential blessing in the desert, and Hagar knows that God will not let her be thirsty or hungry.

Scriptural references to hospitality generally construe hospitality not as simple acts of kindness but as moral imperatives and ethical commands. The stories around Abraham are only one way of exploring the theme of divine hospitality where God himself steps in by sending angels to proclaim news or help. But most cases of hospitality are from one person to another. Here there is no direct divine intervention, but when two people meet, God is always present.

Hospitality should not be confused with contemporary understandings of charity or entertainment. This hosting of a person or people as guests is the closest meaning we can give to the Arabic noun *ḍiyāfa*. While this act is about hospitality in terms of providing food, shelter and conversation, diverse concepts of hospitality amount to something much greater than hosting a guest or welcoming a stranger, however challenging and significant this may be. Islamic piety extols extensively the virtues of feeding guests and feeding the poor, often going into great detail as to the correct manner in which hosting and welcoming should be done. Feeding another person, especially the hungry, is always the most significant and the simplest act of hospitality, but hospitality is a multi-layered concept. It is not about institutional charity, but rather a virtue or a combination of virtues which go beyond giving. Rather, it involves a sacred duty to think beyond our immediate selves in a wide variety of contexts and relationships. This includes charity and alms, but is not defined only through the giving of material wealth.

The most concrete form of hospitality familiar to most of us very often does involve inviting, welcoming or being with others, and the etiquettes associated with these kinds of encounters. We invite those who are our friends or those with whom we wish to nurture and develop

29

friendships. It is a preferential kind of hospitality, a form of social interaction for the purpose of mutual pleasure. But hospitality towards others in scripture and in ancient societies was often commanded towards those who were nameless strangers and not just invited guests. These strangers could be wealthy or poor, travellers or our fellow citizens, and indeed those living on the margins of society. It demanded a commitment reflected in showing dignity and care to those who are unknown rather than welcoming those whom we wished to know. Our contemporary lives may not be characterized by welcoming strangers or becoming vulnerable strangers ourselves. Nor do most of us rely on the charitable giving of others, the generosity of others to feed or clothe us, but hospitality is not only about giving and receiving; it's essentially about the transformation of persons and societies.

Furthermore, it is a universal virtue and we should not reduce this virtue as simply entertainment of others. If we reduce it to entertainment, we think of it as something we do in the private sphere where we are more concerned with preparing the house than welcoming someone into our life. If we think of hospitality as pleasure or entertainment first, our house is never ready; there is always more to do and invariably more to prepare. Hospitality is a flexible concept even if it is always about crossing thresholds. It never really ends, for there are always more guests, more strangers with whom we may not always become friends but towards whom we have duties. If we view hospitality as a way of life, as a way of being, then the distinction between private and public becomes less visible and hospitality transcends into that which we embody for the love of God.

Hospitality should not be reduced to a quaint sentimentality. Hospitality costs not simply in financial terms in how much we spend on others, but more significantly in psychological and emotional terms. It demands that we make our lives visible to others and urges us not to be complacent about the society around us. There is a universality to this topic, even if like other forms of human relationship, its significance varies over time, space and different cultures. Judith Still's examination of hospitality draws attention to theorists lamenting a decline in standards of hospitality; she quotes Ben Jelloun:

> Some people are more hospitable than others: generally speaking, they are those who have remained close to the soil and live in wide open spaces, even if they are poor. The industrialized countries, obedient to a cold rationality, have had to unlearn hospitality. Time is precious and space limited. There's a shortage of accessibility, or in other words of generosity and freedom, because everything is calculated and measured. Doors are shut and so are hearts.[12]

The Qur'ān and the Prophet's *Sunna* (way of the Prophet) often align hospitality with charity and where the act of hospitality is framed largely in the act of giving. Giving was always seen as an act of hospitality and narratives of hospitality often focused on the poor and poverty. It is said that someone once came to the Prophet and said 'I love you, O Messenger of God', to which he replied, 'Be ready for poverty.'[13] This did not necessarily or always mean destitution, but a life of lowliness before God and loving those who were poor. In writing on poverty in the Qur'ān, Michael Bonner claims that the Qur'ān provides a blueprint for a new social order in which the poor will be treated more fairly. But he poses the question, 'Who were the poor mentioned in the Book and who were their benefactors?' Bonner rightly states that other than the Qur'ān itself, few written records survive from seventh-century Arabia, which makes finding answers to such questions quite elusive. However, regarding the poor, 'Not only did the Qur'ān provide guidance for dealing with the poor; it also dominated much of the thought and behaviour concerned with economic activity. Indeed, poverty and economic activity were closely tied in early Islam. A kind of "economy of poverty" prevailed in Islamic theory and practice.'[14] The Qur'ānic notions of the purification of wealth and distribution of excess illustrate a distinctive Islamic way of conceptualizing charity, generosity and poverty. Later on, the jurists and exegetes attempted to distinguish between the destitute as in *fuqarā'* and the poor as in *masākīn*, where a popular view is that *fuqarā'* means the passive poor, those who ask for nothing, whereas *masākīn* refers to those who beg.[15] One could argue that the poor were those who had nothing to expect from this world and who had everything to expect from God. The notion of seeking 'refuge in God' for all of one's needs is a strong theme running throughout Islamic thought.

Much of the Qur'ānic emphasis is on giving to those in need, whether through tax, alms or charity, as a way of creating new relationships, a new and more generous social order. But the themes and persons around which this ethical imperative to give and share is framed are to be found in a pre-Islamic milieu where Bedouin societies already laid an enormous emphasis on hospitality as central to a noble character. Generosity (*karam*) is part of hospitality, and consists first and foremost in providing food. In its pre-modern and pre-industrial

Arabian context, hospitality is regarded as something fundamental to the desert environment and nomadic wanderings. As Miriam Shulman and Amal Barkouki Winter explain the important role that hospitality plays in the harsh environment of the Middle East:

> The virtue seems an ineluctable product of the landscape ... to refuse a man refreshment in such a place is to let him die, to threaten the openhandedness nomadic peoples must depend on to survive.[16]

Snjezana Akpinar emphasizes the pre-Islamic emphasis on hospitality as a humanizing element and writes that along with honour and chivalry, 'hospitality was considered as an act of unconditional surrender to the needs of others'.[17] But Toshihiko Izutsu writes that generosity and hospitality were themselves synonymous with the pre-Islamic (*Jahīlī*) concept of 'honour' and that generosity was not so much a 'virtue' as blind irresistible impulse that was deeply rooted in the Arab heart, a 'master passion of the Arabs'. Personal liberality towards guests and strangers was a mark of genuine nobility:

> For a pagan Arab, charity was not simply a natural manifestation of his feeling of tribal solidarity, for very often it extended beyond the members of his own tribe to the strangers who happened to be there. Nor was it always dictated by the motive of benevolence and kindness. It was first and foremost an act of chivalry. A man who could make a royal display of his generosity was a true dandy of the desert.[18]

We have several examples of individuals who reached the highest point of generosity and hospitality in the pre-Islamic period. Perhaps the most famous and most proverbial is the Arab poet Ḥātim ibn ʿAbd Allah ibn Saʿd al-Ṭāʾī. Stories of his generosity have passed down the centuries across Islamic lands and cultures. In his famous *adab* compilation, *The Unique Necklace*, Ibn ʿAbd Rabbih writes that Ḥātim was the one who would order his slave to light a fire on a hill when the winter was very harsh, so that anyone who had lost his way, might be guided to him:

Kindle the fire for the night is severely cold
And the wind is gusty and biting, O kindler.
Perhaps your fire will be seen by a passer-by;
If it will bring a guest to me, you will be free.

The only things which Ḥātim did not give away in any act of generosity were his horse and his weapons. However, his generosity was so great that one bad year when the earth was very dry and the crops had been wiped out and there was no food, he killed his horse in response to his neighbour's cry for help to feed her children. Ḥātim's own children and others nearby also ate the meat, but he himself did not take a single bite and recited the following verse, 'A Miser sees only one way for money, while a generous man sees many.' Stories of such icons of the pre-Islamic as well as the Islamic world are central to the formation of *adab* literature, where the didactic tone is often about extolling themes of both manners and virtuous behaviour. Here, man's nobility was often equated with his magnanimity to those of his own tribe as well as to strangers who could be hostile.[19] Yet as Geert Jan van Gelder writes in his exploration of food and literature, 'Extreme and extravagant liberality is neither the expression of unselfish charity, nor a means to get to Heaven, but the appropriate way to gain honour and glory for oneself, one's clan and one's tribe. Thus one acquires a form of immortality, not in the Hereafter but on earth, in stories and poetry.'[20] Of course, being considered a niggard also brought its own immortality, but this was an immortality of shame and dishonour that stained not only the individual but also his kin and tribe for generations.

The outlook of the pagan Arabs was Islamicized, so generosity and hospitality became to be seen as distinct virtues, religious duties, but not virtues with a simple narrative. If we turn to the Qur'ān itself, there is no one particular narrative about hospitality nor does the concept feature in any singular way. The concept of hospitality is not one concept but several concepts involving various kinds of people and various kinds of relationships. We may begin with the notion of guests (ḍayf/ḍuyūf), where we see only a few references in the Qur'ān. Derivatives of the verb ḍāfa from which we derive ḍiyāfa are mentioned on a few occasions, once through the verbal form 'offer them hospitality' (yuḍayyifūhumā) and five times through the noun ḍayf:

They refused to offer them hospitality (Q18:77)

So fear God and do not disgrace me concerning my guests (Q11:87)

Has there reached you the story of the honoured guests of Abraham? (Q15:24)

And tell them about the guests of Abraham (15:51)

35

Lot said, 'Indeed these are my guests, so do not shame me'
(Q15:68)

They demanded from him his guests, but we blinded their eyes
saying, 'Take my punishment and my warning' (Q54:37)

In addition to guests, the Qur'ān contains numerous references
to wayfarers/travellers (*ibn al-sabīl*, literally 'son of the road') and
neighbours (*jār*), and their frequent mention points to ethical directives about doing good towards others within a particular taxonomy
of duties

Worship God and associate nothing with Him, and to parents do
good, and to relatives, orphans, the needy, the near neighbour, the
neighbour farther away, the companion at your side, the traveller,
and those whom your right hands possess. Indeed, God does not
like those who are self-deluding and boastful. (Q4:36)[21]

The Qur'ānic phrases for the two different kinds of neighbours
are *jāri dhī l-qurbā wa l-jāri l-junūbi*. Yusuf Ali translates 'the near
neighbour' and 'the neighbour farther away' as 'neighbours who are of
kin' and 'neighbours who are strangers'. He elaborates that 'neighbours who are near' includes those who are not just local, but those
with whom we have some intimate relationship. Equally, 'neighbours
who are strangers' includes those who live far away as well as those
whom we do not know.[22] In his seminal article analysing the concept
of stranger in medieval Islam, Franz Rosenthal writes that the words
'strange' (*gharīb*) and 'stranger' (*ajnabī*)[23] are both absent from the

Qur'ān, although as we shall see, the word *gharīb* is used frequently in the *ḥadīth* literature to mean stranger. The concept of hospitality always involves the concept of a stranger. But as Rosenthal points out, despite there being strangers everywhere in Muslim societies, 'within the community of believers and wherever Muslims were in political control, there was in theory no such distinct category as a "stranger"'.[24] Thus, the ideal was that every Muslim was always at home with other Muslims and so could not be seen as a separate category. Neither *ajnabī* nor *gharīb* had the connotation of stranger as enemy that is found in some languages, and Rosenthal adds that whilst *ajnabī* today may mean a foreigner, i.e. belonging to a different nationality, this was not a known category in medieval Islam. All of this contrasts with the concept of the stranger in Classical Antiquity where the stranger was often seen as a problem.[25] However ambiguous the concept of stranger and the status of the stranger was in the Muslim world, the attitude to strangers was not xenophobic. In medieval Islam, then, the stranger was everyone who had left his original place of residence and gone to live abroad. Rosenthal adds, 'no distinction was made between leaving home for good, or staying abroad for some time and gradually losing any intention to return, or just travelling with no thought of permanently changing one's residence such as was done by pilgrims, merchants and fortune seekers; here we may include groups like beggars, crooks and wandering low-class entertainers who often had no place they could call home'.[26]

However, the word *ajnabī* is assumed in the category of 'the neighbour farther away' or 'neighbours who are strangers', the latter implying one who is an outsider.[27] Some commentators put forward the possibility of the 'neighbour who is near' as being the neighbour who is Muslim or the neighbour who is a relative of sorts. Others such as Ibn Kathīr state that neighbour here includes those from the Jewish and Christian faiths. Ibn Abbās explains the distinction as well as the rights of the neighbour:

> … and unto the neighbour who is of kin (unto you)) the neighbour who also happens to be your relative has three rights over you: the right of kinship, the right of Islam, and the right of being a neighbour (and the neighbour who is not of kin); the neighbour who is not a relative has two rights: the right of Islam and the right of being a neighbour (and the fellow traveller); a fellow traveller has two rights: the right of Islam and the right of companionship.[28]

While there is a distinction made by some between the nearness of the neighbours, whether it be physical, biological or spiritual, the Qur'ānic command does not distinguish in how they are to be treated. Stating that there are many *ḥadīths* about the rights of the neighbour, Ibn Kathīr elaborates:

> Once the Prophet asked his companions, 'What do you say about adultery (*zinā*)?' They replied. 'It is forbidden as God and His Prophet have forbidden it and it will remain forbidden until the Day of Judgement.' The Prophet replied 'Listen, a man who has committed adultery with 10 women has committed a lesser sin than one who commits adultery with his neighbour's wife. The Prophet then asked, 'What do you say about theft?' They replied, 'This too God and his Prophet have forbidden and it will remain forbidden until the Day of Judgement.' The Prophet replied,

38

'Listen, a man who steals from 10 houses has committed a lesser sin than one who steals from his neighbour's house.'[29]

The neighbour is a contested category in Islamic thought, and while much is owed the neighbour both morally and materially, there is also present a hierarchy of the neighbour. The eight-century Shāfi'ī scholar Dhahābī lists 'Offending One's Neighbour' as the fifty-second major sin in his list of seventy major sins.[30] He quotes a tradition that 'He who believes in God and the Last Day does not harm his neighbour.' Two further *ḥadīths* quoted in this work show the significance of the rights (*ḥuqūq*) of the neighbour, but also the distinction in the concept of neighbour:

> If your neighbour is a relative and a Muslim, he has threefold rights on you: that of being a neighbour, that of being a Muslim, and that of being a relative. If the neighbour is a Muslim but not a relative, he has twofold rights, while if he is a non-Muslim, he has a single right – that of being a neighbour.

> A man came to the Prophet and asked him, 'O Messenger of God, guide me to something which if I do it, will take me to the Garden.' The Prophet replied, 'Be good to others.' He replied, 'How will I know if I am being good to others?' The Prophet replied, 'Ask your neighbours. If they say you are good to others, you are good, and if they say you are bad to others, you are bad.'[31]

Relationships with neighbours are central to the theme of hospitable goodness in Islamic thought. It is not enough to emphasize the virtues of one who is good to his neighbour; one also has to be appreciative of his neighbour. Neighbours and guests are often mentioned in the same sentence in many sayings. Mālik's famous legal compendium, the *Muwaṭṭa'*, mentions this in several ways:

> The Messenger of God, may God bless him and grant him peace, said, 'Whoever believes in God and the Day of Judgement should speak good or be silent. Whoever believes in God and the Day of Judgement should be generous to his neighbour (*yukrim jārahu*) and whoever believes in God and the Day of Judgement should be generous to his guest. He is to be welcomed for a day and a night and his hospitality is for three days. Anything after that is *sadaqa*. It is not permitted for a guest to stay with him [his host] until he becomes a burden to him.[32]

According to Lane, the word *jā'iza* can mean a draught of water, a gift, provisions or an act of kindness. Lane refers to this *ḥadīth* and explains, '[The period of] the entertainment of a guest is three days, during the first of which the host shall take trouble to show him large kindness and courtesy, and on the second and third he shall offer him what is at hand, not exceeding his usual custom; then he shall give him that wherewith to journey for the space of a day and night; and what is after that shall be as an alms and an act of favour, which he may do if he please or neglect if he please.'[33]

> The Messenger of God said: 'Putting up a guest for one night is obligatory. If you find a guest at your door in the morning, then this (hospitality) is (like) a debt that you (the host) owe

him. If he (the guest) wants, he may request it, and if he wants, he may leave it.'[34]

Despite the emphasis given to neighbour, the distinction between neighbours and other guests can be quite blurred. The result is a universalizing of the neighbour and a universalizing of benevolence, but also understanding that it is very often the neighbour who is our biggest stranger. In the Christian tradition, John Calvin argued that 'to make any person our neighbour, therefore, it is enough that he be a man; for it is not in our power to blot out our common nature'. For Calvin, in the parable of the Good Samaritan (Luke 10: 29–37), Jesus redefines neighbour and love for neighbour, and broadens out our moral obligations to one another.[35] In her comments on Calvin and the necessity of translating abstract notions into concrete hospitality, Christine Pohl writes:

> The practice of hospitality forces abstract commitments to loving the neighbor, stranger and enemy into practical and personal expressions of respect and care for actual neighbors, strangers and enemies. The twin moves of universalizing the neighbour and personalizing the stranger are at the core of hospitality. Claims of loving all humankind, of welcoming "the other," have to be accompanied by the hard work of actually welcoming a human being into a real place.[36]

Welcoming often requires material wealth or goods to be given away or to be spent on others. One of the commonest themes of the Qur'ān in its definition of goodness and piety is found in the exhortation to spend on others and to give to the poor. While the institution of almsgiving (*zakāt*) in the Medinan period remains in the sphere of compulsory obligations, a basic pillar of Islam, giving one's wealth away voluntarily (*sadaqa*) to a certain category of people, demands a different kind of generosity and attitude. In his seminal work on reciprocal gift giving, Marcel Mauss claims that justice was a prior meaning of *sadaqa* encompassing the twin moral ideas of gifts and wealth, and sacrifice. He states, 'Generosity is necessary because Nemesis will take vengeance upon the excessive wealth and happiness of the rich by giving to the poor and the gods. It is the old gift morality raised to the position of a principle of justice; the gods and the spirits consent that the portion reserved for them and destroyed in useless sacrifice should go to the poor and the children.'[37]

There is undoubtedly in Islamic thought a strong ethic of purifying the wealth one has through just distribution. In some passages the voluntary aspect of this kind of giving assumes an obligatory tone, though remaining distinct from *zakāt*. In other passages, both *zakāt* and *sadaqa* are blurred, simply sharing the imperative to give and do good. These kinds of lists often follow commandments of belief and doctrine. Here, the traveller/wayfarer (*ibn al-sabīl*) remains a recipient of this wealth alongside widows and orphans:

Righteousness is not that you turn your faces toward the east or the west, but [true] righteousness is [in] one who believes in God, the Last Day, the angels, the Book, and the prophets and gives wealth, in spite of love for it, to relatives, orphans, the needy, the traveller, those who ask [for help], and for freeing slaves; [and who] establishes prayer and gives zakah; [those who] fulfill their promise when they promise; and [those who] are patient in

42

poverty and hardship and during battle. Those are the ones who have been truthful and God-fearing (Q2:177).

They ask you, [O Muhammad], what they should spend. Say, 'Whatever you spend of good is [to be] for parents and relatives and orphans and the needy and the traveller. And whatever you do of good – indeed God knows of it' (Q2:215).

Ibn 'Abbās explains that giving charity to parents was abrogated by the verse on inheritance and there appeared a greater stress on giving to the orphans and the poor.[38] Even the spoils of war must be divided in such a way that the traveller is entitled to a rightful portion:

And know that anything you obtain of war booty – then indeed, for God is one fifth of it and for the Messenger and for [his] near relatives and the orphans, the needy, and the [stranded] traveller (Q8:41).[39]

So give the relative his right, as well as the needy and the traveller. That is best for those who desire the countenance of God, and it is they who will be the successful (Q30:38).

However, it should also be noted from this that whilst giving to the poor and the traveller is a repeated Qur'ānic command, so are our duties to look after our relatives; in fact relatives, especially if they are poor, must be a priority when giving away wealth. Dhahābī relates several *hadīths* emphasizing this religious imperative and lists the abandonment of relatives as the ninth major sin:

Allah's Messenger said, 'One who breaks the ties of family relationship (*qāti'u raḥm*) will not enter the Garden. Those rich people who break ties of family, abandon their poor and weak relatives due to pride in their wealth or status, not treating them with kindness nor helping them in their need, will be deprived of the garden unless they repent towards Allah.

The Prophet said, 'If someone has poor relatives and instead of spending on them he gives charity to others, his charity will not be accepted by Allah, and Allah will not look at him on the Day of Resurrection. However, if he himself is poor, he should keep ties with them by visiting them and keeping informed of their situation.'[40]

The Qur'ān remains silent on the details of poverty and need, and the question of who exactly are the poor; the dominant command is to give. It neither permits nor prohibits asking questions from the recipient. Compassion cannot be expressed if it questions first. This was a theme expressed with some force by the Church Fathers such as John Chrysostom, for whom repentance without almsgiving was a corpse and without wings. He wrote a sermon on almsgiving when he passed through the marketplace during winter and saw the poor and the beggars and the ill uncared for. Chrysostom stated that we should always make sermons about almsgiving. He called for mercy and forgiveness of sins as part of the act of philanthropy, asking the question 'Why are you a busybody and why do you meddle with other folks' affairs? God did not command us to investigate the lives of others and demand of them accounts, and to be curious after others' way of life.' For Chrysostom, God does not withdraw his benefits from those who steal, plunder or commit prostitution, rather his philanthropy means that we all share the 'sun and the rains and the crops of the earth'. In Chrysostom's view, the exhortation to give requires asking no questions:

> If we are going to examine lives, we will never have mercy upon any human being; rather hindered by this opportune meddlesomeness, we will remain fruitless and destitute of all help, and we shall submit ourselves to great toil to no purpose and in vain. For this reason I now beg you truly: to banish far from us this ill-timed curiosity, and give to all who have need, and do this abundantly, so that we may obtain much mercy and the philanthropy of God on that day.[41]

In an earlier homily, Chrysostom had encouraged giving to the poor as almsgiving takes the side of the giver and pleads on their behalf. He explains that almsgiving is the 'salvation of the soul' and writes:

> For this reason, just as washbasins are found before the church's doors filled with water so that you may wash your hands, the poor sit outside of the church so you may wash the hands of your soul. Have you washed your physical hands with water? Wash the hands of your soul with almsgiving. Do not use poverty as your excuse.[42]

Similarly, almsgiving could even be compared to baptism itself as expressed by the bishop of Turin, Maximus of Turin, at the end of the fourth century:

Almsgiving is another kind of washing of souls, so that if perchance anyone has sinned through human frailty after baptism there is still the possibility of being cleansed by almsgiving, as the Lord says: Give alms and behold, everything is clean for you. But, with due regard to the faith, I would say that almsgiving is more indulgent than baptism. For baptism is given once and provides pardon once, whereas as many times as alms are bestowed, pardon is granted.[43]

In his exploration of how God in Christ gives meaning to the meaningless, the Swiss theologian and Catholic priest Hans Urs von Balthasar (1905–1988) writes that 'genuine Christian charity prefers to tend the dying, the helpless, the lepers, the mentally defective. Again: Christian compassion for men does not wish to begin, nor ought it to begin, there – thus allowing itself to be more and more ousted by increasing non-Christian welfare institutions. It begins, rather, at the heart of common, human social-welfare work, but must distinguish itself – because it knows about God's ultimate way with men – by always proceeding in tranquillity and by going on when others give up.'[44] Thus almsgiving is not really about giving, it is about transforming. It is not a momentary act but an attitude to life and humanity itself which always demands going further.

In the lives of the great saints, the boundaries between helping the poor and living a life of poverty oneself were often blurred. St Francis of Assisi (1182–1226) had accepted poverty as an ideal, but also as a source of joy. He clothed poverty with human flesh by calling it 'Lady Poverty' and made poverty the object of his desire. He also encouraged his fellow friars to embrace poverty in the absolute assurance that God would provide for them. To some extent, his attitude reflects the words in Luke 9:3, 'He said to them, "Take nothing for your journey, no staff, nor bag, nor bread, nor money – not even an extra tunic.' Jesus advises his disciples to go with nothing so that they would have to ask for hospitality, become dependent, even surrender themselves to the generosity of others.

Beds were not allowed and he was adamant that the clothes the friars wore should be 'ragged, patched and shabby' so that they did not appear in any way better off than the poorest beggars they might meet on the streets. Poverty meant a life of simplicity and of contemplation because it was poverty which had been Jesus' companion in his earthly life; it was the ultimate jewel. It is poverty which lifts all impediments away from the soul and it is the virtue which makes the soul 'while still retained on earth, converse with the angels in heaven'. It is said that during a missionary journey with Brother Masseo, they both stopped at a town to beg for some food as they were very hungry. St Francis said in his gratitude that he did not think they were worthy of such great treasure, to which Brother Masseo responded by asking how this could be when they lacked all the essentials of life and had to beg. St Francis replied that he called this great treasure because 'there is nothing here provided by human industry, but everything is provided by Divine Providence'.[45]

While saints and mystics often embraced poverty as a premise for a God-centred life, the physical endurances of their own lives never diminished the obligation on ordinary believers to give to virtually anyone in need. In this sense, the duty to give *zakāt* and *sadaqa*, i.e. obligatory and voluntary almsgiving, is also to be portioned to the traveller as well as other deserving categories such as the poor and the widows:

Alms are for the poor and for the needy and those who collect
them and for those whose hearts are to be reconciled, for freeing
captives and for those in debt and in the cause of God and for the
traveller/wayfarer – this is ordained by God and God is Knowing
and Wise (Q9:60).

The Qur'ān commentator and historian Ṭabarī explains that
there is a difference of opinion as to whether *ibn al-sabīl* is just
a traveller or a guest and whether he is to be afforded the rights
of the traveller or the rights of the guest.[46] In the *Mukhtaṣar*, the
eleventh-century Ḥanafī jurist al-Qudūrī explains these categories of
deserving people and adds that the traveller/wayfarer (*ibn al-sabīl*) is
one 'who has wealth in his own land but he himself is currently in
another place in which he has nothing'.[47] Thus, again it is not the
fortunes nor the background of the traveller which should affect
what he is due, rather the simple fact that he is in a foreign land and
also a stranger in that land. The emphasis lies on the current homelessness of the traveller so that he is seen as someone uprooted and
without shelter.

The Qur'ān and *ḥadīths* give little account of the different types
of traveller, but travel including pilgrimage is important for Muslim
self-expression and formed an essential part of desert and nomadic
life. It is worth pausing here to briefly look at the significance of the
travel narrative as an expression of Arab identity, especially during
the pre-Islamic period. This Jāhilīyya literature was invoked as being
an amoral or lawless prelude to the history of the Arabs, and the
post-Prophetic generation characterized it as godless and barbaric,
but as Ilse Lichtenstadter writes:

Yet, the Arab still looks back to this age with a certain nostalgia, a certain pride. The silence of Arabic poetry on religious beliefs and the lack of expressions of religious emotions in it and other forms of pre-Islamic literature were taken as proof that the Arab did not possess religiosity. But that lack was due to the censorship of the Islamic scholars who, generations later, purged all expressions of pre-Islamic beliefs from their literary written records and substituted the name of Allah for those of pre-Islamic deities.[48]

Poetry served as the medium through which the pre-Islamic ideologies were transmitted to the wider population. Poetry both informed the collective consciousness of the people and was memorized as part of the culture of nomadic ideologies. Khurshid Fariq summarizes the diversity of topics covered in poetry which was a way of lessening the tedium of a monotonous desert life:

Through it they drove camels fast or slow and inspired and disciplined their children. Through it they advised friends, thanked benefactors, censured wrongdoers, remonstrated with unkind relatives and expressed sorrow at mishaps. Through it they rebuked and threatened enemies and circulated their personal and tribal merits. Memory and poetry mean to them what books and journals mean to us.[49]

Writing of the pre-Islamic poets such as the renowned Imru al-Qais who composed the most famous hanging odes, Muhammad Bakalla comments that the major theme which is characteristic of the pre-Islamic ode is the description of the poet's journey by horse or by camel. He says that this is usually termed the 'travel theme'. In the section, 'the poet gives an account of his adventures in the wild life of the desert, the hunting scenes, the difficulties he might have experienced and the danger he may have come across'.[50]

In the post-Islamic period, the traveller could be the migrant as well as the pilgrim, hoping for both rational and spiritual transformation. Surveying the motives of three famous travellers, Ibn Jubayr (1145–1217), Ibn Battuta (1304–1368/9) and Ibn Khaldun (1332–1406), Fathi el-Shihibi cites Thomas J. Abercrombie's conclusion of Ibn Battuta's travel motives:

> Ibn Battuta never dwells on what drove him. Curiosity? Perhaps it was to the stars with a sage on a remote mountain top, to suffer the majesty of a turquoise horizon aboard an equatorial isle, to seek spiritual shelter with the pious throngs of Mecca, to breathe the white winter winds of the Russian steppes or the spices of a Persian bazaar, to dine with kings or share a crust with a passing nomad. More likely it was a quest for knowledge. One never seduced by a foreign culture can never appreciate the fetters of his own. Life, after all is a journey, a voyage of discovery.[51]

Travel was a way of recording history, and those who travelled carried ambitious aims, to cover as much land as possible and to survey different cultures in all their richness. They saw in this endeavour a scholarly duty to leave truth and wisdom for posterity, 'a memorial built with art and skill'. For example, even a small introductory fragment from *The Meadows of Gold* by the Baghdadi historian

Mas'ūdī illustrates the imperative to witness cultural and geographical diversity first hand as he travelled the world by land and sea, and consorted with kings:

> He who has never left his hearth and has confined his researches to the narrow field of the history of his own country cannot be compared to the courageous traveller who has worn out his life on journeys of exploration to distant parts and each day has faced danger in order to persevere in excavating the mines of learning and in snatching precious fragments of the past from oblivion.[52]

Travel for trade, for faith and in search for knowledge are all reflected in Islamic literature. While traveller and wayfarer are fairly generic concepts, it is worth noting that a particular kind of travel was always held in high esteem in Islamic thought. If travel is essentially a journey of the mind, Sam Gellens writes, 'the *ḥadīth* literature reminds the believer that the search for knowledge is intimately tied to the act of travel'. He points out the high merit of seeking knowledge, of travelling to acquire knowledge, all encapsulated in the *ṭalab al'ilm*:

> Travel as a meritorious activity is endowed with an ancient pedigree in the Muslim tradition. A rich vocabulary of words related in one way or another to travel is found in the Qur'ān and the *ḥadīth*. Embedded deep in Muslim consciousness is an identification of travel with pious activity, an appreciation that achievement in such endeavour is a sign of divine approval and munificence.[53]

Travel also has a psychological and emotional impact on our sense of ourselves and others:

> As in other civilisations and traditions, travel is particularly impor-
> tant when considering changes in Muslim imagined communities
> past and present. Travel creates boundaries and distinctions even
> as travellers believe they are transcending them. In the hope of
> creating new horizons, travellers set off from home, encounter
> 'others' and return with a sharpened sense of difference and
> similarity.[54]

To a certain extent, the merits of travel are romanticized in connection with the hospitality of the ancients. This is reflected in more contemporary notions of commerce and travel which have had a negative impact on hospitality. Here, it is argued that while the spirit of commerce may have united all nations, it has also unfortu- nately broken 'the links of beneficence between individuals':

> It has produced countless commodities, more extensive knowl-
> edge of things and people, easy access to luxury and love of self-
> interest. That love has taken the place of the secret movements of
> nature, which used to bind men together with tender and touching
> attachments. Wealthy travellers have gained the enjoyment of all
> the pleasures of the countries they visit, joined with the polite
> welcome given to them in proportion to the amount they spend.[55]

Yet travel has often been seen as participation in a bigger enter- prise, and in the early Islamic context it spoke of a social and political endeavour. It is perhaps best encapsulated in the concept of *hijra*, most commonly translated as the Prophet's migration journey from Mecca to Medina in the year 622 C.E. This brought in a quasi-revolutionary spirit of brotherhood within the groups of migrants (*muhājirūn*) who had left their homes and possessions to support the nascent Muslim community in Medina. As Khalid Masud explains, many of the meanings like rejecting or banishing invoke 'a distancing – physical or otherwise – from evil and disbelief'. He summarizes that certain points can be inferred: '*hijra* was an obligation of physical movement towards self-definition, refusal to migrate meant exclusion from the society and *hijra* established a bond of relationship among Muslims'.[56] Much of this is encapsulated in the following verse:

> Indeed, those who have believed and emigrated and fought with their wealth and lives in the cause of God and those who gave shelter and aided – they are allies of one another. But those who believed and did not emigrate – for you there is no guardianship of them until they emigrate. And if they seek help of you for the religion, then you must help, except against a people between yourselves and whom is a treaty. And God sees what you do (Q8:72).

Emigrating and fighting for one's faith are often juxtaposed in the Qur'ān. The references to both the emigrants and those who helped them (*ansār*) convey the strong bond which emerged through faith, migration and community. People left their homes in Mecca to follow the Prophet in Medina, but those who helped them in Medina spent of their own wealth giving shelter and aid, and thereby formed new alliances. This kind of hospitality linking travel for the sake of God features frequently in the Qur'ān. It points to the collective efforts made by groups leaving the comfort and tranquillity of their homes 'in the way of God' to those who welcome them for the sake of God. New relationships emerge as a consequence of migration where the migrant and the traveller must always be provided for. Thomas Michel adds an interesting contemporary dimension to the Qur'ānic and biblical migration accounts:

> The experience of being forced to leave one's home because of poverty, threats, or fear of violence is one that most of us have fortunately not experienced, but it occurs so frequently in the lives of the principal characters of the Bible and the Qur'ān that it is clear that this experience is fundamental to God's message for humanity. Abraham forced to leave his father's house, Moses and his people fleeing Egypt in the middle of the night, the baby Jesus carried off to Egypt by his parents a step ahead of Herod's soldiers, Muḥammad's early disciples taking refuge in Ethiopia, and the prophet Muḥammad's own *hijra* to Madina – these dramatic stories show the centrality of the refugee experience for God's word.[57]

In connection with travel, brief mention must be made of the places where people could also stop for lodging and food. This was the foundation of hostelries, which were often couched in religious, philanthropic or economic rhetoric. In her work on the changing nature of institutions of hospitality in the Mediterranean world, Olivia Constable writes about the *funduq*, the hostel for travellers which was similar to the Catalan *fondaco*, both words sharing their long heritage going back to the Greek word *pandocheion*, an inn or hostelry, literally meaning 'accepting all comers'. These three words signified places which accommodated travellers' needs across the Mediterranean, because from its earliest history the Mediterranean has been the realm of travellers. This included merchants, warriors, pilgrims and vagabonds who moved by land and sea, and travellers needed shelter, food and security to make their voyage possible.[58] This family of institutions provided these facilities and was critical in enabling the cross-cultural exchange which fuelled a healthy commercialism in medieval Europe. In the eleventh and twelfth centuries western European merchants encountered the *funduq* when they did business in Muslim markets. The arrival of foreign Christian traders led to the development of specialized facilities called *fondacos*, which were modelled on the *funduq*, but which allowed *foreign* communities some autonomy, albeit under the oversight of local Muslim authorities. While they may have been owned and maintained by local administrators, 'western merchants were allowed to practise their faith, follow their own customs and even drink their own wine from within *fondaco* walls'.[59]

Travellers and wayfarers are a distinct category of people with specific needs, but the Qur'ān often blurs the distinctions between various groups. It does so often because everyone who is in some way vulnerable or uprooted needs food and shelter, and individual giving allows this to happen; it is a personal as well as civic obligation. The Qur'ānic verses which speak of giving to the poor and the needy and to the traveller can be considered as multiple ways of creating a relationship with those outside our immediate family and friends.

The distinctions between *zakāt* and *sadaqa* and hospitality are often blurred and emphasis is upon the individual to give according to ability. Rich and poor are not defined in any categories, and wealth and poverty are not measured in any systematic way. But giving what one can to others went beyond a one-way obligation on the rich towards the poor. Giving to others is both a personal as well as institutional way of expanding our social conscience and recognizing that others have a stake in our wealth. If one had nothing to give, then doing good for others and to others was also an act of charity. But even though the Qur'ān does not elaborate beyond the act of giving in multiple ways, as part of a wider narrative of hospitality to the stranger and the needy, Muslim societies developed a culture of ubiquity of charity. Observers who travelled to Islamic societies encountered and admired the variety of charitable works and the diversity of benefactors. The sixteenth-century scholar and mystic Guillaume Postel travelled more than once to the Ottoman Empire as a translator for an official French Embassy to the Ottoman Sultan and to other parts of the Middle East to collect manuscripts. Clearly moved by what he saw, he wrote:

> You find poor people who have nothing to give who understand that offering help to people consists not only of food and drink, but all kinds of needs: some spend their lifetime repairing bad roads by bringing stones, wood, filling holes and improving their surfaces; others arrange the course of streams and water sources, bringing water to the roads; and some dig wells, or bring water to the road in a shed of some sort, and there invite [the passersby] to drink with such enthusiasm that I was certain they drank wine

that was to be found flowing from the streams. In North Africa, because water is scarce close by the cities, you find foundations for water built at the tombs of some Muslims and there is some sufi who is maintained by the foundation to keep the cisterns full of water, and to encourage passersby to pray for the soul of the departed and the living family. Such foundations for water on the roads are a common project of poor people. There are rich people more in Anatolia than any other part of Turkey, who when they see travellers coming on the roads, they invite them to eat, drink and sleep in their homes for the sake of their of their [own] souls, and take nothing for it from anyone; neither rich nor poor pays anything, and the next day one thanks them heartily, invoking God's blessing on them in recompense. And these kind of people are most respected among the Muslims because they send their charity to Paradise ahead of them.[60]

Giving through wealth, actions and words is encouraged because God himself holds such acts in esteem and our acts of generosity will always bring us closer to God.

When we look at Christian reflections on hospitality, the whole obligation to welcome the stranger and the narrative of hospitality is built around Jesus himself. The force of Matthew 25:35–36 (within the larger context of Matthew 25: 34–40), 'For I was hungry and you gave me food, I was thirsty and you gave me drink, I was a stranger and you welcomed me', became the common ground between strangers and hosts as 'Jesus, the most desired guest comes in the form of the vulnerable stranger'. Writers in the New Testament portray Jesus as a gracious host who welcomed all kinds of sinners into his presence. But Jesus is also portrayed as a vulnerable guest and needy stranger, in that 'He came to that which was his own, but his own did not receive him. Yet to all who did receive him, to those who believed in his name, he gave the right to become children of God – children born not of natural descent, nor of human decision or a husband's will, but born of God' (John 1:11).

Those who turned to him found welcome and the promise of being received into the Kingdom; such are the rewards of welcoming the stranger and feeding the poor or the hungry. Such biblical passages became the main incentive behind offering hospitality where welcoming the stranger would be rewarded with eternal life and a place at the heavenly table. Such verses had a profound impact on the understanding of hospitality in the Middle Ages and were often the rationale for monastic hospitality in twelfth-century texts. These verses influenced the *Rule of St Benedict* and in chapter 53, 'On the reception of Guests', he warns about the importance of welcoming everyone as 'Christ himself'. Prayers should be said together and humility shown to the guests at all times when he is arriving or departing. If necessary, the Superior should break his fast for the sake of a guest, unless it happens to be a principal fast day. Moreover, the Abbot will give the guests water for their hands and both 'Abbot and community wash the feet of all guests'. It was especially in the welcoming of the poor and the pilgrims that the greatest solicitude was to be shown for in their presence, 'Christ is received'.[61] Hospitality became of particular significance in the monasteries not only because it was seen as a Christian duty but 'the correlation between Christ and the outsider meant that whoever refused the stranger effectively refused Christ and risked damnation'.

While Jesus was identified with the outsider, whether as stranger or even when Jesus begins an encounter as a guest, he often ends up as a host.[62] In the last supper, taken as the pattern for the Eucharist (Matt. 26, Mark 14, Luke 22), Jesus' role as host takes on an even deeper dimension. Laura Hartman writes that 'His Christ status makes his hospitality holy and nourishing to the spirit as well as the body. Indeed, given his parables speaking of the reign of God as a banquet, Jesus' food miracles offer a glimpse of the alimentary dimensions of his eschatology – a delicious foretaste of the world to come.'[63] Jesus is therefore central in diverse ways to the ethics and imagination of Christian hospitality. As Pohl writes:

> The intermingling of guest and host roles in the person of Jesus is part of what makes the story of hospitality so compelling for Christians. Jesus welcomes and needs welcome; Jesus requires that followers depend on and provide hospitality. The practice of Christian hospitality is always located within the larger picture of Jesus's sacrificial welcome to all who come to him.[64]

As noted above, one of the main categories of people who are to be afforded hospitality are travellers or wayfarers, or in the biblical context, strangers. Providing such hospitality assumes a different dimension when we turn to the *ḥadīth* literature. The obligation of hospitality towards the traveller or the wayfarer similar to the guest, means that all have rights over a potential host; *ibn sabīl* is used frequently in *ḥadīths* to speak of travellers and their rights. The traveller or wayfarer must be acknowledged irrespective of his character, his origins or his destiny, and this acknowledgement can be expressed in specific acts:

59

There are three to whom Allah will not speak on the Day of Resurrection, nor will He look at them or purify them, and theirs will be a painful torment: A man who has surplus water in the desert but refuses to give any to a wayfarer; a man who sells a product to a man after ʿAsr and swears by Allah that he bought it for such and such amount, and he believes him, when that is not the case; and a man who swears allegiance to a ruler, and only does so for worldly gains, so if he gives him some of (these worldly benefits) he fulfils his oath of allegiance, and if he is not given anything he does not uphold his oath of allegiance.[65]

The *ḥadīth* comprises a list of acts incurring divine condemnation and this includes one who has surplus water (*faḍl*) but does not give any to the traveller. Presumably, if there was no surplus water, the person is not remiss in not giving the water to the traveller; it is only when there is extra that the obligation to give to another should be observed. Hospitality is an obligation, a kind of debt to the rightful recipient, and yet the host's own circumstances should be taken into account.

Islam like all other scriptural traditions has been enriched with stories and anecdotes about prophets and saints who shed light on how God works and tests humankind. A famous hospitality tradition is related to Abraham, who was one of God's chosen messengers, but who was rebuked by God for refusing hospitality to a stranger:

It is said that a Zoroastrian asked hospitality from Abraham, the friend [of God]; so he said: If you become a Muslim, I will give you hospitality. So the Zoroastrian passed on, and God revealed to him [Abraham]: you would not give him food except with his religion changed, and I have fed him for seventy years notwithstanding his unbelief. If you had given him hospitality for a night, what responsibility would have fallen on you? So Abraham set off running after the Zoroastrian and brought him back and gave him hospitality. So the Zoroastrian said to him: By what means did it become plain to you? So he mentioned it to him. And the Zoroastrian said to him: Does he deal with me in this way? Show me Islam so that I can become a Muslim.[66]

Travellers and travelling are associated with disparate themes in the Qur'ān and often mentioned in relation to purity, prayer and other rituals. But the miscellany of *hadīths* on the traveller reflect a philosophy of empathy and sympathy for those crossing from one land to another. Very often the traveller is simply one whose life is to be made easier whether it's in the shortening of prayers, exemption from fasting as part of a group of people who deserve material or financial help. This is why there is in these *hadīths* both an assumption and exhortation to do right by the traveller. As Valerie Hoffman writes, 'The harshness of the desert environment and the serious risk of bodily harm encountered when travelling without the protection of one's tribe were mitigated by the common courtesy of offering any traveller hospitality for at least three days'.[67] Benevolence towards the traveller can also be seen in the following *hadīth*:

(When he died) Messenger of Allah left neither a dinar nor a dirham nor a male slave nor a female slave, nor anything else except his white riding mule, his weapons and his land which he had given in charity to wayfarers.[68]

There are also *ḥadīths* which speak of the life of the traveller as the ideal life, never rooted and never attaching itself to anything in a foreign place however long they may stay.

The messenger of God took me by the shoulder and said: 'Be in the world as though you were a stranger or a wayfarer.' The son of Umar used to say: 'At evening do not expect [to live till] morning, and at morning do not expect [to live till] evening. Take from your health for your illness and from your life for your death' (related by Bukhāri).[69]

The Arabic for stranger here is *gharīb*, which as noted is not found in the Qur'ān. The concept of the transience and impermanence of human life is captured in the life of the traveller, *'ābir al-sabīl*. Rosenthal also elaborates on another strongly held theme in the Islamic tradition which is that the ancient use of travel as a metaphor to describe man's sojourn on earth had the obvious implication in Islam 'that human beings are strangers always and everywhere'. The Muslim Ṣūfīs appropriated this metaphor to reflect an inner religiosity whereby being a stranger turned into a lifestyle:

If life on earth was a journey, this fact had to be made apparent by constant travel, and if, further, this meant being a stranger, its outwards manifestation was for Sufis to present themselves as stranger. They should not stay in one place.[70]

The themes around 'strangeness' in this world also led many devotees to claim that the soul too is a stranger in this world. The believer is one whose heart does not become attached to anything in the world and who longs for the Hereafter which is the permanent abode and the final return.

If generosity and hospitality were already central features of pre-Islamic societies, the advent of Islam turned generosity into a genuine Islamic virtue by emphasizing that wealth should be spent with pious motives and 'in God's way'. Generosity could not be boastful and excessive, but more restrained. As Izutsu writes:

> The duty of almsgiving was offered to the Muslims as the most suitable mould into which they might pour their natural generosity without being led into the satanic vices of haughtiness and extravagance. Almsgiving provided in this way a new outlet for the old instinct of generosity that was deeply rooted in the Arab soul, but it was so calculated at the same time, as to work as a powerful regulator of its excessive energy.[71]

The transition from giving to almsgiving as a legalized tax is present in the Qur'ānic concept of *zakāt* which brings together personal ethics with religious duty. The noun *zakāt* appears 32 times in the Qur'ān, often placed immediately after ritual prayer in terms of the believer's duties:

> The believing men and believing women are helpers of one another. They enjoin what is right and forbid what is wrong, and establish prayer and give *zakah*, and obey God and His Messenger.

Those – God will have mercy upon them. Indeed, God is Exalted in Might and Wise (Q9:71).

And remember when We took the covenant from the Children of Israel, [enjoining upon them], 'Do not worship except God; and to parents do good and to relatives, orphans, and the needy. And speak to people good [words] and establish prayer and give *zakah*.' Then you turned away, except a few of you, and you were refusing (Q2:83).

The payment of *zakāt* is one of the five canonical obligations on the adult Muslim, although the Qur'ān does not provide much detail as to how this is collected or distributed. The corpus of legal manuals was at the forefront of elaborating and expanding when and on what goods *zakāt* was due, as well as explaining who should give and more importantly who were the rightful recipients. *Zakāt* is not meant to be a solitary act, expressed in some void from one believer to another; it was always seen as the concrete expression of faith (*imān*) for the good of the social order of the Muslim community. As Amy Singer writes, 'the obligation is realized through people by virtue of their interaction, and not by an individual facing God alone as in prayer'. Despite the official tone implied in payment and collection, Singer is also right in pointing out that concerning both *zakāt* and *sadaqa*, where 'one is an obligation and the other a choice, in practice the responsibility to carry out both seems to have been left often to individual initiative throughout much of Islamic history'.[72]

There are around another 68 verses which quite simply extol spending on others through a form of the verb *anfaqa*:

64

They ask you, [O Muhammad], what they should spend. Say, 'Whatever you spend of good is [to be] for parents and relatives and orphans and the needy and the traveller. And whatever you do of good – indeed, God is Knowing of it' (Q2:215).

Those who spend their wealth [in God's way] by night and by day, secretly and publicly – they will have their reward with their Lord. And no fear will there be concerning them, nor will they grieve (Q2:274).

But again, there is a caution about giving one's wealth away to the point of self-perdition:

Spend your wealth in the way of God and make not your own hands contribute to your destruction; but do good, for God loves those who do good (Q2:195).

The multiple ways of understanding charity and generosity formed the substance of much of the major theological treatises of the Islamic world. The theological works differentiated between themselves as to where giving to others should feature in the hierarchy of virtues and the formation of good character; Ghazālī writes:

Luqman the Wise once asked his father, 'Father, what is the finest single trait in a man?' 'Religion', he replied. Then he asked, 'And what are the finest two traits?' 'Religion and wealth,' said he. 'And the finest three?' 'Religion, wealth and modesty.' 'And if they should be four?' 'Religion, wealth, modesty and good character'. 'And if they should be five?' and he replied, 'Religion, wealth, modesty, good character and generosity'. 'And if they should be six?' 'O my son,' he replied, 'When these five traits come together in a man, then he is pious and pure, one of God's saints, and is quit of Satan.'[73]

In his celebrated work on remembering God, the fourteenth-century theologian and jurist Ibn Qayyim al-Jawziyya wrote firstly about what the Prophet said in relation to charity:

Tirmidhi related on the authority of Anas ibn Mālik, that the Prophet said, 'Charity truly extinguishes the wrath of the Lord and wards off affliction.' Charity extinguishes the Lord's wrath and a servant's sins and iniquities as water extinguishes the fire. Tirmidhi relates that Mu'adh ibn Jabal said, 'I was with the Prophet [may God bless him and grant him peace] on a journey, and one day I came close to him as we travelled, and he said, 'Shall I not direct you to the gate of goodness? Fasting is a shield. Charity extinguishes sins as water does fire. And the prayer of a man in the middle of the night is the sign of the truly pious.'[74]

The first deed which should accompany faith is charity, but if one does not have anything material to give or is too weak to help someone else, the very least a person can do as a charitable act is 'restrain himself from harming others'.[75] Charitable giving therefore is not only about helping another with material offerings, but a particular attitude, a fundamental virtue in the character of the believer.

Charity and generosity are applauded and encouraged, but ostentation is to be avoided, for 'ostentation, however little, annuls good deeds and enters [by any one of] countless doors' and 'boasting in one's heart to God of some good act done, spoils it'.[76] Generosity must never become wastefulness and the excess of lavishness was also seen as a moral defect. The believer is encouraged to 'spend in the way of God', but this spending must be kept in balance. There is in Islamic thought a constant reminder that wealth is to be shared, but this sharing must exist alongside prudence. Yet, as a general theme, there is quite clearly in the Qur'ān a preference for spending one's wealth, on oneself but especially on others. There is an account from the life of the Prophet, who, it is said, gave so generously even to those who were rude, that one recipient of his generosity urged his countrymen to become Muslims, 'for Muhammad gives like one who has no fear of poverty'.[77] Many of the great saints spoke of limitless generosity, claiming that the truly faithful, the ones who are close to God, keep nothing for themselves, 'neither the reputation of being good nor the hope of a reward in the hereafter'. This is because such a person 'is in the state of total bankruptcy, because he is truly generous'. The famous Rābi'a al-'Adawiyya used to pray, 'O Lord, give all my share of this world to the non-believers, and if I have any share of the hereafter, distribute it among Your faithful servants. All I wish for in this world is to yearn for You, and all I wish for in the hereafter is to be with You.'[78] For these saints, need and want was not limited to material goods, but rather they wanted to give away everything as nothing of this world, not even good character meant anything to them. Their desire was for God alone.

Miserliness or niggardliness (*bukhl*) and hoarding of one's wealth, especially if it means ignoring the needs of the poor and the needy, are seen as moral flaws. The Qur'ān condemns such people to terrible punishment on the day of judgement:

> And let not those who [greedily] withhold what God has given them of His bounty ever think that it is better for them. Rather, it is worse for them. Their necks will be encircled by what they withheld on the Day of Resurrection. And to God belongs the heritage of the heavens and the earth. And God is well acquainted with what you do (Q3:180).[79]

Ibn Qayyim emphasizes the effects of miserliness through an image of physical bodily constriction:

> His breast is constricted, unable to expand. His stomach contracts. His soul is small, his happiness paltry. But his cares and woes are many. Rarely will he help the needy or the beggar. He is indeed like a man in a robe of iron, his hands so bound to his neck that he can neither move them nor free them. Whenever he tries, the coils spring back in place. For whenever such a man wishes to give, his miserliness holds him back and his heart remains imprisoned. But each time a charitable person gives, he feels his heart expanding and his breast relieved, as if a robe of iron were loosening for him.[80]

God himself is magnanimous, so miserliness is the opposite of God's attribute. The issue of miserliness was discussed in great detail by the ninth-century master of prose and philosopher Jāḥiẓ, whose satirical account of all varieties of misers is peppered with philosophical musings:

I have never seen a community hate and despise a generous man; on the contrary, they love and respect him. Indeed, they love his posterity and because of him, they respect his kinsfolk. Nor have I found them hate or despise a generous man because of his exceeding the bounds of generosity to the extent of extravagance. On the contrary, I have found them study his virtues and make enquiry of one another into his fine qualities, even crediting him with extraordinary kindly actions he never did, and incorrectly attributing to him prodigious acts of generosity to which he never aspired. [As for the miser], one moment I find them hating him, the next despising him and – in their intense hate of him – hating his sons, and – in their utter contempt of him – hating his kinsfolk.[81]

The emphasis on generosity lies in the belief that the generous person is close to God and heaven while the miser is far from God and near to hell. Giving to others only increases God's bounty on the giver, even though the giver should give out of a sense of justice and not from the desire to be rewarded by God:

A miser wrote to a generous man advising him to save and scaring him about poverty. The generous man replied, '"Satan threatens you with poverty and commands you to commit abomination, whereas God promises you forgiveness and bounty from Him" [Q2:268]. I hate to abandon what has already happened in order to do what may never happen.'[82]

The Islamic imperative to give to the poor and the needy in various ways is based on the idea that while wealth divides humankind into rich and poor, it is only through consideration of the poor and the needy that the rich 'purify' their wealth. Wealth accumulation is not in itself a sin, for wealth is simply matter and matter should be seen as morally neutral. In the same way, imposed poverty is not a virtue. However, wealth can be enslaving and simply *having* material fortune is a morally inert life. If we show an unwillingness to spend on others or to give through compassion and faith to both the needy and relatives through various forms of charity, only then will our wealth be seen as a sin. There is no denial of the principles of private property and individual ownership, but owners of wealth must manage their wealth in relation to God. The spiritual life is a movement away from the self to others, and giving from what we have, however little, shapes and gives meaning to our material life. In this respect some of the most eloquent diatribes against the rich who refuse to share with the poor appear in the writings of the Church Fathers. Chrysostom in his sermon on the First Letter to Timothy asks where the rich obtain their wealth and continues:

> The beginning and root of wealth must lie in injustice of some sort. And why? Because, in the beginning, God did not create one person wealthy and another to go wanting; nor did he, at some point later in time, reveal great heaps of gold to one person and cheat another searcher. He gave one and the same earth to all alike. And in as much as the earth is a common possession, how is it that you have acres and acres of land while your neighbour has not the tiniest fraction of the earth? . . . How can a rich person be a good person? He is a good person when he shares his wealth;

70

by no longer being wealthy he becomes good – by giving it to others. As long as he hoards it for himself, he is not good.

St Ambrose has similar accusations against the rich:

How long, O wealthy, will you draw out your insane desires? Shall you alone live upon the earth? Why do you cast out those whom nature has made your companions and claim for yourselves the possession of nature? The earth was made in common for all, rich and poor. Why do you alone arrogate an exclusive right to the soil, O rich? Nature, which brings forth everyone poor, knows no rich. For we are not born with clothing, nor are we conceived with gold and silver. Naked she brings us into the light, needing food, covering and drink. Naked the earth receives those whom she brought forth not knowing how to enclose their property in the sepulchre. The narrow sod is equally generous to both rich and poor, and the earth, which did not contain the desire of the rich when he was alive, now contains him whole and entire.[83]

Patristic literature tries to articulate a conception of poverty and wealth in right relation, which can bring spiritual balance. For the Church Fathers, there are no rich or poor, we are all born the same and die the same way. But the poor were always identified with Christ, and the problems caused by wealth inequalities are created by human injustices towards one another. Wisdom lies in recognizing the ability of each person to limit their needs and desires and avoid overabundance. In Islamic thought and practice, giving was a religious obligation, the right of the poor, as well as a form of voluntary charity. Both aspects of giving were not simply about the rich giving to the poor with all the challenges that might pose, but more importantly, about creating a desired social and moral order. The moral obligation to give was present within one's family, and among strangers and travellers, but the distinctions are, in my opinion, deliberately blurred. Charity was one way of framing human obligations and entitlements to a whole host of people, despite the hierarchy often created around the more deserving. Giving of one's wealth, of one's time, is in essence about creating radically different kinds of relationships with people. Only by recognizing the right measure of one's own needs and avoiding the over-indulgence which leads to deprivation for others do we appreciate that we exist for each other – the fundamental premise of hospitality.

CHAPTER 2

Ghazālī and Others on Hospitality

To invite people to dine with us is to make ourselves responsible
for their well-being for as long as they are under our roofs.

(Jean-Anthelme Brillat Savarin, 1755–1826)[1]

The judge and gourmand Jean Antheleme Brillat-Savarin (1755–
1826) wrote in his classic book, *The Physiology of Taste*, that it was
because man, amongst all of nature's creatures, endures the most
pain, that 'he gives himself up completely to the small number of
pleasures which Nature has permitted him'. He states that while the
pleasure of eating is one which we share with animals, it is also 'the
actual and direct sensation of satisfying a need'. Eating demands
either appetite or hunger, whereas 'the pleasures of the table are most
often independent of either one or the other'. Furthermore, 'the
pleasures of the table are known only to the human race; they depend
on careful preparation for the serving of the meal, on the choice of

place, and on the thoughtful assembling of guests'. For Brillat-Savarin, all animals ate, but only humans cultivated eating to a pleasurable state, a form of aesthetics where by the end of the meal, both body and soul were nourished. Man's spirit grows more perceptive and his imagination flowers as 'clever phrases fly to his lips'. Brillat-Savarin sees the beginning of hospitality, the concept of the meal, as part of the second stage of human development, 'when man ceased to nourish himself on fruit alone'. Families ate together as a result of the hunt and it was these gatherings which gradually extended to include neighbours and friends. Later, as the human race had spread out, 'the bored traveller came to join in such primitive feasts, and to recount to all peoples, for one of the strongest of human laws is that which commands respect for the life of any man with whom one has shared bread and salt'.

For this French gourmand, the second stage of human development also saw the birth of language:

It is during meals that language must have been born and perfected, whether it was because they were constantly recurring necessity or because the relaxation which accompanies and follows a feast leads naturally to confidence and loquacity.[2]

The pleasures of the table as opposed to the pleasures of eating rely on conversation to nourish both body and soul. At the beginning of most meals, people eat hungrily, without much talking, but as these needs are satisfied, 'the intellect rouses itself, conversation begins, a new order of behaviour asserts itself, and the man who was no more than an eater until then becomes a more or less pleasant companion'.[3]

For Brillat-Savarin, gourmandism itself is wrongly confused with gluttony or voracity. But social gourmandism is the 'enemy of overindulgence' and 'morally, it is an implicit obedience to the rules of the Creator, who having ordered us to eat in order to live, invites us to do so with appetite, encourages us with flavour, and rewards us with pleasure'.[4] A similar sentiment was expressed by the thirteenth-century Arab scribe Muḥammad b.al-ḥasan b. Muḥammad b. al-Karīm, al-Kātib al-Baghdādī. He wrote in the introduction of his famous cookery book, *Kitāb al-Ṭabīkh*, *A Baghdad Cookery Book*, that there should be no blame in taking pleasure in food and he himself preferred this pleasure over all others. He quotes the Qur'ānic verses encouraging humankind to eat that which is lawful and good, and added that 'the pleasures of this world are divided into six classes. They are food, drink, clothing, sex, scent and sound. The most eminent and perfect of these is food; for food is the foundation of the body and the material of life. There is no way to enjoy anything else but with health, which it supports.'[5] Geert Jan Van Gelder comments on this particular theme prevalent in the Islamic world, contrasting it with Christianity:

> The Koranic passages in favour of enjoying food as one of God's blessings have done useful service in the justification of culinary pleasures in Islam, as can be seen, for instance, from the preambles of cookery books. The mortification of the body, so prominent in many strands of Christianity, finds little encouragement in the Koran, although like any civilisation Islam had its share of it.[6]

For Baghdādī, food was a pleasure but also a legitimate pleasure. The Qur'ān speaks in several places about food as part of God's bounty and encourages the believer to 'Eat and drink, but avoid excess'(Q7:31). The observation to eat from God's beneficence is an ethical imperative and assumed under a general principle of observing moderation in life. Thus, there is no blame in enjoying food, nor is there any blame in specializing in it to perfect it as art. He remains confident in his choice of his preferred pleasure: 'Men disagree in their choice among the pleasures we have mentioned, some of them preferring food over the rest and some preferring others, such as clothing, drink, sex and sound. I am one who prefers the pleasure of food over all the other pleasures and so I composed this book for myself and for whoever may want to use it in the making of dishes.'[7]

Human eating is always more than just feeding oneself. Thus, how and what we eat and give hospitality to others are considered ethical issues often discussed as part of a wider narrative on virtuous living. Everyone must eat, but in every age our attitude towards this basic fact of life is complicated by the ideas which shape our society. We can try to imagine a world in which no creature ate, but this is not God's world. Creation thrives because its members eat, and the food God provides is an expression of God's desire that creatures find creation a good and beautiful place. People come together to eat, united by many things including family, kinship and religion. They form communities which eat together, because in eating we are not just filling our stomachs, but often participating in a kind of worship where God is remembered in the food we eat and the people with whom we eat. The Acts of the Apostles records that early Christian communities participated in a common life together: 'Day by day, as they spent much time together in the temple, they broke bread at home and ate their food with glad and generous hearts, praising God and having the goodwill of all the people. And day by day the Lord added to their number those who were being saved' (Acts 2: 46–47). As Norman Wirzba writes, 'Food is a sign of God and when creatures cannot eat, or when they find that economic systems prevent groups from enjoying food that God otherwise provides, it is a clear sign that God's order has been violated or that our backs have been turned against God.'[8]

In the medieval period people looked to the Church for guidance, but the Church's attitude to food and eating were mixed and its teachings consequently confused. Fasting was part of Jesus' eating practice (Matthew 4:2), although he admonished his followers who fasted not to be ostentatious about it (Matthew 6:16–18). In Mark 2:19, when he is asked why his disciples do not fast, Jesus' response is, 'The wedding guests cannot fast while the bridegroom is with them, can they? As long as they have the bridegroom with them, they cannot fast.' The suggestion is that there are times to feast and times to fast.[9] As Bridget Henisch writes, 'On the one hand, eating and fasting were sanctified by biblical example; on the other, Christianity was shot through with desire to detach the soul from the world, to help it grow impervious to life's enchantments; only a saint could hope to reconcile the two ways of thinking in his life. Ordinary man had to be content with uneasy compromise and endless tug of war.'[10]

But if the Bible is brimming with references to food and meals which elicited a variety of attitudes towards food and eating, it also contains many references to meals, feeding others, including the most important image of God himself as the ultimate host on earth as well as in heaven. In the seventeenth century George Herbert's poem drew on the image of God as the master and host who knew exactly what his creatures needed to sustain themselves, for '[God's] cupboard serves the world' where even 'flies have their table spread, ere they appear'.[11] Hospitality, notwithstanding the moral imperatives around fasting austerity and asceticism, was to be honoured, and meanness and niggardliness condemned. Hospitality and charity went hand in hand as both were actions which recognized need in others. Leon Kass writes about the civilizing effects of hospitality in political communities, as hospitality requires necessity, generosity and self-consciousness. Kass makes the point that while 'nature's beneficence is silent and (perhaps) unintended, human hospitality is deliberate and self-aware':

> It may seem strange to suggest that exclusive and sectarian communities, if they are to be civilized, depend radically on acknowledging the existence and dignity of the broader and universal human community, most of which they exclude. Yet if civilisation is to be civil, the otherwise arbitrary and largely conventional division of mankind into heterogeneous and multiple sects or associations must pay homage to the non-arbitrary and natural sameness of the human species and its dignified place in the natural whole.[12]

From the beginning of Greek history, the meal and its guests played a major symbolic role in society. As Michel Jeanneret writes, the banquet had many functions, political, social and cultural, and it was always the end product of a high degree of organization. Jeanneret continues, 'In the houses of Homer's princes, the banqueting table is the centre of communal life: a place to meet and welcome others, a place where warriors make alliances. A little later, the Athenian *symposion* becomes an important nexus of pleasure to which Dionysos, the Muses, wine, dance, music and poetry all contributed their charms.' Pleasure and rules, moderation and immoderation, are the paradoxes determining the banquet, and Plato talks of the banquet as a *pharmakon*, both poison and remedy, malevolent and benevolent. But when we come to Plutarch we see that the aim of table conviviality is both etiquette and ethics. There is a desire to align the banquet with the noble joys of the intellect. Here sensual pleasure is no longer the objective, rather the guests at a Plutarch banquet 'derive no pleasure from eating, drinking or playing, but rather from chatting about serious things ... wise people, removed from material impulses and opposed to luxury'.[13]

In both forms of dining, good manners and the quality of conversation were considered essential to conviviality. As has been noted, animals can gorge themselves in silence, but men had to feed both the body and the mind. As Jeanneret points out, 'Words complement cooking; like a well-prepared sauce, they represent the specifically human contribution of a culture capable of keeping the excesses of nature in check.' Convivial discourse had to be elegant, and meant, amongst other things, allowing everyone to feel comfortable, removing hierarchy and difference, 'where there is laughter but no mockery ... jokes but no provocation'.[14]

From a different perspective, the contemporary philosopher Julian Baggini speaks of the virtues of the table and the pleasures of convivial indulgence, but also critiques the common perception that eating well and being single do not go together. Developing a rich interior life is central to living well and Baggini writes of the importance of interiority in all aspects of our lives whether or not we live on our own:

For most people, cooking and eating do not greatly feed their inner lives. For some of us, they do. If you are remotely interested in food, however, then no meal is simply an opportunity to refuel. You will be attending to what is pleasant or unpleasant about the dish, how you might do things differently next time or how you might reproduce it yourself at home. These are not high-minded thoughts, but they have a role to play in a life that is enquiring and attentive to the richness and value of quotidian experience.[15]

Hospitality is more than eating and conviviality, but eating together and conviviality are the most obvious ways most of us understand this practice. Furthermore, we do not just engage in hospitality at home or receive it in other people's houses. Societies have always had places where people go in search for company and conversation. In contemporary society, we can see the convergence of table, eating and friendship in the multiple coffee houses which have appeared in cities as reflections of a city's culture and aspirations. This is not new, for people have always found places outside the home to be together and share conversation where food and drink creates the desired atmosphere. Taylor Clark writes that this kind of gathering is vital to a culture's health, so historically London had its pubs, Paris its cafés, Beijing its formal teahouses, and 1950s America its soda fountains:

Today, we have the cosy, indulgent coffeehouses as our social hub, and Starbucks is the first company ever to have taken this kind of communal place, standardized it, branded it, and sold it to the world at large. In effect it's turning America's living room into the planet's living room.[16]

Thus meals and drink, however frugal or lavish, are central to the practice of hospitable relations. Even when we do not wish to spend time cooking and preparing food for guests or friends, we find ways of being with them in other places for the betterment of our emotional life. As Taylor writes, the thing Starbucks provides, 'feelings of extravagance and invigoration, of social connection, of safe refuge – are things people desperately want'.[17]

The Qur'ānic narrative on food contains very many verses which encourage eating of the good things which God has created as intrinsic to worshipping God as the provider. Many of the verses are long, detailing the various crops and foods which grow as a consequence of God who in his mercy 'poured down water in torrents' so that food could grow (Q80:25). All of them encourage reflecting on food as God's blessing:

It is He who has made for you the earth as a bed [spread out] and inserted therein for you roadways and sent down from the sky, rain and produced thereby categories of various plants. Eat [therefrom] and pasture your livestock (Q20:53–54).

O messengers, eat from the good foods and work righteousness (Q23:51).

Say, 'Is it other than God I should take as a protector, Creator of the heavens and the earth, while it is He who feeds and is not fed?'

Say, [O Muhammad], 'Indeed, I have been commanded to be the first [among you] who submit [to God] and [was commanded], "Do not ever be from among the polytheists"'(Q6:14)

The linking of God and food is to see God as the ultimate provider and our need as mortals to eat. When we eat we should remember that we are dependent on God, and the food in front of us is a result of God's goodness, 'Oh you who believe, eat of the good things which we have provided for you and give thanks to God if it is him you worship' (Q2:172). Gratitude (*shukr*) here is not only thanks for the food but essential to the whole belief system of the Muslim. Belief cherishes the conviction that life has a purpose and the goodness of our existence for which we should be continually grateful flows from an infinite goodness which is God. We are reminded to be grateful, but our gratitude to God can never equal his goodness towards us. Again Baggini makes an interesting point about the religious rituals of grace and gratitude over meals. As an atheist, he does not think that expressions of gratitude are indispensable, but argues that 'the main problem for atheists and agnostics is not that we have no one to thank, it's that we don't have a ready-made framework for doing so'.[18] For Baggini, gratitude is bigger than saying thanks and is expressed in the way we live.

Hospitality which centres on food has arguably been a central feature of religious piety from an early stage, but was extolled not so much for the purpose of aesthetic pleasure, but rather for feeding those in need, and cultivating relationships with friends, strangers or travellers. In the monotheistic religions, the food and drink one served to a guest was a sign of God's grace, but it was also a sacred duty; there is nothing quite so simple and yet quite as profound as in the giving and serving of food to others. We ourselves are all guests of God's hospitality and have an obligation to show hospitality to others. Thus, our hospitality to others is a sign of our love for God as God is always present when guests are present at the table. The Qur'ān reminds us that hospitality cannot be a transaction or a contrived exchange; it must be given freely and accepted freely, 'And they feed, for the love of God, the indigent, the orphan, and the captive, [saying] "We feed you for the sake of God alone: no reward do we desire from you, nor thanks"'(Q76:8–9).

Yet serving others also relies on a practical wisdom, knowing that humility and generosity had to be balanced in the act of being hospitable. One of the key proponents of this kind of piety was the theologian al-Ghazālī. Abū Ḥāmid al-Ghazālī (d.1111), the foremost Sunnī Muslim scholar, mystic, jurist and theologian of the medieval world, devotes a significant section of his famous *Revival of the Religious Sciences* to matters relating to eating and hospitality. This chapter will explore this subject by a close reading of Ghazālī's particular text, *Manners relating to Eating (Kitāb ādāb al-akl)*.[19] It is preceded by a very brief look at the concepts of disciplining the soul in *Al-Ghazali on Disciplining the Soul, Kitāb Riyāḍat al-nafs & On Breaking the Two Desires (Kitāb kasr al-shahwatayn)*.[20] Ghazālī's concern is that man must discipline his soul for the sake of the righteous life, for a gradual detachment from worldly temptations which allows us to become nearer to God. This *jihād* against the soul is mentioned in multiple ways:

The Emissary of God (may God bless him and grant him peace) said, 'The believer is beset with five afflictions: a believer who envies him, a hypocrite who hates him, an unbeliever who makes war on him, a devil who misguides him and a soul which struggles against him.

Man has three enemies: the world, the devil and the soul. Be on your guard against the world through renunciation, against the devil by disobeying him, and against the soul by abandoning desire.

It is said that God (Exalted is He) revealed to David: 'O David! War and caution your companions about indulging in desires, for hearts which are attached to worldly desires are veiled from me.

Abu'l-'Abbās al-Mawṣilī used to say to his soul, 'O soul! Neither do you revel in the world with the sons of kings, nor do you struggle for the Afterlife with the ascetics. It is as though you had imprisoned me between heaven and hell. O soul, are you not ashamed?'[21]

The last citation is a call of desperation as humankind remains suspended between the two worlds, caught in the desires for this world and the hopes of the afterlife. Ghazālī's conclusion towards the end of this book is that the purpose of self-discipline, this long inward strife, is to find oneself 'constantly in the presence of God'.

In *Breaking the Two Desires*, Ghazālī writes that 'the greatest of the mortal vices which man may harbour is the desire of the stomach'.[22] The first section of this book explores how hunger and thirst are good for our spiritual awareness and satiety should be avoided. While fasting (*sawm*) and eating frugally were established as pious practices early on in Islamic history and regarded as beneficial to humankind, it would seem that very soon, hunger itself was seen as a sort of virtue. This was not because hunger and fasting were ends in themselves, rather they were a means to a higher ideal, purification of the heart and nearness to God. In these books, Ghazālī extols the virtue of frugality, recounting the stories of saints and prophets who ate little or fasted most of the time in order to purify their hearts and minds and thereby draw nearer to worship and prayer. In Ghazālī's view, the renunciation of certain kinds of food or the merits of hunger were multiple, including the purity of one's heart and sharpening of the mind; overindulgence or even just a satiated stomach made one lazy, slothful, causing the intellect to sleep. He quotes a Prophetic *ḥadīth*, 'the light of wisdom comes from hunger, while remoteness from God comes from satiety, and proximity to Him comes from loving the poor and being close to them'.[23] The way to master one's soul, to empty it from desire, is through hunger as hunger breaks one's desire for sin. He writes, 'all sins originate in one's desires and strengths, the stuff of which is food in every case: when one eats less, every one of one's desires and strengths will be enfeebled'.[24]

The desires of the stomach were issues concerning both Muslims and Christians and by 200 C.E. Tertullian was one of the first to link flesh with lust and carnal desire. In the fourth century St Jerome stated that a stomach filled with too much food and wine leads to lechery; indulging in food incited lust, and for this reason 'fasting was seen as a way of both cleansing the body and controlling sexuality'.[25] In *The Rule of Benedict*, chapter 39 speaks specifically of the desired amount of food for the table and advises 'two cooked dishes', with fruit and fresh vegetables as a possible third. Above all things, however, it is overindulgence which must be avoided as overindulgence is opposed to the Christian character, 'And see to it that your hearts be not burdened with overindulgence' (Luke 21:34).[26] Food was important for the body and the mind, and it was always a divine blessing. Yet, consumption required moderation for the development of the spiritual life and ascetic practices.

Fasting in the early church did not always mean abstaining from all food, but only certain food and until certain times, and by the fourteenth century the Lenten fast ended at midday, and people also ate a small meal in the evening. The dry fasts of some Christian sects which excluded meat, fish, eggs, milk and dairy products, wine and oil soon proved too rigorous for many Christians and so from the beginning of the Middle Ages, fish was already permitted.[27] Over time the list of forbidden foods was trimmed down further.

Many of the Church Fathers related these temptations to their views of the fall. The fifth- and early sixth-century Syrian monastic writer Philoxenus of Mabug considered the first sin to be the 'desire of the belly' and writes that the clever tempter

Saw that this was the most powerful of the passions and that it occupied the first place in us. He drew near to it, stirred it up and afterward sowed laxity and, after that, desire. And that is how the passion of fornication made its appearance as well: As soon as they had eaten, the eyes of both were opened, and they knew that they were naked. . . . See how the beginning of the universal sin and the transgression of the first commandment was the desire of the belly; it is through that that all the sins and every punishment have come upon us.[28]

Tim Winter claims that in the formative period of Islam we can see 'substantial and verifiable Christian influence upon certain forms of Muslim piety'.[29] This seems to include the practices of abstention such as hunger and fasting in the way of God. Of course, fasting is present also in the Hebrew Bible, 'Is not this the fast that I choose?' the author writes, 'to share your bread with the hungry and bring the homeless poor into your house' (Isaiah 58:6–7). The purpose of fasting is to be in pursuit of humility and justice for the poor and downtrodden. As Laura Hartman says, 'To fast means to recognize human bodies as frail, as dependent upon food and upon God, but also to recognize humans as more than their bodies.'[30]

There is a strong theme running in both Christian and Islamic thought that the believer should not be too greatly concerned about the food which fills the body but leaves the soul to die. Fasting and partial abstention from certain foods are in both Christianity and Islam essentially about subordinating the lower appetites so as to have a greater God consciousness. But the ascetical motive was not the only one which led to the practice of fasting in early Christianity. Rudolph Arbesmann writes that at a very early time, fasting began to play an important part as a general preparatory rite in the liturgy and a fast could be prescribed for all those who, after a careful preparation, were admitted to the solemn ceremony of baptism. A similar fast was demanded of the recipient and minister of holy orders as well as those receiving the Eucharist. He states that 'In one of his exegetical homilies on St Matthew, St John Chrysostom describes the Christian who combines prayer with fasting as having double wings and being lighter than the very winds; and in another homily of the same series, he goes so far as to say that fasting without almsgiving is not even considered as fasting.'[31] In both Christianity and Islam, fasting, prayer and almsgiving were virtues of abstention and generosity which turned the believer's heart and mind towards higher goals than the trappings of material life in this world. Even though they might be observed on different occasions and times in both religions, these practices were cultivated as virtues helping to conform man's will to that of God.

For the Ṣūfīs, it was not just the spiritual effects of fasting or partial fasting that were significant but also the virtues of humility and patience which developed through exercising such temperance. Many practised what might be seen as extreme forms of fasting, and Valerie Hoffman illustrates the varying attitudes to food and fasting in the way of God:

> We get a glimpse of the severity of fasting practised by early Sufis in a saying of Abu ʿUthmān al-Maghribï: 'The one devoted to the Lord eats only every forty days, and the one devoted to the Eternal eats only every eighty days.' Another Sufi commented, 'If the Sufi says after five days (of fasting), "am hungry", then send him to the marketplace to earn something' (Qushayrï 1990: 81–2) – that is, he is unworthy to live the Sufi life. Sahl al-Tustarï was asked, 'What do you say of the man who eats once a day?' He replied, 'It is the eating of the believers' – that is, of the average faithful but non-Sufi Muslim. 'And three times a day?' He retorted, 'Tell your people to build you a trough!' (Qushayrï 1990:81).[32]

Even for those who did not practise or encourage this level of abstention, eating and fasting were not neutral acts, but rather character-forming, sacred acts in themselves. If indulgence made it easier to give in to temptation, fasting was seen as a primary tool for subduing the soul and strengthening worship of God. In this respect, Ṣūfīs often distinguished physical fasting from spiritual fasting:

> The fasting prescribed by religion is to abstain from eating and drinking and sexual intercourse from dawn to sunset, while spiritual fasting is, in addition, to protect all the senses and thoughts from all that is unlawful. It is to abandon all that is disharmonious inwardly as well as outwardly. The slightest breach of that intention breaks the fast. Religious fasting is limited by time, while spiritual fasting is forever and lasts throughout one's temporal and eternal life. This is true fasting.[33]

Physical fasting ends with the intake of food, but those who understand the inner meaning of fasting say that 'the joy of breaking the fast is the day when the believer will enter paradise'. For many Ṣūfīs, eating might break the physical fast, but fasting continued even after eating for those who 'keep their senses and their thoughts free of evil and their hands and tongues from hurting others'.[34] Notwithstanding the relevance of this distinction, physical fasting was a reality in the lives and wisdom of many ascetics. This conception of fasting or partial fasting has a contemporary resonance, not just through an increased interest in the food we eat, but ideas of the good life outside of religious virtues. The philosopher Julian Baggini considers fasting in a secular context today and sees its worth as being a check on our desires. If eating has become a compulsive activity, reflected too often in the 'bored snack and the peckish peck', it is because human beings have become used to acting on desires almost automatically. He writes that if we act unthinkingly on whatever desire we want fulfilled, we are not governing ourselves, rather we are letting ourselves be governed by our impulses. He cites monastic discipline as a way of thinking about autonomy:

> True freedom therefore requires the ability to exercise self-control rather than simply being carried by whatever desires and impulses arise in you. Only eating certain things at certain times, as monks do, is a way of countering our tendency to slavishly follow our desires, breaking the link between desire and action, impulse and acting on it.[35]

This virtue of frugality to crush one's passion is also combined with the other prominent Ṣūfī feature of being hospitable to guests in which the serving of food becomes central to the devotional life. The obligation to be hospitable to a guest and the practice of frugality create a distinct ethos in Ghazālī's short treatise on the etiquettes of hosting a guest. Both hospitality, properly conducted, and abstinence should be seen as practices which draw us near to God, for in both we are thinking beyond our immediate selves. In his Introduction to his translation of the *Kitāb ādāb al-akl*, Denys Johnson-Davies writes that 'Sharing a meal with others is an opportunity for companionship. Even before the coming of Islam, the obligations owed by a man to his guest were strictly laid down. Similar teachings were enjoined by the Qur'ān and the *Sunna* of the Prophet. Thus we find numerous examples of *ḥadīths* which deal not only with what would today be termed "table manners" but also with the host–guest relationship.'[36] Similarly, Christian reflection on food is about not only abstention but a seeing of food as a material sign of God's providence. In his recent article on food, Norman Wirzba writes that food cannot be reduced to a commodity, but should be seen as 'God's love made delectable'. He explains:

One might try to imagine a world in which no creature ate, but this is not God's world. Creation thrives because its members eat, and the food God provides is an expression of God's desire that creatures find creation a good and beautiful place. We might say that one of the clearest and most basic signs of God's presence in the world is that there is nutritious and tasty food to eat. When creatures cannot eat, or when they find that economic systems prevent groups from enjoying the food that God otherwise provides, it is a clear sign that God's order has been violated or that our backs have been turned against God. Good food is a witness to God because good food is God's love made delectable. God creates food as the material, most sensory promise of God's abiding and celebratory presence among us.'[37]

For Ghazālī, the primary evidence for God was not *per se* rational; there was no way to certain knowledge except through prayer and the development of the inner life, a virtuous life. The answer lay in the mystical paths which meant devoting oneself to rituals of the faith, to prayer and worship. The goal of human life was to prepare oneself for the ultimate meeting with God and this purpose required both mind and body. Thus it makes sense for Ghazālī to begin the Prologue:

Now, the goal of those with understanding is to meet God exalted in the abode of reward. But there is no way to meet God without knowledge and deed, and it is impossible to devote oneself to these without a healthy body. The health of the body is attained only through food and the partaking of food in necessary quantities over periods of time. On this matter, one of the pious *salaf* (predecessors) has said, 'Eating is part of religion' (*al-akl min al-dīn*)[38]

Eating therefore carries meaning in this life and the next. It is a universal human requirement for survival. Eating is not a sin of self-indulgence, rather eating well is encouraged as a blessing from God. Drawing upon a wide range of *hadīths*, Ghazālī explores eating alone, eating in company, preparation of food for visiting brethren and finally, the manners of hospitality. Some of the most salient points Ghazālī makes in respect of the food we eat are that it must firstly be lawful *(halāl)* in itself and in the manner in which it is acquired. Ghazālī stresses that God has ordered the eating of that which is good *(tayyib)* in a broader sense than simply rightful slaughter. This is encapsulated in the Qur'ān, 'O you mankind! Eat of what is on earth, lawful and good; and do not follow the footsteps of the devil, for he is to you an avowed enemy' (Q2:168). Food must be lawfully obtained and lawful for consumption, and this marks belief from unbelief. This is a theme explored in greater detail in book 14, *On the Lawful and the Unlawful*. Ghazālī discusses the significance of eating what is lawful and also spending from what has been lawfully obtained. Lawful consumption and how we obtain food and buy food is a matter of individual piety; it affects our very being and the way we understand our relationships with those around us:

Aḥmad ibn Ḥanbal and Yaḥyā b. Maʿīn were friends for many years until one day, Yaḥyā said, 'I would never ask anyone for anything. If [I were desperate and] Satan offered me something to eat, I'd take it [rather than beg].' Thereafter, Aḥmad refused to meet Yaḥyā, until Yaḥyā said he was sorry, explaining that he had only been joking. At that, Aḥmad replied, 'Do you joke about religions? Do you not know that eating is part of religion that God has given precedence over good deeds?' Then he recited the verse of the Qur'ān, 'Eat of the good things and work righteousness' (Q23:51).

If one gains wealth through wrongdoing, and then uses it to improve family ties, or gifts it as charity, or spends it in the way of God; God will gather it together, and then he will throw it into the Fire.

One who spends unlawful earnings in acts of devotion to God is like one who attempts to purify an unclean garment with urine. An unclean garment may not be purified except by means of pure water, and wrongdoing may not be rectified except by means of the lawful.[39]

Eating lawful food is a theme which resonates in various forms of Islamic literature and is emphasized in the traditions pertaining to the Prophet's ascension narrative (miʿrāj). Here the Prophet witnesses a table-spread containing pieces of good meat which no one is eating and rotten meat which many are enjoying. When he asks Gibrīl who these people are, the reply is, 'These are of your community who abandon what is lawful and proceed to what is unlawful.' Food becomes a potent metaphor for human actions and always reflects more than simply feeding ourselves. How and what we eat speaks of the connection between the physical, psychological and spiritual. In this context, Muḥammad also witnesses a group of people whose lips resembled the lips of camels and who were being stoned. When he asks about these people, Gibrīl replies, 'They are those of your community who eat up the property of orphans and commit injustice. They are eating nothing but a fire in their bellies, and they shall be roasted in it.'[40]

Ghazālī also states that the Prophet encouraged ablutions before and after eating, 'because eating as a support for religion is a form of worship, it is proper that one approach it in the same state as for prayers'.[41] Thus, food and eating must be respected. Among the many descriptions of how the Prophet ate is that he would place food on the ground as it was a reminder of humility. If not, then it 'should be on a *sufra*, as a reminder of travelling, and travelling puts in mind travelling to the Afterlife and the need of provision in the form of pious deeds'.[42] While eating lawful food was seen as part of religious observance, the manner of consumption was always a reminder of life's impermanence and that life is synonymous with a journey. It is true that many Muslim households will still spread a large dining cloth on the floor inside the home, especially when there are many family members and guests eating at the same time; it is easier and more humbling for everyone to sit on the floor than squeeze round a table. Yet today the more universal norm is that of eating at a table. The evolution of table manners is linked to the gradual emergence of the table as the physical focal point for family and social convergence. Kass's comments on the emergence of the table as an elevated place argues that human beings usually take food higher up so that they can enjoy the pleasures of the table. Table manners are learned first in childhood around the family table and 'whether at home or away, whether as host or guest, being at table and eating with others obliges proper conduct'. He continues:

> To be at a table means that one has removed oneself from busi-ness and motion and made a commitment to spend some time over one's meal. One commits oneself not only to time but also to an implicit plan of eating. We sit to eat and not just to feed, and to do so both according to a plan and with others.[43]

Food eaten at a table is not just about consumption, but about eating together. In her survey of food and manners during the medi-eval period, Melitta Adamson writes how tables were central to a good meal and eating around a table had a civilizing effect on public manners. One such example, albeit taken from the dining habits of the upper crust, is as follows:

> In the hierarchical society of the Middle Ages in which one's status and good manners determined one's place at the dinner table, being a glutton and looking after one's own belly without any consideration for one's fellow diners was unacceptable behav-iour. In fact, it was expected that the diner offer the best pieces to others and that women should appear disinterested in food. Sharing with diners of lower rank was seen as gracious courtesy, but it did not mean sharing the actual dinner table with the really poor and destitute.[44]

Ghazālī outlines how one sits near to food, helps oneself to food, and also how we should be content with what is served before us. He stresses the *ḥadīth* that one should try to eat with others and not alone. He then cites several traditions which explain how we should act when we have to choose between prayer and meal time:

The Emissary of God (may God bless him and grant him peace) said, 'if the time for evening prayers and that of supper coincide, begin with the supper'. So long as one does not yearn for food and there is no harm in putting off the time for food, it is more seemly to give preference to prayer. But if the food is ready and the time for prayer has come, and by putting off the meal, the food will become cold or spoiled, giving it preference is more desirable when there is time, whether one craves it or not – according to most Traditions. This is because one cannot abstain from thinking about food even when one is not very hungry.[45]

Much of this exploration is about recognizing the basic human need for food accompanied by the human desire for company. The sharing of meals signals an assumption of benevolence as this social manner of eating is essentially about cultivating relationships. We can eat alone, but more often than not, we choose not to. The cultivation of a relationship lies in the little acts such as not eating until precedence has been given to others who are present either because of their age or superiority (*faḍl*). Furthermore, Ghazālī encourages people to talk amicably while they eat, as conversation creates bonds of friendship. As Kass rightly says, 'It is shared speech, even more than the shared food, that makes a community of diners.' For Kass, our conversation is enriched when others take part, and in the course of 'privately restoring the (necessarily private) body with food, the soul keeps its head erect, taking and giving nourishment in conversation'.[46] The way we eat and show respect for guests does not only say something about who we are as people, but is seen as part of worship itself.

Yet while food may be fundamental to the guest–host relationship, one should refrain from any affectation. This means that if a person possesses nothing and has no money to buy any food, he should not take out a loan for the purpose of feeding a guest. If he has only enough food for himself, then he need not feel compelled to present it to the guest if it causes him any difficulty. This is stressed at some length on the basis that if we put ourselves out for our guests, then we would tire of inviting people and dislike the whole process, and Ghazālī writes:

A man said, 'I used to go to the house of one of my brethren and he would put himself out for me. I said to him, "You do not eat this when you are alone, nor do I. Why, then, do you think that meeting up with each other, we should eat it? Either you stop this affectation or I shall stop visiting you." He stopped his affectation and for this reason we continued to meet.'

He cites the *ḥadīth*, 'the Emissary of God (may God bless him and grant him peace) ordered us not to put ourselves out for a guest with something we did not have, but to present him with what we had'.[47] There should be no shame in presenting whatever food one has to a guest, nor should the guest make any particular demand when offered a choice. While this sounds like practical wisdom, it seems to me counterintuitive to what most of us do in real life. That is, many people go to great lengths to buy and prepare extra food with much labour for their guests precisely because they wish to be more hospitable. When I was growing up, so much of the celebration of Ramadan and the day of Eid was about food. My mother's outlook was that the joy of Eid lay in the build-up to the day, not the actual day itself. It was the fasting and praying in the month of Ramadan, the last few days of frenzied activity to ensure everything was ready, and the rigorous cleaning and tidying that were all part of Eid. Then there was the food, copious amounts of food cooked during Ramadan, *iftars* for so many friends and relatives, and then the special cuisine reserved for Eid. But as a family, we never went anywhere for Eid. We always stayed at home and invited others, whether for breakfast, lunch or evening dinner. As children and even as young adults, we just helped out, never quite understanding why we always did the inviting, why we always had to cook so much and why my mother was so insistent that it was better to have guests than be a guest. It wasn't simply because my mother enjoyed cooking that she insisted on this kind of hospitality; it was her way of giving to others, of being a good presence in some small way in other people's lives; cooking and serving for others was a worthy medium for doing this. The idea that one should not put oneself out for guests was a complete anathema to her. As far as I could see, it was neither affectation nor ostentation which drove her, but rather the desire to be able to indulge her guests who had made time to come. Yes, she loved hearing praise for her cooking and took pride in the food she served, but I also think having people in your house, taking the time to cook for them, being a good host, demands certain qualities. We have to be patient, diligent and hope that in doing for others, we can bring out the best of what is within us. This requires hard work and more importantly that we think of others, that we share with others and that we make time for others. Hospitality therefore assumes a different meaning in the lived reality of people's lives, and while it may not always be about ostentation or affectation, it is seldom satisfied with simplicity.

In his seminal work, *The Gift*, Marcel Mauss writes of his family friends in Lorraine who were forced to live quite frugally, but nevertheless 'would face ruin for the sake of its guest on Saints Days, weddings, first communions and funerals. You had to be a *grand seigneur* on these occasions', because, as he writes, 'we must always return more than we receive, the return is always bigger and more costly'.[48] There is within us, I think, a strong sentiment and willingness to do for others, a desire which even if susceptible to our own egos and leanings for ostentation, remains at the core of hospitality.

Bridget Henisch refers to this tension in her survey of medieval society, where the religious ideal of private austerity was coupled with public generosity. It is said that Thomas Becket, the Archbishop of Canterbury in the mid-twelfth century, was highly praised by his contemporaries for curbing his own appetite but keeping a superb table for any guests. At dinner he himself, as a mortification, drank 'water used for the cooking of hay', but as host he served wine and was 'always, however, the first to taste the wine before giving it to those who sat at table with him'.[49] The Emperor Charlemagne's ninth-century biographer, Einhard, wrote that some of the emperor's officials were worried by the number of foreign guests entertained at court, but Charlemagne 'considered that his reputation for hospitality and the advantage of the good name which he acquired more than compensated for the great nuisance of their being there'.[50] As Henisch writes, 'To err on the side of reckless extravagance might bring financial embarrassment; to err on the side of frugality could achieve nothing but contempt.'[51]

In the fourth section of his book, Ghazālī explores themes relating to hospitality towards guests (ādāb al-ḍiyāfa). The first issue in hospitality is the invitation itself. It is noteworthy that Ghazālī begins with a tone of caution on the limits of hospitality:

The Emissary of God (may God bless him and grant him peace) said, 'Do not go out of your way for a guest that you will come to dislike him, for he who dislikes a guest dislikes God, and he who has disliked God, God has disliked him.' He said, 'There is no good in someone who is not hospitable.'[52]

So while there is an imperative to be hospitable, to the point where the attitude to a guest is compared to liking or disliking God, hospitality comes with its own ethics for both host and guest. Citing several traditions, Ghazālī nevertheless stresses the importance of giving food to others as part of faith such as when asked 'What is faith?' the Prophet replied, 'the giving of food and the exchange of greetings'. He ends on a most dramatic saying, 'A house which is not entered by guests, is not entered by angels.'[53] In Islamic thought, while angels are often associated with eschatological and apocalyptic material, they are also an integral part of the human world. Islam has generally viewed angels as present with human beings in this life in various guiding roles, which means that human actions can affect their relationships with the angels. Indeed, Islamic tradition states that the Prophet himself was greeted by Gibrīl for the very first revelation and it was Gibrīl's request by which began the transformation of his destiny as man and prophet. Although heaven and earth are separated, God creates a way for his will to be communicated to his earthly creations: there may be division and space between the divine and human, but 'God ensures that separation does not cause abandonment and isolation'.[54] Angels in this respect carry out an extremely important duty – conveying God's wishes and thereby connecting the human to the divine. It is worth elaborating here on a particularly poignant non-Islamic depiction of this angelic visit by the German poet Rainer Maria Rilke. Rilke's sympathies towards Islam have also been observed elsewhere, but in this poem, 'Mohammed's Calling', the encounter between angel and messenger speak of a transformation of them both:

When into the hidden cave the angel stepped –
he was unmistakable, so towering and radiant –
the lone man there shed all claims
and asked only to be permitted
to remain the simple man he was,
a merchant confused by his travels.
He could not read – and now a word like this
was too much for even a wise one.

But the angel, imperious, pointed over and over
to what was written on the page he held,
and would not yield and kept insisting: read.

101

Then the man read, and when he did the angel bowed.

It was as if he had always been reading,

and now was able to obey and bring to pass.[55]

Angels are not invited by human beings. They are always on a divine mission, and this is Gibrīl's ultimate divine mission. He descends upon Muḥammad in his solitude, and while Muḥammad is fearful and resists, his fear is met with Gibrīls' imperious persistence. Only when Muḥammad began to read, did the angel bow before God's messenger, no longer imperious, but in humility and obeisance. Rilke wrote in a letter that in doing this, Muḥammad 'breaks his way through to the one God with whom one can converse'.[56] There is no mention of Gibrīl bowing in reverence in the Qur'ān, but Muḥammad is now God's prophet and his new status and destiny changes his relationship with the angels themselves.

Angels act as intermediaries for God and there are many *ḥadīths* which reflect the visit of angels as a sign of holiness, of sacred time and special bonds:

> Allah's Messenger was the most generous of all the people, and he used to be more generous in the month of Ramadan when Gabriel used to meet him. Gabriel used to meet him every night in Ramadan to study the Holy Qur'an carefully together. Allah's Messenger used to become more generous than the fast wind (*rīḥ mursala*) when he met Gabriel.

> Allah's Messenger asked Gabriel, 'Why don't you visit us more often than you do?' Then the following Holy Verse was revealed

(in this respect): – 'And we (angels) descend not but by the order of your Lord. To Him belong what is before us and what is behind us, and what is between those two and your Lord was never forgetful' (Q19.64).[57]

Angels can bring dread to human beings even as they keep a watchful eye over God's creation, commending those who have prayed and remembered God; they themselves are always subservient to God's commands and wishes. In the hagiographical literature we find that angels often serve as instruments of God's care and protection for the young Ṣūfī destined very early on in his life to follow a particular mystical path. The mystic may be frightened in his ignorance, but he is always learning the Truth from this powerful angelic presence. A simple but poignant story comes from the writings of one of the most powerful saints and scholars, ʿAbd al-Qādir al-Jīlānī:

> When I was a small child, every day I was visited by an angel in the shape of a beautiful young man. He would walk with me from our house to school and make the children in the class give me a place in the front row. He would stay with me the whole day and then bring me back home. I would learn in a single day more than the other students learned in a week. I did not know who he was. One day I asked him and he said, 'I am one of Allah's angels. He sent me to you and asked me to be with you as long as you study.'

He continues with the same story:

Every time I felt a desire to go and play with other children I would hear a voice saying, 'Come to Me instead, O blessed one, come to Me.' In terror I would go and seek the comfort of my mother's arms. Now even in my most intense devotions and long seclusions, I cannot hear that voice clearly.[58]

Thus, if angels are absent in a house where there are no guests, it would appear that their absence is really about the more lamentable absence of God's presence. Angels act as intermediaries, but in so doing they bring God's presence into our lives. Ibn Qayyim relates a tradition in which the Prophet asked of people 'to roam the meadows of heaven'. When asked what that meant, he replied, 'The gatherings of remembrance'. He went on to say that 'the gatherings of remembrance are gatherings of angels, who assemble on earth only where God is remembered'.[59]

All hospitality assumes some remembrance of God and there is a qualification for the kind of guests one should invite. Ghazālī speaks of pious people, by which is meant poor rather than rich people, and Ghazālī states, 'The worst food is the food of a banquet to which the rich have been invited in place of the poor.' While Ghazālī encourages inviting the poor and the pious rather than the rich, he still maintains that in hospitality one must not forget one's relatives, for their 'neglect creates loneliness and the severing of kinships'. Even when one invites friends, one should be cautious not to single out individuals as this may 'cause loneliness in the hearts of the rest'.[60] Ghazālī is always careful to define real piety as a balance between ordinary acts of duty towards those who are near to us, and extraordinary acts of hospitality towards those who are distant from us in all kinds of ways. This qualification of the kind of guest one should invite resonates in a slightly different manner in New Testament verses such as Luke 14:12–14, where Jesus makes a clear distinction between rich and poor:

> He said also to the one who had invited him, 'When you give a luncheon or a dinner, do not invite your friends or your brothers or your relatives or rich neighbours, in case they may invite you in return, and you would be repaid. But when you give a banquet, invite the poor, the crippled, the lame, and the blind. And you will be blessed, because they cannot repay you, for you will be repaid at the resurrection of the righteous.'[61]

The purpose of hospitality is not only to solidify existing relationships, but rather to reach out to those who are on the margins of our communities and very often people who are not only materially poorer, but suffer other disabilities and disadvantages. In offering them hospitality, we are not expecting any immediate benefit or any reciprocal invitation, but as Christine Pohl writes, 'The poor and the infirm come with their inconvenient needs and condition, with their incapacity to reciprocate. But in welcoming them one anticipates and reflects the welcome of God.'[62]

The issue of wealth and social standing plays a large role in Ghazālī's analysis, a discussion issue he expands in his rules of accepting an invitation. The first rule is that the rich should not be given preference over the poor in accepting an invitation, for that is arrogance and arrogance is prohibited.[63] He explains in more detail:

> A man ought not to decline [an invitation] because of distance or because of the host's poverty or lack of social standing. A distance

105

that can normally be endured should not cause one to abstain. This is why it is said in the Torah or one of the sacred books, 'Walk a mile to visit a sick person, two miles to take part in a funeral, three miles to accept an invitation and four miles to visit a brother in God.' Precedence was given to accepting an invitation and paying a visit because through these one fulfils the right of the living, who are more deserving than the dead.[64]

Ghazālī's exploration of accepting invitations is qualified by the obligation on the Muslim to have certain intentions when replying yes to an invitation. The intention should not be simply to fill one's stomach, but also to please the host by the visit and so that they are both people who 'love one another in God'. Good intentions should precede the visit as this is fundamental to host–guest hospitality. Yet, if the guest knows that by accepting an invitation, he will eat food that is of 'dubious origin or silk and silver will be spread out, or that people will be engaged in slander, defamation and lying, then it becomes obligatory to consider such invitations unlawful'.[65] Accepting an invitation therefore is not simply a virtue in itself, but requires reflecting on what will be the implications for one's faith. An invitation should not be declined because of distance, and if one is observing supererogatory fasts, then accepting this invitation should take precedence over the fast. In Ghazālī's view, 'for if breaking the fast should give pleasure to his brother, then let him break his fast, and let him expect a reward in the Afterlife for having broken his fast with the intention of bringing joy to his brother's heart'.[66] A similar story is told of a Christian hermit who along with his disciple visited a monastery and accepted an invitation to dine with the monks. Once they left and were on the road again, they passed a well and the disciple wanted to have a drink of water, but was stopped by his master who said 'today is a fast'. When the disciple protested, 'But Father, did we not eat today?' the master acknowledged this and replied that they had broken their fast earlier because 'That was love's bread, my son: but for us, let us keep our own fast.'[67]

For Ghazālī, the brother can be seen as a fellow believer and honouring the invitation from another believer is as if 'one had honoured God'.[68] It is difficult to see whether one's behaviour should be any different if one is invited by a non-believer, i.e. a non-Muslim in this context, but this distinction is not really discussed. Related to the topic of eating with Muslims, the *Kitāb al-Athār* contains only a few *ḥadīths* on whether one should ask about the source of the food one is given when invited by a Muslim:

Muhammad said, 'Abu Ḥanīfah informed us saying, "Muḥammad ibn Qays narrated to us that Abū'l-'Awjā' al-'Ishār was a friend of Masrūq and he would invite [Masrūq] and [Masrūq] would eat of his food and drink without asking him [about the source of the food and whether it was *ḥalāl* or *ḥarām*]."'

Muhammad said, 'We adhere to this. There is no harm in it as long as one does not know of a specific wrong. That is the verdict of Abū Ḥanīfah, may God, exalted is He, have mercy on him.'

Muhammad said, 'Abū Ḥanīfah informed us from Ḥammād that Ibrāhim said, "Whenever you go to see a man, eat of his food and drink of his drink and do not ask about it."'

The above is qualified in another saying attributed to Abū Ḥanīfa that one should not ask about the source of the food when invited by another Muslim not just anyone else, but also that if there is any doubt as to the origins of the food, it is better not to eat it.[69] It would seem that any doubt concerning what is eaten must be expressed even if it might be uncomfortable for the host. A tradition is narrated in which a companion of the Prophet invited him to eat, and when the food was brought to the Prophet, he sat down to eat but couldn't quite swallow the very first morsel. He took the morsel of meat out from his mouth and asked the host from where he had got the meat. The owner's reply was, 'Messenger of Allah, it is a ewe which belonged to a friend of ours, but we did not have that with which to buy it from him. We hurried and slaughtered it and made it for you before its owner could come and we could give him its price.' The Prophet is reported to have asked for the food to be removed as it had been obtained through wrongful means. However, it should also now be seen as *sadaqah* or charity and could be fed to prisoners as they are needy inhabitants.[70]

Ghazālī returns to the theme of food, stating that there should be plenty, but not an ostentatious amount of food, and that the best food should be served first. Furthermore, the host should not be in a hurry to remove the dishes before the guests have stopped eating or had their fill. He writes:

Ibrāhīm ibn Adham once brought plenty of food to his table and Sufyan [al-Thawri] said to him, 'O Abū Ishāq, do you not fear this is extravagant?' Ibrāhīm replied, 'There is no extravagance in food unless the intention is to be extravagant; abundant provision would [then] be an affectation.' Ibn Mas'ūd said, 'We have been forbidden to accept the invitation of someone who boasts about his food.' A group of the Companions disliked eating food that had been boasted about.[71]

Thus food and hospitality must contain an authenticity and integrity which implies a commitment to living well and not to pretence. Finally, accompanying a guest to the door as he leaves is a sign of respect and the guest should also leave in good spirits even if he does not feel he was treated as well as he expected. Ghazālī concludes with the obligation on the guest to leave only with the permission of the host and not to stay for more than three days because that may burden or bore the host. He repeats the *ḥadīth*, 'Hospitality is for three days, anything more is charity (*sadaqa*).'[72]

There is a certain tension which runs throughout this work, namely between the duty of hospitality on the host and the obligations on the guest. There is no requirement to reconcile the two positions as a good relationship is premised on both guest and host knowing how to be and act in consideration of each other. There is a civility in this interaction which forms the basis of the relationship. Hospitality has spoken as well as unspoken rules, and in purely human terms it is not limitless. An amusing anecdote of guest hospitality of more recent times is attributed to the writer and *pīr* (spiritual guide) Khwaja Hasan Nizami ((1873–1955). It is said that on a very cold December night when the Khwaja and his family had all gone to bed, he was woken by shouting and knocking on the door and found five men standing at the door, wet and cold. He invited them in, and as well as ordering his servant to get some bedding, he gave them dry loincloth to change into. The visitors were annoyed and angrily settled for what the Khwaja gave them and added that they wanted hot tea for now and later on would be wanting eggs. The Khwaja had initially ignored their rudeness, but their bad behaviour and lack of consideration for others increased his annoyance and despite their requests for food and his own generous reputation in that town, he said:

> When I intend to visit someone I inform my host eight days beforehand. I tell him that I will arrive at such and such a time and that I will have my servant with me, that I don't eat rice and don't drink tea, and that I shall bring my bedding with me and stay only one night. And I expect anyone who wants to stay with me to do likewise. That is what courtesy means or in other words 'behaving like a gentleman'. And when people go against these standards, come without warning at an inconvenient time, without previous acquaintance, I call them not guests but pests.[73]

Returning to Ghazālī, he details the etiquettes of welcoming the guest and the obligations on the host to make the guest feel welcome. Ye throughout this work, there is a strong emphasis on hospitality as a virtuous act only if done with the right intentions and not for affectation or boasting. Humility is central to his thinking. In this kind of writing, we find a certain type of discourse on hospitality which may seem somewhat removed from the way we envisage and do guest hospitality today, especially in urban settings. By this I mean that there is a virtuous tone and an inherent simplicity to this narrative, where the complexities and tensions inherent in receiving, cooking and the physical labour of looking after guests are subsumed under the overall imperative to cultivate particular etiquettes. It is also depicted as a rather male world and the presence of the female and the feminine in the whole process of hospitality is missing. It is, after all, women who often bear the primary burden and the joy of cooking, cleaning and preparing for guests. Theirs is a hidden labour, but they are indispensable to the whole process of doing hospitality, whether it's a meal for one guest or a whole feast for several guests. Furthermore, there is no mention of complimenting the food or the hosts, even though it is inconceivable that this did not happen and that it goes against the essence of this kind of hospitality. This would be the case whether the one who prepared the meal was male or female. It is interesting to note that in his work on the Jewish communities who lived in the Islamic Mediterranean as portrayed in the Cairo Geniza documents, Goitein writes that much is said on hunger but little on food, despite the culinary delights of Jewish cuisine. Furthermore:

> The hostess, if mentioned at all in a letter of thanks, would be referred to in general terms, or lauded for her piety and charity, never for her cooking. In general, a woman would be praised as efficient and tidy, not as a good cook. This is somewhat surprising, since cooking and baking were duties incumbent on a housewife by law. But among the many virtues possessed by the biblical woman of valour, excellence in the preparation of food is not mentioned.[74]

This is echoed somewhat in Elizabeth Warnock Fernea's (1927–2008) account of her two-year stay in a tiny Iraqi village called El Nahra. Fernea, a writer who had accompanied her anthropologist husband to conduct ethnographic studies, recounts her daily life in the village where one day she invites the local 'sheik' Hamid to lunch. Having worked very hard over what turns out to be a successful meal, she wished that her helper Mohammed had been more forthcoming with appreciation:

> I felt let down and disappointed. I suppose I had expected Mohammed to comment enthusiastically on the excellence of each dish which we had presented for the sheik's pleasure. He didn't. No one ever did such a thing I found out later. If the food was good, it was obvious; people ate it, and there was little of it left. Why should one talk about it? I half realized this, even at the time, but I needed reassurance.[75]

But alongside this premise of welcoming guests, Islamic literature is replete with anecdotes and treatises stressing the virtue of generosity, which includes generosity of meals, as indispensable to cultivating hospitable relationships. For the faithful, God is generous and likes generosity in others. Generosity is not affectation, rather it demands a level of selflessness. It requires us to give what we have in the belief that God himself will provide.

Ghazālī's views on hospitality include exploring the virtues of charity, almsgiving and the details of guest hospitality. Many other essayists and thinkers of the classical era spoke less about the details of the host–guest relationship, but included hospitality within a wider narrative of *adab* literature where wealth and personal generosity were often themes of ethical discussion. *Adab* meaning literature, belles-lettres, manners and etiquette regularly contained a moralistic component which could be entertaining rather than obtrusive. As Van Gelder writes about the *adab* anthology, it was 'more or less thematically arranged compilation of bits of prose and poetry, with or without commentary or connecting texts between the quotations; in short, a kind of literary banquet'. The variety of maxims, poems and anecdotes reflected many themes, including generosity and piety. These were seen as virtues central to a noble character, and lack of generosity in any individual was not only condemned, but despised as going against cultural and religious sentiments. One such example was the tenth-century Andalusian writer and poet, Ibn ʿAbd Rabbih, who writes in his introduction to the Book of the Chrysolite:

> The noblest quality in the world, the most beautiful, the most praiseworthy, and the best by which to guard oneself against blame and shield defects – is for anyone to have an innate generosity that adorns his munificent nobility and open-handed liberality. If generosity has nothing else to commend it but the fact that it is one of the attributes of God Most High by which He has named Himself, [it is a worthy quality]. . . . The Prophet, may God bless him and grant him peace, said, 'When a generous man comes to visit you, be generous to him.'[76]

Many of the sayings deplore miserliness, such as 'What malady is worse than miserliness?' He relates the saying of the Arab sage Aktham ibn Ṣayfi, who encouraged people to train their characters to achieve high aims and praiseworthy deeds and to be 'kind to those inclined to you, adorn yourselves with generosity and it will bring you others' love, and don't be stingy for you will accelerate poverty'.

Ibn ʿAbd Rabbih follows this with a poem, 'Is it for fear of poverty, you've hurried it up, and delayed spending what you gathered? Thus, you've become poor, when you're really rich, and now you're no more than what you've done.'[77] In another anecdote, it is said that a man who has both reason and generosity is the best, but 'Don't break relations with a generous man, although you do not like his reason; benefit from his generosity and let your reason be of use to him. But by all means, flee from a stupid and miserly man.'[78]

Human beings can be blessed with many qualities, but generosity of heart which shows itself not only through what one spends on others but how one is with others, always surfaces as the most noble of all human virtues. Ibn ʿAbd Rabbih cites from a sermon by Saʿid ibn al-ʿĀṣ that if God has given you abundance, you should spend from it openly because after your death, you will leave it only to two kinds of people, 'either a doer of good who belittles nothing, or a doer of evil who will spare nothing'. He cites a poem, 'Make others happy with your wealth during your lifetime, for only a doer of good or a doer of evil will succeed you. If you amass wealth for a doer of evil, this will not enrich him; whereas the doer of good will make a little wealth increase.'[79]

Often, the generosity of giving away wealth and the generosity expressed through doing good deeds overlapped. For many of these writers, good deeds brought us near to God and God always rewards good deeds. But doing good also gave the individual the right reputation amongst his friends. For some, human beings were defined by what their deeds amounted to, either good or bad. Abu Bakr Muhammad ibn Durayd said, 'A man is only a story that follows [his death]. So, be a good story to those who heed.'[80]

114

The eighth-century Persian writer and translator Ibn al-Muqaffa' wrote a major treatise concerning practical wisdom and right conduct, called *al-Adab al-Kabīr*, in which he extolled the merits of learning and living by the right principles rather than detail. He provides general exhortations about what is and is not important:

> Know that your mind cannot encompass everything, so free it up for what is important. Your wealth does not suffice for all people, so direct it specifically to those entitled to it. Your liberality cannot extend to the common people, so single out virtuous people.

> Know that whatever time you spend thinking about unimportant things is to the detriment of what is important; that whatever money you spend on trivial things you can no longer use for things of true value you may want to do; that whatever generosity you divert to unworthy people will harm you by making you fall short toward virtuous people; and that whatever time of your night and day you devote to unnecessary things will make a mockery of necessities.[81]

Ibn al-Muqaffa' is also mentioned by al-Tawḥīdī, the eleventh-century Arab/Persian essayist in a debate about the superiority of the Arabs. After insulting the Byzantines, the Chinese, the Indians, the Turks and the Africans, Ibn al- Muqaffa' explains to a group of Arabs that while the truth is not to his liking, it is the Arabs who are the most intelligent. He explains that Arabs inhabited a desert and desolate country relying only on their own reason and ability to survive and understand the physical world around them. They had neither a book to instruct them nor a model to follow, and aside from the many things they understood about vegetation and the changing seasons, they also created rules refraining people from bad deeds and encouraging good:

> Thus, you may meet any one of them on some mountain road, who will extol noble deeds, omitting nothing, and condemn foul deeds at great length. Whenever they speak they exhort one another to do good, to protect neighbours, to spend their wealth and to adopt praiseworthy qualities.[82]

In Ibn al-Muqaffa''s opinion, the Arabs were not instructed in these qualities, rather they learnt them through their 'well-educated instincts and knowing intellects'. In almost any list of virtues or qualities attributed to the Arabs, both of the pre-Islamic and post-Islamic eras, one always finds generosity and the willingness to spend of their wealth.

The importance of generosity as a central trait of good character is highlighted in many of the celebrated works of the essayists of the classical age. Generosity was not only about sharing wealth, but implied a particular attitude to life as a whole. As James Lindsay writes, 'Poets were fond of men who slaughtered herds of camels to provide stupendous feasts to win the love of a woman, to celebrate a great victory in battle, or simply to demonstrate one's open-handedness.'[83] Some of the most memorable names became those who slaughtered their last camel to feed an enemy or stranger who happened to pass by their tent; this action may have left the host destitute, but the act of generosity ensured that he along with his kin became immortalized in poetry through the generations. Kinship was the glue that kept Arabian society together, and what happened to the individual, happened to the whole tribe. Conversely, stinginess and niggardliness were deplored. The ninth-century prose writer and essayist al-Jāḥiz writes of countless tales, both serious and light-hearted, of miserliness in his comical masterpiece, *Al-Bukhalā', The Book of Misers*. He begins by asking the question:

> How indeed can a man who has marked himself out for misery lead (others) to happiness, how can one who commences by defrauding persons of note set to offering good advice to common folk? Why do they proffer as plea in (their) justification, notwithstanding their powerful intellects, something that the community by common consent finds repugnant?[84]

He later comments on the relationship between those of a less generous nature and God:

> Misfortunes are the swifter to befall the properties of misers and calamities damage them the more severely, simply because they rely less upon, and have poorer expectation of, Allah. A generous man is either reliant upon or has better expectations of Allah. In every circumstance he is closer to one trusting in Allah and more sympathetic to one of that kind.[85]

For al-Jāḥiz, miserliness is not simply a moral defect, going against the Arab virtues of generosity and nobility, but affects the very nature of one's faith in God. A miserly person is neither trustworthy nor trusting. God himself is magnanimous, generous and merciful, and would only want us to cultivate these qualities. However, many of his stories are reflections on certain tribes or places and one of the people al-Jāḥiẓ singles out are the people of Khurāsān:

> My friends allege that a group of Khurāsānīs shared a lodging and did without the benefit of a lamp as long as they could. Then they contributed equally to the expense (of one), sharing in it, but one of them refused to help them out and join in defraying the cost. So when the lamp came they would bandage his eyes with a cloth, and he and they would stay like this until they went to bed and extinguished the lamp. Then when they put it out, they would free his eyes (of the bandage).[86]

The opposite of miserliness was expressed in physical and spiritual displays of God's bounty and benevolence. A most common way to speak of someone's miserly nature was in their treatment of guests and the food they served. Ibn ʿAbd Rabbih writes of an Arab Bedouin who, while eating at his host's house, had a hair stuck to his mouthful. When the host pointed out the hair, the Arab Bedouin retorted that his host had been watching him eat so closely that he would never eat with him again, and he left saying, 'Death is indeed better than visiting a stingy man who deliberately observes the edges of a morsel to be eaten.' In the same collection of anecdotes, he also mentions Bakr ibn ʿAbd Allah, who said that a person who approaches food to which he has not been invited is worthy of one slap. The person who wants to sit somewhere other than where the host advises, is worthy of two slaps, and the one most worthy of three slaps is 'he who has been invited to food and says to the host, "Invite the housewife to eat with us." '[87] Human relations, morals and etiquette could all be observed and written about with either food or guests as the main focus of the discussion. This often included details about washing one's hands, eating with the right hand, but also how one ate meat and left the bones on the plate. Food was physical nourishment, but eating especially with guests was a visual, emotional and intellectual exercise. Offering food to one's guest was fundamental to all hospitality, but the dynamics of how everyone ate, talked and behaved with one another, could break the host/guest relationship or deepen its value in the eyes of all involved.

Food and animals were often used in parables and stories of Ṣūfīs to express saintly power and define those who had reached a certain goal. Central to the spiritual journey, the life of the ascetic, is the ability and desire to control one's physical appetites. Only when one has reached a particular spiritual status is moderation no longer necessary, as the saint has already been able to conquer his passions, so that they do not keep him away from God and worship. There is a story told by Ṣūfīs about a man who read that certain dervishes, on the orders of their Master, never touched meat and did not smoke. The man made his way to the place where he could sit at the feet of the illuminated ones; they were all over ninety years old. He did not spot nicotine or any shred of animal protein among them, and he was delighted to sit amongst them and breathe in the unpolluted air and taste the bean-curd soup, hoping that he would at least live to a hundred. Suddenly one of them whispered, 'Here comes the great Master!' They all stood up as the sage entered, and he smiled benignly and went into the house, heading for his quarters. This benign sage did not look a day over fifty. The man asked how old this sage was and was told, one hundred and fifty years old. One of the other Ṣūfīs then commented, 'I don't suppose any of us will reach that venerable age and station, he is allowed twenty cigars and three steaks a day, since he is now beyond being affected by frivolities and temptations!'[88]

Food also appears in stories of saints and miracles. There is a story relating to ʿAbd al-Qādir al-Jīlānī that on hearing of his fame and wealth, a woman from Baghdad decided to leave her son in his care. She said to him, 'Take this child as your own – renounce all right to him – and raise him to become like you.' After a while, when the mother came to see her son, she found him thin, pale and eating a crust of bread. She was angry and wanted to see the shaykh, who was well dressed and eating a chicken. She protested, 'While you eat your chicken, my poor son, whom I left in your care, has nothing but a piece of dry bread.' The shaykh placed his hands over the chicken bones and said, 'In the name of Allah who revives bones from dust, rise!' He lifted his hands and the chicken was alive. It ran about the table saying, 'There is no god but Allah and Muhammad is His Messenger and shaykh ʿAbd al-Qādir is the friend of Allah and His messenger.' The shaykh turned to the woman and said, 'When your son can do this, he can also eat whatever he wishes.'[89]

CHAPTER 3

Divine Hospitality

Christian reflections on hospitality emphasize that hospitality is the way that should characterize meeting with strangers because hospitality is the concrete expression of love. Such reflections usually centre on mirroring God who is the ultimate host. It is God who creates, gives, embraces and loves. As Lucien Richard writes, 'The central image of the vision of life sustaining the law of hospitality to the stranger for Christianity is that of the Kingdom of God.'[1] Thinking through God's hospitality and what it means for our relationships in this world takes us into all kinds of directions and in recent years there has been a steady growth of literature in this area. Biblical sources have laid the foundations for a variety of theological perspectives on the meaning of stranger and welcoming the stranger, but they also provide a rich spectrum of thought on sharing of meals and God's bounty. John Navone S. J. expresses the hospitality of God through God's creative being:

We are all guests of God's hospitality. The world in which we live is pure gift. Our own existence, our human nature, our essential human consciousness, intelligence and creativity are all gift. The companionship of other human beings like ourselves is gift. So is the presence on earth of plant and animal life, of water and air and mineral resources, of light, of the firm earth beneath our feet and the blue-sky overhead. We did not make these things nor cause them to come into being. Moreover, we would not exist for one moment if all these things were not around us to sustain our existence. God is the Host Exemplar of all his guests. Creation expresses God's hospitality.[2]

In writing about Christian hospitality as worship, Elizabeth Newman sees hospitality as an 'extraordinary adventure', one which involves participation in the 'triune life of God':

Just as God provided manna for the Israelites in the wilderness, Christians acknowledge that God continues to provide living bread in the body and blood of Christ and living water in the pools of baptism. God provides for us and always will. The question is, are we prepared to receive? The question rightly frightens us as it did the ancient Israelites in images, indeed our own lives. But God's triune hospitality calls us to a different place, a place where we practise living lives determined by God's giving across the grand sweep of time rather than our own limited grasp of the way things are.[3]

Christian faith understands the dynamics of hospitality as a Christomorphic trace in the universe. God welcomes us to share not only in the humanity of his son, but also in his divinity, the meaning of sacramental life and the basis of Christian spirituality. As Christine Pohl writes, 'New Testament discussions of hospitality continue and extend, but also transform basic Old Testament understandings. In Romans 15:7, Paul urges believers to "welcome one another" as Christ has welcomed them. Jesus' gracious and sacrificial hospitality – expressed in his life, ministry and death – undergirds the hospitality of his followers. Jesus gave his life so that persons could be welcomed into the Kingdom and in doing so linked hospitality, grace and sacrifice in the deepest and most personal way.'[4] Thus, our hospitality to one another is a re-enactment of God's hospitality. And focusing on the importance of home as the place where we do hospitality and break down barriers, Rosemary Haughton writes, 'To invite another person into the space I regard as my own is, at least temporarily to give up a measure of privacy. It is already to make a breach in the division between the public and the private to create the common – and it happens in the space called home.'[5]

The phrase 'hospitable God' is not a phrase one hears in Islamic thought and there is no similar Christology in Islam whereby God's self-giving is made manifest in the sending of his son and Holy Spirit. In the Qur'ān, the dominant sense is one of provision where God provides for his creation in multiple ways; the Qur'ān is replete with such verses. One of the emphatic epithets of God is *al-Razzāq* – the Provider, 'O mankind, remember the favour of God upon you. Is there any creator other than God who provides for you from the heaven and earth?'(Q35:3) God himself carries the responsibility for provision, 'And there is no creature on earth but that upon God is its provision, and he knows its place of dwelling and place' (Q11:6).

There is mention of specific people who are nourished and protected by God, 'When Mary is born, she serves in the *mihrāb*, the sanctuary of the temple which emphasizes a separate physical location where she could devote herself to worship, a place where men had no access. She stays there under the care of Zakariah, who is surprised to find Mary receiving food miraculously from God:

> Every time Zakariah entered upon her in the prayer chamber, he found her with provision. He said, 'O Mary, from where is this [coming] to you?' She said, 'It is from God. Indeed, God provides for whom He wills without account'(Q3:37).

God's mercy therefore provides for all. The fifth *sūra* of the Qur'ān, *Al-Mā'ida/*The Table encourages believers, amongst other things, to eat of the good things God has provided and also warns believers not to prohibit upon themselves the good things which God has made lawful (Q5:87). There is a particular section in Q5:48 telling the believer that God could have made all people into one nation, but gave us each different laws and ways (*shir'a, minhāj*) so that he could test humankind. It is quite possible that the fundamentals of what is being tested are our own goodness and hospitality to one another as well as our obedience to God.

It is to God we turn for all our needs, for God is always the ultimate refuge. If the structural context implicit in the devotional vocabulary of Christianity is different than that of Islam, the practical obligation to show care and hospitality remains the same. I would contend that offering hospitality as a way of imitating the divine, as well as being obedient to God, is embedded in the rich vocabulary of charity, generosity, mercy and compassion which permeates the entire Qur'ān and is found in so many of the *ḥadīths*. An example of this lies in the following:

The Messenger of God said, 'Verily, God the Exalted, and Glorious will say on the Day of Resurrection: "O son of Adam, I was ill but you did not visit Me." He would say: "O my Rabb, how could I visit you and You are the Rabb of the worlds?" Thereupon He would say: "Did you not know that such and such a servant of Mine was ill but you did not visit him? Did you not realize that if you had visited him (you would have known that I was aware of your visit to him, for which I would reward you) you would have found Me with him? O son of Adam, I asked food from you but you did not feed Me." He would submit: "My Rabb, how could I feed You and You are the Rabb of the worlds?" He would say: "Did you not know that such and such a servant of Mine asked you for food but you did not feed him? Did you not realize that if you had fed him, you would certainly have found (its reward) with Me? O son of Adam, I asked water from you but you did not give it to Me." He would say: "My Rabb, how could I give You (water) and You are the Rabb of the worlds?" Thereupon He would say: "Such and such a servant of Mine asked you for water to drink but you did not give it to him. Did you not realize that if you had given him to drink you would have found (its reward) with Me?" [6]

The vocabulary of compassion/mercy (*raḥma*) and giving in the Qur'ān always points to the fundamental attribute of God himself as well as inspiring a vision of a particular state of human relationships in which doing for one another means doing for God. We are always in God's presence, and when we think and act generously towards someone else, we are being the way God wants us to be, because this is how God himself relates to us. The richness of the Qur'ānic vocabulary which points to giving and generosity as virtues that take us closer to God also implies the welcome and waiting which reflects the God–human relationship.

I'd like to draw on two particular ways of showing this – the first is through the beautiful but often complex language of divine mercy, compassion and justice which all essentially point to divine hospitality in their own ways. The second is through exploring the Qur'ānic and Islamic images of paradise. Here bounty and plenty are promised to the faithful through the mention of food, lush landscapes and other sensual delights. In some ways this is God's welcome par excellence, but in both kinds of narratives there is a sense of a forgiveness and a welcome which is yet to come. Both narratives point to the eschaton, but they say something about a God who gives and whose generosity is expressed through the mercy with which he listens and hears his creation, inviting us to be in a certain way.

In both Christianity and Islam, God reveals of himself in different ways. In developing the relationship between the divine and the human, Muslims focused on God's modes and purpose in revelation, the human obligation to submit to reading God's presence in the Qur'an, and obeying God's will in response to a revealed text. Christianity saw in revelation an aspect of God's self-giving, so that the meaning and fulness of revelation is found in Jesus Christ. But Muslim theology also wrestled with how transcendence could be reconciled with immanence and how God, who does not reveal himself in his interaction with humankind, could be known. How could human beings understand a transcendent God who exists in pre-eternity as well as post-eternity, whereas human life, intellect and perception are all finite? The issue, it seems, is that transcendence does not mean distance, for God does want to be known. God is near man, 'nearer to him than his jugular vein' (Q50:16), he can be known by his attributes of which he speaks directly through the Qur'ān, he is 'light upon light' and he is defined by his 'most beautiful names' traditionally numbering ninety-nine. It is God's will and goodness which allows us all to be and grow.

Prophecy and scripture are inextricably tied to divine communication, so that it is principally through Muḥammad and the Qur'ān that Muslims come to see God as a moral and eschatological reality. This in itself is a particular understanding of God's mercy whereby throughout history, it is owing to his mercy that God sends and humanity receives different forms of God's communication. It is in this receiving that humankind understands something of God, a God who both hides and reveals of himself, but always acts out of mercy for his creation. The paradigm of the divine–prophetic relationship is often construed as a struggle, a history in which God has sent prophets as guidance and a call for communities to return to righteous living and prepare for the life to come, and yet the message continues to be contested and rejected.

One of the greatest Ṣūfī saints explained that the reason why these varying revelatory signs became necessary was because all the created souls forgot their origin in God and needed to awaken from the sleep of unconsciousness. 'Abd al-Qādir al-Jīlānī wrote of the

127

gradual descent of the created souls who forgot the days when they were in union with God:

A time came when these souls started binding themselves to the flesh and forgot their source and their covenant. They forgot that when God created them in the realms of souls, He had asked them *Am I not your Lord?* And they had answered, *Indeed!* They forgot their promise, they forgot heir source, their way to return home: but God is merciful, the source of all help and security for His creation. He had mercy upon them, so He sent divine books and messengers to them to remind them of their origin.[7]

Thus, the prophets kept coming and the divine message kept coming until the final event of Muḥammad, whose mission it was to awaken people from the 'sleep of unconsciousness'. This prophetic paradigm is central to the Islamic understanding of revelation, but so is the paradigm of divine mercy. Our journey is caught between obedience and disobedience, where sorrow and affliction are as present as joy and pleasure. Both are intertwined throughout the course of our lives, but the end is a new beginning with God. It is this new beginning which is understood not so much in terms of salvation but *falah*, a reaching of a certain state.

By contrast, scripture and prophecy play a secondary role in Christianity in the sense that through Jesus Christ, God no longer offers us a prophetic message pointing to an eschatological reality, but rather offers himself, the Incarnation being central to the Christian conception of God. Thus God acts as the Infinite in the finite and the Absolute in the relative. However we understand divine revelation as immanent or transcendent, God intercedes in human history at some level to communicate with humanity about humanity and about himself; God does this because he is merciful and loving. The Qur'ān is replete with the vocabulary of compassion as the defining essence of God:

> God the Most Compassionate (al-raḥmān)! It is He who taught the Qur'ān; He who created man and taught him speech (55:1–4).

> Say, 'O my servants who have transgressed against themselves, despair not of the mercy of God (raḥma Allah), for God forgives all sins: for He is oft-forgiving, most merciful (ghafūr al-raḥīm) (Q39:53).

> My mercy (raḥmati) extends to everything (Q7:156).

> God is truly compassionate and merciful to mankind [ra'ūf al-raḥ īm] (Q22:65).

> He has at heart that which you suffer, He has care for you, for the believers, compassionate and merciful [ra'ūf al-raḥīm] (Q9:128).

Creation is the result of this mercy, but creation is also the result of God's own desire to be known. Nowhere is this more explicit in Islam than in the famous hadith qudsi, 'I was a hidden treasure, then I desired to be known, so I created a creation to which I made myself known; then they knew me.'[8] The very purpose of creation is for God to reveal himself. For Ṣūfis such as Ibn 'Arabī and Hallāj this is not because God needs creation in any way to realize his fulness, but because God's creative love is so strong that it triggers the whole process of creation. God's self-identity is timeless, he does not become less God or more God in the act of creation, but something within God inspires a movement of creative freedom. Before creation, God contemplates the splendour of his essence in itself and the essence of his self-admiration is Love:

> In his perfect isolation God loves Himself, praises Himself, and manifests Himself by Love. And it was this first manifestation of Love in the Divine Absolute that determined the multiplicity of His attributes, and His names. Then God by His essence in His essence desired to project out of Himself His supreme joy that Love in aloneness, that he might behold it and speak to it. He looked in eternity and brought forth from non-existence an image, an image of Himself, endowed with all the attributes and all His names: Adam. He created Adam in His own image, thus the human became the place of His manifestation.[9]

For Ibn ʿArabī, love becomes a universal principle encompassing the actions of all creation, the basis by which all phenomena are explicable. It is the movement of love which creates the existence of the world. According to Ibn ʿArabī's cosmogony, there are two focal points in being, that of Creator and Creation; both are essentially one. These two focal points are perpetually involved in a downward and upward movement of attraction. This is the force of Love which is the cause behind our ostensible existence. It is the secret of creation (*sirr al-khalq*).[10]

Human beings may not be able to attribute a beginning or purpose to God's love, but he writes, 'We came from love, we are created in love.'[11] William Chittick explains that for Ibn 'Arabī, it is God's radiance which we witness in this life and not his being or *wujūd*. Only God is the truly Real and the cosmos is 'everything other than God':

> For Ibn 'Arabī, the word *wujud* carries both the Sufi and the philosophical meanings. No matter how 'ontological' his discussions may appear to modern readers, he never loses sight of the fact that *wujud* designates not only the incomparable and ineffable Reality of the Real, but also the immanent presence of God in the knower's awareness. The gnostics look with both eyes, and they perceive *wujud* as both absent, because it is none other than the Divine essence, and present, because it is none other than God's self-disclosure as the selfhood of the knower.[12]

It follows from this that God is generous and bountiful by nature, because his being is infinitely full and effusive. Human beings love God's self-disclosure in the form of the universe. We can say that the world is God's glory made manifest. The world exists to draw everything into the contemplation of his beauty, but in his essence God remains unknowable. Thus even when we say 'God rejoices' when someone has repented, 'the intent is merely to express satisfaction with the repentance of the one in question, and it is not possible to believe about God, Glorified and Exalted be He, the sensation that is experienced by created beings. For surely, the attributes of the One True God, Exalted be He, are beginningless. None of His attributes are created.'

It is worth pausing here to further explore another aspect of this particular *ḥadīth* which expresses God's desire to be known and that is the idea of the 'pathetic God'. Islamic Gnosis speaks of both the unknowable God, 'the God who is not', i.e. the *Theos agnostos*, and the revealed God who thinks and acts, and is capable of relation. In his study of Ibn ʿArabī, Henry Corbin explains that a more faithful translation of this famous *ḥadīth* is 'I was a hidden Treasure and I yearned to be known. Then I created creatures in order to become in them the object of my knowledge.' He continues with his analysis of Ismailian Gnosis which suggests the Arabic word for divinity *ilāh* may come from the root *wlh*, 'connoting to be sad, to be overwhelmed with sadness, to sigh toward'. The Name *Al-Lāh* therefore expresses sadness, nostalgia 'aspiring eternally to know the Principle which eternally initiates it; the nostalgia of the revealed God yearning to be more *beyond* his revealed being'.[13] Schimmel gives a succinct expression when she says, 'Ibn ʿArabī developed the myth of the longing Divine names which, utterly lonely and, so to speak, "non-existent", that is, not yet actualized in the depths of the Divine, longed for an existence, and burst out in an act comparable to Divine exhalation.'[14] Corbin states that these names which are the divine essence itself, though not identical with the divine essence, have existed from all eternity and are the means by which God reveals himself to us 'a succession of *tajalliyāt*, of theophanies'. The names are designated as 'Lords' (*Arbāb*) and God describes himself to us through ourselves, i.e. the divine names are relative to the beings who name them, they manifested themselves in the universe which thus became their mirror. They have always longed for 'concrete being *in actu*'. It is the sigh of compassion, *Nafas Raḥmānī* (the breath of the Merciful), which marks the release of the divine sadness and this breath releases the divine names which have remained unknown for so long.[15] Creation therefore is the work of divine love, but also divine self-love, and it is only by this merciful breath that Creation came into existence; mercy therefore is the cause of Creation and her substance. Corbin speaks of a 'God whose secret is sadness, nostalgia, the aspiration to know Himself in the beings who manifest His Being. Also, a passionate God, because it is in the *passion* that his *fedele d'amore* feels for him ... only the knowledge that his *fedele* has of his Lord is the knowledge which this personal Lord has of him.' Thus, there is a reciprocity here in that God knows himself through myself, the knowledge I have of him, 'an alone with him alone'.[16] But if the divine name is associated with sadness, Ian Almond is right to state that 'the idea that Allah should feel the discomfort of solitude, that God should have need of company, certainly veers towards the unorthodox and heretical'.[17] Almond eloquently summarizes this relationship that if 'God is an expression of our loneliness, then equally we are an expression of God's'.[18]

What God reveals of himself and what can be known is a paradox. Divine names as ways of knowing and confirming, as well as not knowing the nature of God, are contained in the tension between apophatic theology (theology of denial) and cataphatic theology (theology of affirmation). Both have their reference to the one God. In the writing ascribed to the late fifth-/early sixth-century Christian theologian and philosopher Denys the Areopagite, we have an explanation of this paradoxical relationship which bears some resonance to the theological wresting faced by Muslim mystics:

Therefore God is known in all things and apart from all things; and God is known by knowledge and unknowing. Of him there is understanding, reason, knowledge, touch, perception, opinion, imagination, name and many other things, but he is not understood, nothing can be said of him, he cannot be named. He is not one of the things that are, nor is he known in any of the things that are; he is all things in everything and nothing in anything. . . . The most divine knowledge of God happens when the mind turning away from all things, including itself, is united with the dazzling rays, and there and then illuminated in the unsearchable depth of wisdom.[19]

As Louth says, both kinds of theologies apply to the one God and 'represent the movement by which the intellect grasps God's revelation of himself by affirming it, and then penetrates beyond knowledge about God to God himself, by denying and transcending what he has revealed of himself'.[20] God therefore is revealed in many names, but remains in himself, beyond all names.

The Qur'ān mentions human worship of God as the reason for creation:

I created jinn and mankind only to worship me. I want no sustenance from them nor do I want them to feed me (Q51:56–57).

Thus, God has defined his desired relationship with humankind, and yet we have the freedom not to respond. Against this freedom to reject the signs of God, is the Qur'ānic exhortation to turn to God in worship. This is not because God gains anything by human obedience, but because humanity realizes its ultimate goals through recognition of the sovereignty of God, rejection of false gods, and development of divine-like attributes. In all of creation, human beings alone have been made distinct for these qualities and possibilities. As Leon Kass writes, 'Only here has the lifeless blood acquired the breath of life; only here has the cosmos through life finally become conscious of itself'.[21] Seyyed Hossein Nasr saw this tension in humankind in the concept of man as pontiff, *pontifex*. Here, 'pontifical man is aware of his role as intermediary between heaven and earth and his entelechy as lying beyond the terrestrial domain over which he is allowed to rule'. But as Nasr writes, while pontifical man lives in awareness of a spiritual reality which transcends him, this is his own inner nature against which he cannot rebel, 'save by the paying the price of separation from all that he is and all that he should wish to be'.[22] For Nasr, Promethean man is a creature of this world who 'feels at home on earth'. Promethean man has lost the sense of the sacred and is 'drowned in transience and impermanence and becomes a slave of his own lower nature, surrender to which he considers to be freedom'.[23] Yet even here there is a nostalgia for the sacred which humankind struggles to satisfy with worldly distractions.

Human worship may be just one reason behind human creation. To be human is to seek that limitless knowledge which enhances our awareness of our self. If the concept of the divine breath remains largely elusive in determining theomorphism, monotheism stresses that it is our special relationship with God which makes us distinct. It is God himself who has confirmed this special relationship with humanity and it is God's forgiveness which makes him always our ultimate refuge. Prayer, the essence of worship, develops a person's sense of themselves and a yearning for God. God commands us to pray and prayer is an instinctive desire for nearness in solitude, where the believer is transfixed on a God to whom he hopes to feel intimately connected even though God remains a veiled presence. Indeed, Ibn al-Qayyim writes that when the believer stands up to pray, God commands, 'Remove the veil between me and my servant'. When the believer turns his heart to God, the devil cannot find a place 'between that heart and God'.[24] As for the believer whose heart is brimming with faith when he stands to pray, God protects him more than the heavens for 'Surely no heaven is more sacrosanct than the believer'. Heaven is a place for angels and the repository of revelation, but 'the believer's heart is the repository of *tawḥīd*, the love of God and gnosis'.[25] A most poignant image of prayer is given by Rūmī, for whom prayer was the centre of his life in his search for the divine, 'I have prayed so much that I myself turned into prayer, everyone who sees me begs a prayer from me'.[26] Prayer is the supplication of the created to the creator. An early Ṣūfi, Abū Ḥāzim al-Makki, said, 'To be deprived of prayer (*du ʿā*) would be for me a much greater loss than to be deprived of being heard and granted.' Annemarie Schimmel notes that 'This is the keynote for an understanding of the moderate Sufic point of view concerning prayer. Prayer is an intimate conversation between man and God which consoles the afflicted heart even if it is not immediately answered.'[27] For others, the goal of prayer is not in asking of God, but praising God. For the Ṣūfis, the whole world is created for the sake of worshipping, adoring and praising the Creator; whatsoever may happen, happens on account of God's praise. The Qur'ān itself says, 'There is nothing that does not praise him, but you do not understand their praise' (Q17:46).[28]

136

For the Church Fathers, prayer was the ordinary way of touching the divine and they varied in their attitude between formal prayers and their observance at different times of the day, and prayer as a constant interior event. In his analysis, Boniface Ramsey writes of the various ways the Fathers understood the problem raised by Paul in 1 Thessalonians 5:17, who told his readers to 'pray without ceasing'. Among the many who interpreted this was Cyprian of Carthage, who wrote of unceasing prayer for those who are in Christ:

> There should be no hour in which Christians do not frequently and always worship God, so that we who are in Christ – that is, in the Sun and in the true Day – ought to be constant throughout the day in petitions and prayer. And when by the law of nature the night comes around again, those who are praying cannot be harmed by the nocturnal darkness because, for the children of light, day exists even during the night. For when is he without light who has the light in his heart and when is he without the sun and the day whose sun and day is Christ?[29]

Origen's views on unceasing prayer meant uniting prayer with works and virtuous deeds which are part of prayer. In his treatise *On Prayer*, he wrote 'if praying without ceasing means anything humanly possible, it can only mean this: that we call the whole life of a saint a great synthesis of prayer. What we normally call praying is only a small part of prayer.'[30] For St Francis of Assisi, prayer was the fourth foundation stone of his life, along with poverty, simplicity and humility. He was often torn between his duty to preach and his growing desire to spend more time in prayer and quiet contemplation. He saw prayer as purifying 'the desires of the heart', while preaching was distracting and allowed 'dust to enter into the soul'. For St Francis, in prayer one talked and listened to God and 'lived the life worthy of the angels', but in preaching 'one had to descend to the level of human beings'.[31]

But perhaps one of the most beautiful and moving insights into prayer is Augustine's comment on Psalm 38:9, 'O Lord, all my longing/desire is known to you; my sighing is not hidden from you.' For Augustine, the spiritual life began with desire and he writes of prayer as desire, that as long as we continue to desire, we continue to pray:

> For the apostle did not say in vain: Pray without ceasing. Is it possible that we should unceasingly bend the knee or prostrate our body or raise up our hands, that he should tell us, Pray without ceasing? Or if we say that we pray in this manner I do not think that we are able to do it unceasingly. There is another prayer that is unceasing and interior, and it is desire. Whatever else you do, if you desire that Sabbath [namely, eternal life], you do not cease to pray. If you do not wish to stop praying, do not stop desiring. Your unceasing desire is your uninterrupted voice. You will grow silent if you stop loving.[32]

It is desire (*irāda*) that calls out to God. Qushāyri wrote that 'Desire is the beginning of the path of the wayfarers and the name of the first station of those who aspire to God Most High. This feature is called "desire" because desire precedes every matter.' True desire is the absence of all desires other than God. For Qushāyri, one who desires God (*murīd*) is also the one desired by God (*murād*). Nothing happens unless God desires it, and thus, one who desires is 'not other than he who is desired'. This again shows a God in waiting, for the *murīd* is the disciple on the path to God, while the *murād* is the one who is assisted and protected by God. According to al-Junayd, the difference between them is that 'the *murīd* walks, while the *murād* flies'.[33]

The mystery of prayer lies in the desire to be heard always, it is timeless and endless. God is always present for he desires that we desire him. It is our own human despair which cannot always see this. A story from Rūmī's *Mathnawī* brings this to light:

A certain man was crying 'Allah' till his lips were becoming sweet with the mention of his name. 'Why now, chatterbox,' said the Devil, 'where is the answer "Here I am" to all this "Allah" of yours? Not one answer is coming from the Throne: How long will you grimly go on crying "Allah"?' The man became broken-hearted, and laid down his head to sleep. He saw in a dream mystic Khazir all in a green garden. 'Look now,' Khazir called, 'why have you desisted from the mention of God? How is it you repent of having called upon Him?' 'No answering "Here am I" is coming to me,' the man replied, 'and I therefore fear that I may be repulsed from His door.' Khazir answered, 'Your cry of "Allah" (God says) is itself My "Here am I"; your pleading and agony and fervour is My messenger. All your twistings and turnings to come to Me were My drawing you that set free your feet. Your fear and love are the lasso to catch My grace. Under each "Allah" of yours whispers many a "Here am I."'[34]

God prays in the heart of man; he is both worshipper and the object of worship. The Dominican mystic Meister Eckhart claimed that in true obedience there should be no 'I want it so and so', but rather 'a pure going out from what is yours'. For Eckhart, the best prayer was not in asking God for something good or virtuous, but in receiving from God what is God's will. 'Lord, give me nothing but what you will, and do, Lord, whatever and however you will in every way.' True obedience meant 'wholly entering in to God'. He quotes Augustine, 'God's faithful servant has no desire for people to say or to give to him, or what he likes to hear or see, for his first and his greatest aim is to hear what is most pleasing to God.' In Eckhart's view, the most powerful prayer and the most honourable works proceed from the empty spirit:

An empty spirit is one that is confused by nothing, attached to nothing, has not attached it best to any fixed way of acting, and has no concern whatsoever in anything for its own gain, for it is all sunk deep down into God's dearest will and has forsaken its own. . . . We ought to pray so powerfully that we should like to put our every member and strength, our two eyes and ears, mouth, heart and all our senses to work; and we should not give up until we find that we wish to be one with him who is present to us and whom we entreat, namely God.[35]

Although Adam's descent on earth is regarded as a new paradigm for human existence, something between the human and the divine has been ruptured in this exile. If human restlessness is essentially a powerful longing to return and find repose, God too is eager to welcome us back. This seems to be the reason behind the prophetic mission, a divine disclosure, but always a partial divine disclosure.

When God does choose to reveal to his prophets and messengers his secrets or that which is hidden (*al-ghayb*), they are only the bearers of the message; they have no knowledge of the unseen:

Say, 'I do not say to you, I possess the treasures of God, nor do I know that which is hidden/unseen (*al-ghayb*), nor do I say to you I am an angel. I follow only that which has been revealed to me (Q6:50).

If I had knowledge of the unseen, I would have multiplied all good, and no evil would touch me. I am only a warner, and a bringer of good tidings to a people who have faith (Q7:188).[36]

This concept of the unseen or the realm of the unseen (*al-ghayb*) is reiterated in the Qur'ān, for God has the keys to the unseen (*mafātīh al-ghayb*). But even though God is the unseen who sees all, it may be that his love for creation cannot be revealed in its fulness on this earth; it remains veiled until the next life.

If God is a God who waits for us, this does not imply any need on his part. God is the host expecting us, waiting for us, his guests. He knows we will turn to him, and when we do, he responds; God's waiting never finishes, because his forgiveness never ceases. We will always be welcomed in his mercy, because there are no limits to his hospitable and forgiving attributes. His generosity remains the context for our welcome, even though his wrath and justice should make us tremble. He desires human worship because man alone can both worship God and also encompass God in his heart. In Ibn ʿArabī's view, this is the true meaning of divine vicegerency which God bestowed upon Adam:

141

Whoever witnesses what he was created for, in both this world and the next world, is the Perfect Servant, the intended goal of the cosmos, the deputy of the whole cosmos. Were all the cosmos – the high of it and the low of it – to be heedless of God's remembrance for a single moment, and were the servant to remember Him, he would stand in for the whole cosmos through that remembrance, and through Him the existence of the cosmos would be preserved.[37]

In response to our worship, God's love knows no limits:

Whoever shows enmity to a friend of mine, I shall be at war with him. My servant does not draw near to me with anything more loved by me than what I have made obligatory upon him and my servant continues to draw near to me with supererogatory works so that I shall love him. When I love him I am his hearing with which he hears, his seeing with which he sees, his hand with which he strikes and his foot with which he walks. Were he to ask [something] of me, I would surely give it to him; and were he to ask me for refuge, I would surely grant him it.[38]

The concept of trying to draw near to God evokes God as a God in waiting, a God almost desperate to respond to human longing. He does not just listen to us, he becomes the ears with which we listen, the sight with which we see, the hand with which we strike and the foot with which we walk. In Ibn ʿArabī's view, this shows that 'the lover hears Him through Him, the lover sees Him through Him, and the lover speaks to Him through Him'.[39]

142

For Ibn ʿArabī, love is the path and the station. Others have spoken eloquently about listening to our inner voice as it takes us towards God where 'the voice of faith (*imān*) calls to integrity, the voice of submission (*islām*) calls to morality, the voice of virtue (*iḥsān*) calls to the contemplation of God . . . the voice of hope (*rajāʾ*) calls to reassurance, the voice of love (*maḥabba*) calls to longing, the voice of longing (*shawq*) calls to passion and the voice of passion (*walah*) calls to God'.[40]

But for those of us whose faith has not reached such depths, the mutual love between God and human beings is premised on the overarching Qur'ānic narrative of divine forgiveness. Despite the call to worship, God's benevolence is not determined by our acts of devotion. The fundamental human condition is that man is created weak and strong, both discerning and ignorant. Human beings are always open to temptation, the cycle of wrongdoing followed by repentance as present in the concept of *tawba* or 'returning' to God. God for his part acting in accordance with his merciful nature will always forgive. As Izutsu points out, the same word *tawba* means repentance on the part of man and forgiveness on the part of God for humankind 'turns' towards God in repentance and God 'turns' towards man in forgiveness.[41] This does not mean that God is not also a God of judgment or the avenger of evils committed, but if God has any weakness, then that weakness must be human repentance. God's mercy is limitless in the face of repentance. This is a continuous correlation of man–God relations. In fact, in two similar traditions, the Prophet says:

> If you had not sinned, God would have created a people who would and would have pardoned them.

143

If you had not sinned, I would have feared of you what is more evil than sins. It was asked 'And what is that?' Muhammad said, 'pride'.[42]

Although the Qur'ān speaks of doing good in the hope of a future reality, it is our present reality which is transformed first by the good that we do. The Qur'ānic concept of human success (*falah*) is to emphasize that in our journey to know God, lies the struggle and desire to do right in spite of all the wrong we do. This is why divine mercy is such a powerful theme in the Qur'ān; it is the attribute of a God eager and desiring for his creation to turn to him always at any time and from any distance:

Say, 'O my servants who have transgressed against themselves, despair not of the mercy of God, for God forgives all sins: for He is oft-forgiving, most merciful' (Q39:53).

Indeed, Ghazālī quotes a tradition where a believer implores God to keep him away from sin. God's response is, 'All my believing servants ask this from me. But if I should keep them away from sin, upon whom will I bestow my blessings and to whom will I grant forgiveness?'[43] It could be argued that God wants human beings to commit sin, but only so that he can forgive; sin and wrongdoing are part of human nature, but also what connects us to God in repentance. Through forgiveness, God gives and gives. Herein lies a mutual dependency between the divine and the human, a dependency which does not limit God nor implies need, but allows him constant opportunities to show the full magnitude of what his being encompasses in all its justice. There is a similarity here to II Peter 3:9, 'The Lord is not slack concerning his promise, as some count slackness, but is long-suffering towards us, not willing that any should perish but that all should come to repentance.' The philosopher and mystic Meister Eckhart also speaks of humankind's relationship to God through sin, but says that God willingly suffers the harm caused by sin. For Eckhart, those who are really rooted in the will of God would not wish that their sins had not occurred. This is because 'you are thereby bound to greater love and are thereby cast down and humiliated. The only regret of the sinner should be that he acted against God. You should have confidence in God, believing that He would not have allowed this to happen to you unless He wanted to promote your welfare by so doing.'[44]

In return, his mercy and his gifts have no bounds. In those Qur'ānic verses and *ḥadīths* which speak so profusely about God's mercy, we find an Islamic doctrine of eternal, indeed radical hope. I would contend that despite the terrible images of hell which are also described in detail in the Qur'ān, the overriding message of divine mercy eclipses the damnation of hell for the unbelievers and wrong-doers. In humankind's wretched but eternal need to love and be loved lies the recognition that belief and non-belief can be the choice between hope and despair.

It is living and dying with hope that brings us closer to God in a constant movement:

It is not expedient that anyone should leave this world except out
of love for God, in order that he may be desirous of meeting with
God. For whoever desires to meet with God, God desires to meet
with Him, and hope joins him to love.[45]

145

What exactly is meant by meeting God is left to be imagined, for we do not know how God is in the afterlife and how he is in heaven or paradise. This is often contrasted with God's panoptic gaze encapsulated most eloquently in the *ḥadīth* that '*iḥsan* is to worship God as if you see him or if not, to know that he sees you'.[46] God who is 'in the heavens and the earth' knows our secrets, the secrets which we keep in our chest (*sadr*) or heart (*qalb*). But he retains the element of secrecy of self by speaking only through inspiration or from behind a veil, never revealing himself directly to humankind. The secrecy motif of how God hides and reveals is presented throughout the Qur'ān in a variety of verses. God's knowledge pervades to all things human and contrasts with the human inability to keep any secret in the reality of divine omniscience. And yet the Qur'ān speaks of the ultimate vision of God for the fortunate when God himself will be revealed, 'On that day, some faces will be radiant looking at their Lord' (Q75:22–23).

It is said that around a third of the Qur'ān is eschatological, whereby belief in the day of judgement and the afterlife became articles of faith. The Qur'ān mentions, in different and overlapping ways, concepts of life immediately after death, the period between death and the day of resurrection, signs of the end times here on earth for all, and images of the various abodes of the afterlife. The two ideas of damnation and forgiveness in God's final judgement dominate this eschatological narrative. At the heart of Qur'ānic eschatology is the conviction that human beings are called to account by God. This is a warning repeated in the Qur'ān that all prophets cautioned their communities about this day, but they were mocked along with people refusing to live in the light of this eschatological dawning. According to the Qur'ān, death is the one event affecting all life, 'Every soul will taste death' (Q29:57), but it is also the event through which human life enters into another stage of its destiny. In Islam, this transformation of earthy life is real and God-ordained. It begins in the grave, but we have no definitive sense of where it ends. We may not comprehend fully what a future life after death means, but the depiction and events of an afterworld form one of the central motifs of the Qur'ān. The ethical teachings of the Qur'ān are to be understood in the light of the reality of the day of judgement, for the whole of human history is a movement from creation to the eschaton. Although the Qur'ān repeatedly mentions a life beyond this earthly existence and events of the eschaton, the relationship between humankind, resurrection and death is a rich didactic theme in the Islamic tradition, capturing the imagination of scholars throughout history.

In her intriguing and detailed analysis of the distinction between a Christian afterlife and a Muslim afterworld, Nerina Rustomji writes:

> Islamic eschatology provides an *afterworld*, while Christian eschatology focuses on an *afterlife*. While some Eastern Christian texts incorporate metaphors of a physical world, Christian texts in general present the quality of future lives through relationships with humans, angels and the divine. By contrast, Muslims enjoy an afterlife within the parameters of a physically described afterworld. The connotation of 'The Garden' and 'The Fire' involves spaces and objects more than states of being.[47]

The two concepts are often conflated, but the afterworld provides a real setting and even a cursory look at some of the Qur'ānic verses shows how they portray this afterworld already in existence waiting for the faithful and the righteous. This world waits for man who must experience being earthly before he can assume the heavenly. The heavenly is the fulfilment of all the desires which remain in him, but most significantly, the vision of God. The themes and images are repeated in various ways, but the descriptions always convey indulgence without sin. These depictions of heavenly bliss are not about activities of entertainment or hedonism, but are about reward, for there is no escaping the Qur'ānic exhortation that life after death makes distinctions between good and bad, virtue and wickedness. God may forgive everyone everything, but heaven and hell provide difficult but seductive ways of thinking about right and wrong in this life. Owing to their patience and constancy, God rewards people with paradise where they will recline on thrones, where there is perfect shade and fruit hanging in abundance and in humility. They will drink from vessels of silver and goblets of crystal:

And they will be given to drink there of a cup (of wine) mixed with Zanjabil – A fountain there, called Salsabil. And round about them will (serve) youths of perpetual (freshness): If you see them, you would think them scattered pearls. And when you look, it is there you will see a bliss and a realm magnificent. Upon them will be green garments of fine silk and heavy brocade, and they will be adorned with bracelets of silver; and their Lord will give to them to drink of a wine pure and holy (Q76:16–21)

[Here] is the description of Paradise, which the righteous are promised, wherein are rivers of water unaltered, rivers of milk the taste of which never changes, rivers of wine delicious to those

148

who drink, and rivers of purified honey, in which they will have from all [kinds of] fruits and forgiveness from their Lord, like [that of] those who abide eternally in the Fire and are given to drink scalding water that will sever their intestines (Q47:15)

This afterworld is divided into two – heaven and hell, or Garden and Fire. Both of these abodes can be entered only at the end of time and their descriptions are conveyed in earthly physical sensual terms. The verses describing heaven and hell are often juxtaposed to compare the fate of the virtuous with the fate of the wicked. So while the wicked enter to burn in hell, the virtuous will realize that this is the abode for those who rightfully worshipped and prayed to God. They will appreciate that their deeds meant they escaped the torments of hell. God himself will tell the righteous entering paradise, 'Eat and drink in satisfaction for what you used to do'. Every wish, whether for food or gazing on human beauty, will be granted to those 'reclining on thrones'.

They will exchange with one another a cup [of wine] wherein [results] no ill speech or commission of sin. There will circulate among them [servant] boys [especially] for them, as if they were pearls well-protected. Round about them will serve, (devoted) to them, young male servants (handsome) as Pearls well-guarded. And they will approach one another, inquiring of each other. They will say, 'Indeed, we were previously among our people fearful of displeasing God. So God conferred favour upon us and protected us from the punishment of the Scorching Fire. But God has been good to us, and has delivered us from the penalty of the Scorching Wind (Q52:23–27).

149

They will not only eat sumptuously, drink and wear luxurious clothes such as silk and brocade, but speak to their ancestors and descendants, greet one another as if this was one blissful banquet full of familiarity and joy. God's hospitality will not be like anything they had imagined, even though paradise is in the reign of the imaginary. Ordinary human beings will be treated like kings as a reward for their piety. Abdelwahab Bouhdiba writes in relation to the descriptions of paradise that Islam is 'an economy of pleasure'. For Bouhdiba, the sexual and the sacral reach greater depth in paradise and 'the image of the Muslim paradise is positive and affirmative. Islam does not repress the libido.' Yet it is not paradise which is materialized, rather man's nature which is immaterilaized and reduced to pure pleasure and sensation.[48]

Sensual images of rivers of milk and honey, pure, non-intoxicating wines in the form of *tasnīm* and *rahīq*, silken couches, jewel-encrusted thrones, black-eyed houris and youths described as 'pearls well-guarded' dominate the popular imagination of heavenly delights. In the Qur'ānic heaven, there will be various distinct flows of drinks and 'wines' in which *tasnīm* appears to enjoy the most elevated status. All these different drinks are united by being pure, which essentially means not intoxicating as is the effect with ordinary wines. The Qur'ān presents no definitive understanding of the various drinks that are only partially encapsulated in the English translation of 'wine', but heavenly wine is the reward for abstention from earthly wine.

Whoever drinks wine [*khamr*] in this world, then dies while he is addicted to it and does not repent, will not drink it in the hereafter.[49]

The language of wine, drinking and intoxication is present throughout the narratives of heaven. Both *raḥīq* and *tasnīm* are interpreted as 'wines' that are not only pure, i.e., devoid of any polluting effect, but reserved for those who are nearest to God or the most beloved of God. The imagery here works on multiple levels to contrast heavenly wine with earthly wine and to portray a particular picture of heaven itself. Firstly, in the case of *raḥīq*, this is drink sealed with musk. Musk is highly esteemed for its precious perfume and flavour, and a seal made with it contrasts with the seal of earthly wines, which are usually made of clay or molten wax. Secondly, *tasnīm* refers to springs of 'waters' or 'wine' that flow down from heaven, an image that parallels 'the rivers of wine (*anhār min khamr*), a joy to those who drink' (Q47:15). Whether such images are to be understood literally or allegorically, Islamic thought is not apologetic about the heavenly fulfilment of human physical desires. Creation is to be enjoyed through the senses because sensual pleasures, far from being associated with primeval sin or redemption, are part of God's creation, and therefore divine blessings. Yet, all these pleasures pale into insignificance when compared with the possible vision of God. This is the real reward, where expectation will rise to ecstasy.

This picture of heaven has historically been the subject of some derision, even disbelief, by certain Christian scholars who accused Muslims of being obsessed with the flesh and for not understanding that in the next life we are all children of God in eternal life, for whom such physical pleasures do not matter. As Frithjof Schuon writes in his classic work *Islam and the Perennial Philosophy*:

Christianity distinguishes between the carnal in itself and the spiritual in itself, and is logical in maintaining this alternative in the hereafter; Paradise is by definition spiritual, therefore it excludes the carnal. Islam, which distinguishes between the carnal that is gross and the carnal that is sanctified, is just as logical in admitting the latter into its Paradise. To reproach the Garden of the Houris for being too sensual, according to the down to earth meaning of the word, is quite as unjust as to reproach the Christian paradise for being too abstract.[50]

For one Christian scholar such a depiction of divine bounty was one more way of seducing people to Islamic beliefs. Thomas Aquinas (1225–1274 C.E.) was an Italian Dominican priest of the Roman Catholic Church who ranks among the most influential philosophers and theologians in the West. Thomas saw Islamic monotheism as a mixture of different falsehoods and wrote that Muslim teachings appealed to desert wanderers. He added to this a specific critique which was the charge of concupiscence and carnal pleasure as a means of enticing people to Islam. In his discussions on life after resurrection, Thomas argued that Islam (and Judaism), unlike Christianity, promised people sexual and other pleasures as a reward for virtue, whereas Christianity offered eternal bliss. Thomas devotes much time to his claim that human happiness does not lie in bodily pleasures, chiefly in food and sex:

By this, of course, one avoids the error of the Jews and of the Saracens, who hold that in the resurrection men will have use for food and sexual pleasure as they do now. And even certain

Christian heretics have followed them; they hold that there will be on earth for a thousand years an earthly kingdom of Christ, and in that space of time they assert that those who rise again shall enjoy the leisure of immoderate carnal banquets, furnished with an amount of meat and drink such as not only to shock the feeling of the temperate, but even to surpass the measure of credulity itself, such assertions can be believed only by the carnal.[51]

The sensual imagery of heaven is a repeated theme in Islamic thought. It remains a significant way of conveying divine expectation and divine hospitality. God awaits the righteous and their reward is beautiful in every sense.

These images and their moral message assume a particular poignancy in the *isrā'* and *mi'rāj* narratives, i.e. the Night Journey and the Ascension of Muḥammad. The *mi'rāj* or Ascension of the Prophet is regarded as a foundational event in his life alluded to in a specific Qur'ānic verse, 'Glory to be to God who took His Servant by night from al-Masjid al-Ḥaram to al-Masjid al-Aqsa, whose surroundings We have blessed, to show him of Our signs. Indeed, He is the Hearing, the Seeing' (Q17:1). The second set of verses (Q53:1–8) refer to Muḥammad being 'in the highest part of the horizon, then he approached and descended'. In his study of the *mi'rāj* narratives, Frederick Colby argues that the vocabulary regarding this celestial ascension is vague, and although there is mention of a night journey (*isrā'*), the Qur'ān makes no specific reference to the term *mi'rāj*. The latter gained momentum in extra-Qur'ānic material.[52] It is in the earliest biography of the Prophet, the *Sīra* of Ibn Isḥāq, where we find the details of the two narratives. The story of the *mi'rāj* went through a number of revisions in the course of the Middle Ages, but it speaks of two main events. The first is the *isrā*, when the angel Gibrīl lifts the Prophet on to a heavenly mount called Burāq to accompany Muḥammad on a journey from Mecca to Jerusalem (the distant shrine, al-masjid al-aqsā), where he led the prayer with the prophets (Abraham, Moses and Jesus) on the Temple Mount; the second part is Muḥammad's heavenly journey, described as climbing a heavenly ladder – *mir'āj*, his ascension in which he meets all the major prophets in the seven heavens, ending with Abraham right before the gates of paradise.[53] As Omid Safi points out, 'The ladder (*mi'raj*) in fact lends its name to the whole episode, as well as providing the crucial imagery of ascending. If God is 'within', He is also 'above'. Religiously, humanity has always imagined infinity through the vertical dimension.

'Divine presence both permeates and transcends this realm of reality.'[54] It is written that the ladder itself had alternate steps of silver and gold, coming down from the highest heaven, encrusted with pearls and surrounded with angels on its right and left.[55] Each time Gibrīl takes Muḥammad to meet with another of the prophets, he stops at the gate and knocks. When the voice from inside asks whether Muḥammad has been sent for, and after confirming, only then does Gibrīl take the Prophet inside. He is then welcomed as a guest by the respective prophet-host and Muḥammad watches. One such example is his meeting with Adam, the 'father of humanity': The Prophet sees to Adam's right 'great dark masses and a gate exuding a fragrant smell, and to his left great dark masses and a gate exuding a foul, putrid smell'. Adam would smile and be happy when he looked to his right, and be sad and weep when he looked to his left. When Muḥammad asks Gibrīl about this, his reply is:

This is your father Adam and the dark throngs are the souls of his children. Those on the right are the people of Paradise and those on the left are the people of the Fire. Whenever he looks to his right he smiles and is glad, and whenever he looks to his left he is sad and weeps. The door to his right is the gate of Paradise. Whenever he sees those of his offspring enter it, he smiles happily. The door to his left is the gate of Hell-Fire. Whenever he sees those of his offspring enter it he weeps sadly.[56]

Thus, despite knowing and accepting that God's judgement is real, the prophets weep for the damned souls in the afterlife. Food is used as an image to convey the plight of those who led unlawful lives, with Muḥammad witnessing many eating decaying meat while good meat is left untouched. He finds out they are the ones who abandoned what was lawful and did what was unlawful on earth. Muḥammad himself becomes thirsty and Gibrīl offers him both a bowl of wine and one of milk. Even though celestial wine is permitted, when Muḥammad chooses the milk, Gibrīl is pleased for this is the 'right way'. God's hospitality and welcome towards human beings is portrayed through different entrances and gates, with tables of varying foods. The terrible images of the gates of hell so near to the gates of paradise depict a judgement for all and a practice that involves saying yes to some people and no to others.

While there was discussion as to whether this was a real physical journey of the body or a dream or a vision, another interpretation was that God himself accompanied 'his servant' on this journey. The event is again mentioned in the Qur'ān when it is said that Muḥammad reached the higher part of heaven, 'then he approached and descended, and was at a distance of two bow lengths or nearer, and he revealed to His Servant what he revealed' (Q53:7–10). Later on it is said that 'the sight [of the Prophet] did not swerve, nor did it turn away/transgress' (Q53:17). These verses taken together led to the creation of a vast body of literature which focused on the Prophet's uniqueness amongst other prophets, and perhaps most significantly whether he actually saw God. According to Ibn Abbās, Muḥammad did not just see the throne of God in this journey but he saw God himself, because he said, 'I saw my Lord'. Others say that he saw God in his dream or that he saw only light. But one *ḥadīth* of which there are several variations states that the prophet's wife Aisha was asked whether he had seen God during the *mi ʿrāj*, to which she replied:

My hair stands on end because of what you have said. Have you no idea of three things? – whoever tells them to you is lying. [First,] whoever tells you that Muḥammad saw his Lord, is lying. She then recited, 'Vision comprehends Him not, but He comprehends all vision' (Q6:103).[57]

Trying to encapsulate all these opinions, it is said:

On the whole, the scholars' interpretations of the Prophet's vision show that whether it took place in his dream or in a wakeful state, 'with the eyes of the heart' or 'with the eyes of the head', does not change the fact that he saw Him in the real sense, as the Prophet's dream-vision or heart-vision is by far sharper, more accurate, and more real than the visions of ordinary people.[58]

No-one can imagine how close the Prophet was to the one he saw in the phrase 'a distance of two bows length or nearer', but for the mystics the story reveals the Prophet's superior psychological strength in that he did not faint but saw what he saw and stayed in the divine presence in full consciousness. The great ʿAbd al Qādir al-Jīlānī writes that when Gibrīl accompanied the Prophet on this night, he could not go any further than the seventh heaven because he would be burnt to ashes.[59]

The *miʿrāj* also illustrates a particular distinction between the prophetic and the mystical journey explained so memorably in the fifth chapter of Iqbal's seminal work *The Reconstruction of Religious Thought in Islam*, where the Ṣūfi Abdul Quddus sighs longingly for what Muḥammad experienced. Muḥammad's return to earth is a sign of prophetic sobriety and responsibility, an obligation to fulfil God's commands here on earth. This contrasts with the words of those great Ṣūfis where one detects a restless desire to do away with that which separates humankind from God in this life. Nowhere has this been expressed more hauntingly than in the words of the great Muslim saint Abdul Quddus of Gangoh:

Muhammad of Arabia ascended the highest Heaven and returned.
I swear by God that if I had reached that point, I should never have returned.

Basing his desire to be with God on the narrative of Muḥammad's ascension to heaven, this Ṣūfi saint questions the Prophet's return. The mystic longs for that vision which the Prophet has already experienced. The prophetic role is always guided by God towards the

157

community and he has no alternative but to return to earth and his mission amongst his people. That is God's prophetic paradigm. The mystic has no such commitment, for his focus and goal is God alone. The Prophet has returned, whereas the mystic would find any other experience now meaningless.[60]

The story is important for Muslims not only because it weaves together history, theology and mystical biography, but because of its narrative on worship. It informs the Muslim about the number of obligatory ritual prayers and importance of Muḥammad's intercessory role. For many of the Muslim commentators on the ascension of the Prophet, the role of intercessor was especially associated with his role on the day of resurrection. Muḥammad was seen as the 'master of intercession'. But as McMichael writes, the belief that Muḥammad has the role of intercession on the day of resurrection was completely rejected by medieval Christians, for whom Jesus Christ will have this role. Christ, who has already been raised at his resurrection after three days in the tomb, 'now sits on the very Throne of God so that he might lead human beings to him through their own resurrection by virtue of the power of his resurrection. Christ is there to intercede for all human beings who hope in the resurrection, where he also draws the hearts of all to himself.'[61]

Most importantly the story presents vivid images of the pleasures of heaven and the pains of hell as a warning. As Rustomji writes, 'Seeing, visiting and dreaming of the afterworld became ways that Muhammad was able to provide a preview of the world to come. Part of the preview also acted as an affirmation for believers.'[62] The *mi'rāj* story captured the imagination of writers, poets, mystics, and ordinary Muslims. All kinds of fantastic and grandiose images as well as rhetorical devices were used to portray this mysterious event. Annemarie Schimmel elaborates further that this brief allusion to the *mi'rāj* in the Qur'an was enlarged but also 'lovingly embellished'. During the fifteenth and sixteenth centuries, Persian painters represented this event in glorious detail, with nearly all later Persian and Turkish epics containing a poetical description of the *mi'rāj*. Schimmel makes reference to Farīd al-Dīn 'Aṭṭār's Persian epic *Manṭiq uṭ-ṭayr*, *The Conference of the Birds*: 'There are two journeys, one to God and one in God, for God is infinite and eternal. And how could there be an end for the journey of the soul that has reached His presence?'[63] As an example of a Ṣūfī poem illustrating the sequence of events in this mystical prophetology, she cites 'Attar:

At night came Gabriel, and filled with joy
He called, 'Wake up, you leader of the world!
Get up, leave this dark place and travel now
To the eternal kingdom of the Lord!
Direct your foot to "Where there is no place"
And knock there at the sanctuary's door.
The world is all excited for your sake,
The cherubs are tonight your lowly slaves,
And messengers and prophets stand in rows
To see your beauty in this blessed night.
The gates of Paradise and skies are open –
To look at you, fills many hearts with joy!
You ask from Him tonight what you intend,
For without doubt you will behold the Lord![64]

The *mi'rāj* is an example of a particular host–guest relationship. God is waiting for Muḥammad to ascend to the heavens, and while there is a range of views on the nature of the beatific vision, Muḥammad was an invited guest; there was a time to be present and a time to leave. Heaven itself is a final culmination, but its glimpses during earthly life are just that – glimpses, even for the Prophet himself.

The story also attracted attention from non-Muslims who were keen to demonstrate its inconsistencies and superfluous nature. In his analysis of the *mi'rāj* as a focus of medieval Christian polemics against Islam, McMichael concludes that Christians recognized no moral dimension to the Muslim narrative, but rather saw in this fictitious tale the differences between the respective views of paradise. They were also afraid lest other Christians would be seduced by the Muslim depiction of heaven:

> Even though Christian writers themselves were also 'intertwining' theology and history, mystical insight and biography in their own Christian spiritual reflection and works, it is certainly the case that Christian authors did not at all appreciate the way in which Muslims engaged the linking of these elements in their telling of the *mi'rāj* narrative. In order to protect their own theological truths about God, Christ, and eternal life, medieval Christians believed they had to debunk this tale because heaven itself depended on it.[65]

The *mi'rāj* narrative provides images of heavenly splendour and God's call, but true devotion to God for some involved neither fear

160

of hell nor desire for heaven. Perhaps the most famous example of love of God alone is contained in the words of the saint and teacher of mystical love, Rābiʿa al-Adawīyya:

> O God, if I worship thee for fear of hell, burn me in hell, and if I worship thee in hope of Paradise, exclude me from Paradise; but if I worship thee for thy own sake, grudge me not thy everlasting beauty.[66]

In whatever way the mystic imagines nearness to God, there is here a desire for total dependence, 'of the nothingness of my being until completed by him'.[67]

The biblical image of God as a host is analogous to that of the human host in that God welcomes us as his guests. If human hosts offered their guests lodging, food and protection in the ancient world, God's actions are seen as similar with references to the provision of food. Scattered in numerous biblical passages are references to food and water as God's provision on this earth, as well as what awaits us at the divine banquet. God is not always portrayed in the language of the host, but as a provider. In Exodus the people of Israel are dependent on God for survival and complain against Moses numerous times for bringing them out of Egypt to such destitution. In their cry for water and food, 'bread is rained from heavens' (16:4), 'quails cover the camp' (16:13), they are given manna, which was like 'coriander seed, white, and the taste of it was like wafers made with honey' (16:30–32), and in Exodus 17:1–7, they cry out for water and are given sweet water from a rock. Psalm 105:39–41 tells us that God 'spread a cloud for a covering, and fire to give light by night. They asked, and he brought quails, and gave them food from heaven in abundance. He opened the rock, and water gushed out; it flowed through the desert like a river.' Over twenty-five times, reference is made to the promised land of milk and honey for Israel, 'But I have said to you: You shall inherit their land, and I will give it to you to possess, a land flowing with milk and honey. I am the Lord your God; I have separated you from the peoples' (Lev 20:24). Isaiah's enigmatic prophecy about the Messiah is of a young woman who will bear a son and 'he shall eat curds and honey by the time he knows how to refuse the evil and choose the good' (Isaiah 7:15). We read of God's own promise of the eschatological banquet on Mount Zion, 'On this mountain the Lord Almighty will prepare a feast of rich food for all peoples, a banquet of aged wine, the best of meats and the finest of wines' (Isaiah 25:6). In Psalm 23, God is again the protector shepherd with his rod and staff as comfort who 'prepare a table before me in the presence of my enemies'. And there is God's own free and generous invitation to 'everyone who thirsts, come to the waters; and you that have no money, come, buy and eat! Come, buy wine and milk without money and without price' (Isaiah 55:1–2).

In the Gospels, Jesus is not just eating, but performing miracles, and some of his most famous miracles involve food. There is the story of the large number of fish caught at the lake of Gennesaret (Luke 5:1–11), the six stone water jars which were turned into wine to keep the festivities going at the wedding in Cana (John 2:1–11), and feeding five thousand men alone with five loaves and two fish which he first blessed (Matthew 14; Matthew 15; Mark 6; Luke 9). These events convey the sense of joy in feasting and sharing food with others, and most significantly, they give a foretaste of the world

162

to come. Meals figure prominently in his parables in order to bring people together, but they often also show how the expected hierarchies were turned upside down, such as the banquet to which all the poor, the crippled and the blind were invited (Matthew 22:1–14; and Luke 14:15–24). Those who were too preoccupied and declined the invitation, declined the feast of salvation and eternal happiness in the kingdom of God. Jesus offers God's hospitality to the world. As John Navone says, 'Jesus is God's eschatological envoy extending God's invitation of heavenly hospitality to Israel and the nations. In contrast to the Pharisees, who seek to restrict the hospitality of God to the righteous, Jesus becomes notorious for a practice of open hospitality that brought him the label "a glutton and a drunkard, a friend of tax collectors and sinners"' (Matthew 11:19; Luke 7:34).[68] Thus, the biblical verses on hospitality and food are not simply about what Jesus eats or feeds to others, but what is more important is the question of how and with whom Jesus ate. As a Jew, Jesus would have observed *kosher* rules, but he transcended the dietary restrictions that separated people from one another within the Jewish sects, and as Laura Hartman writes, his 'controversial practices of eating with tax collectors and sinners and drinking with the Samaritan woman directly challenged society's food practices (Matthew 9:10–11; Mark 2:15–16; and Luke 5:30)'.[69] Jesus' ministry thus subverts accepted structures for behaviour and this may be best encapsulated in his commandment to love our enemies:

> You have heard that it was said, 'You shall love your neighbour and hate your enemy.' But I say to you, Love your enemies and pray for those who persecute you, so that you may be children of

your Father in heaven; for he makes his sun rise on the evil and on the good, and sends rain on the righteous and on the unrighteous. For if you love those who love you, what reward do you have? Do not even the tax collectors do the same? And if you greet only your brothers and sisters, what more are you doing than others? Do not even the Gentiles do the same? Be perfect, therefore, as your heavenly Father is perfect (Matthew 5:43–48).

True welcome and hospitality is not about doing our duty; it always demands a magnanimity which stretches our minds and souls towards ever greater generosity. Only when we can give far more than we receive do we emulate God's giving.

Food is so fundamental to hospitality that it is hardly surprising that scriptures associate banquets with divine hospitality. The association of banquets with salvation sees Jesus' role in the heavenly banquet as the Messiah who would inaugurate eschatological happiness with the poor and the afflicted; they are his banquet community. Luke's gospel portrays the life and ministry of Jesus as a divine visitation to the world, seeking hospitality. The one who comes as guest 'becomes host and offers God's hospitality so that the whole world can know salvation in the depths of their hearts'. Navone describes the banquet as an 'eschatological community-concept' expressing Jesus' mission of restoring communion between God and human beings. At the eschatological consummation the disciples will eat and drink with Jesus in the kingdom of God, 'I confer on you, just as my Father has conferred on me, a kingdom, so that you may eat and drink at my table in my kingdom' (Luke 22:29–30). Jesus serves as servant and as host. The host language comes to the fore in Mark: Jesus as 'the Son of Man came not to be served but to serve, and to give his life a ransom for many (Mark 10:45).'[70]

It is therefore not surprising that it is a communal meal, the Pesach shared by Jesus and his disciples which formed the basis for celebrating the Eucharist, the heart of the church's worship, when believers recall or repeat the words Jesus spoke at the Last Supper:

> While they were eating, Jesus took a loaf of bread, and after blessing it he broke it, gave it to the disciples, and said, 'Take, eat; this is my body.' Then he took a cup, and after giving thanks he gave it to them, saying, 'Drink from it, all of you; for this is my blood of the covenant, which is poured out for many for the forgiveness of sins. I tell you, I will never again drink of this fruit of the vine until that day when I drink it new with you in my Father's kingdom (Matthew 26:26–29).

Eating is the most common thing we all do as human beings. Jesus is the host at this banquet, the host who offers his blood for all humankind. In the first two centuries C.E., this holy meal of bread and wine, representing the body and blood of Christ, was the central act of the liturgy. When Jesus takes the bread, he blesses it and gives thanks for it. But this act intensifies the general sacramentality of the world, for embedded in this hallowing of the mundane staples of a meal 'is an echo of the creational affirmation of the stuff of the earth'.[71] As Adamson writes, 'Eating Christ's body and blood in the form of bread and wine, the products of culture, rather than grain and grape, the products of nature, was designed to create community among the faithful.'[72] The practice of the Eucharist sanctifies eating and human consumption is oriented eschatologically, reminding Christians that their food both embodies something holy and points beyond itself to a reality at the edge of human understanding.[73]

The Last Supper is not really the *last* supper, but the penultimate supper, for Jesus will eat and drink again as when he says, 'I tell you, I will never again drink of this fruit of the vine until that day when I drink it new with you in my Father's kingdom' (Matthew 26:29). The meal is a foretaste of a celestial banquet, and week upon week it serves as an anticipatory meal, reminding Christians that the kingdom and its feast have not yet fully arrived. It has been interpreted wittily as a 'sanctified letdown', because every week that the Eucharist is celebrated, is another week reminding worshippers that the 'kingdom and its feast have not yet fully arrived'.[74]

The Eucharist has been imbued with so many meanings as it lies at the very heart of Christian liturgy. It is in the Eucharist that the death and resurrection of Jesus is remembered and celebrated. As Elizabeth Newman writes, 'the cruciform life of hospitality' is what is prefigured and performed at the celebration of the Lord's Supper. Taken seriously, this can be quite frightening, for who wants to suffer? But this is not suffering for the sake of suffering, rather it is about suffering for the right things and thus living out the death and resurrection of Christ.[75] Some have focused on the Eucharist's power of renewal, where it is the 'supreme ritual expression of brokenness and death, of homelessness and landlessness. It consecrates all the good things of the earth and it promises renewal and rebirth not only for the individual, but for society and the cosmos. And yet it makes us restless on this earth: it makes us see the conditional, and provisional, and broken quality of all human beings.'[76] David Ford speaks of Jesus as welcoming a community that ultimately abandoned him. Even though the community lacks trust and understanding, it is Jesus who does the 'trusting, obeying, suffering and dying. This lack of presumption that they have to do anything right to be the recipients of the bread and wine makes it an Archimedean point of receptivity – and therefore, of potential gratitude.'[77]

Meals require that we share and make space for others, especially those who are the poor and marginalized in society, and vulnerable to humiliation. This is what Paul admonishes in those who come together to eat and forget the poor, for this does not reflect the Lord's Supper, 'For when the time comes to eat, each of you goes ahead with your own supper, and one goes hungry and another becomes drunk. What! Do you not have homes to eat and drink in? Or do you show contempt for the church of God and humiliate those who have nothing?' (I Corinthians 11:21–22).

Yet, at the same time as the theme of the banquet table where God serves as generous host remains one of the most pervasive images of salvation in scripture, Amy Pauw states that 'the scandal is that the guest list for the eschatological banquet appears selective. With unnerving regularity the yes of God's hospitality to some is paired with the no of exclusion to others.' She cites several biblical verses to show how God's redemptive hospitality towards human creatures is often depicted as partial and particular, and that theologians have done away with these depictions. For example, in the parable of the wedding feast in Matthew, a man enters the wedding feast without authorization and is ordered to be thrown out, 'to be bound hand and foot and thrown out of the banquet hall, into the outer darkness where there is weeping and gnashing of teeth' (Matthew 22:13–14). The wedding feast has been interpreted as heaven, while the 'outer darkness' refers to hell or eternal punishment. Darkness can refer to moral depravity or to death and nothingness (Job3:4–6). The 'weeping and gnashing of teeth' refers to both physical and spiritual pain, the lot of those who reject Jesus as in 'Whoever believes in the Son has eternal life; whoever disobeys the Son will not see life, but must endure God's wrath' (John 3:36). Mary sings in praise of God, 'His mercy is for those who fear him, from generation to generation. He has shown strength with his arm; he has scattered the proud in the thoughts of their hearts. He has brought down the powerful from their thrones, and lifted up the lowly; he has filled the hungry with good things, and sent the rich away empty' (Luke 1:50–53). There are those who will receive his hospitality and those who will be denied. And in Revelation, we are given one of most vivid images of divine judgment with its horrifying caricature of the 'marriage supper of the Lamb' (Rev 19:9). Thus, 'With a loud voice he [an angel] called to all the birds that fly in mid heaven, "Come, gather for the great supper of God, to eat the flesh of kings, the flesh of captains, the flesh of the mighty, the flesh of horses and their riders – flesh of all, both free and slave, both small and great . . . and all the birds were gorged with their flesh.' For Pauw, 'the refusal of table fellowship is one of the most haunting images of divine judgment in Scripture, with damnation often depicted in terms of God's ultimate inhospitality'. While decrying the fact that much of Christian eschatology is testimony to the dangers of cutting scriptural images of divine judgment and damnation loose from their moorings in communal practices, Pauw adds that these passages 'about God's ultimate inhospitality to some people function less as a reliable guide to future eschatological events than as a warning or encouragement to a particular community in its practices of hospitality'.[78]

Conversely, in his critique of the American Episcopal Church's practice of admitting those who are not baptized to Holy Communion, Communion without Baptism or CWOB, Michael Tuck explores how Communion without Baptism is a major shift in the Church's historic practice and a profound change to the underpinning sacramental theologies of Baptism and the Eucharist. His critique probes what exactly is being offered to those who are unbaptized in the Eucharist other than a fellowship of the table. While appreciating that CWOB reflects a movement within the church towards more diversity and inclusion in American culture, the 'overemphasis on the narrative of radical hospitality and inclusion present in the practice of CWOB and the "table to font" orientation produces an imbalanced sacramental system that risks limiting the power of both the Eucharist and Baptism to speak to and support the Church today.' For Tuck, the problem with CWOB is that while God's grace is affirmed in this practice, the practice does not reflect the Passion, Crucifixion, Resurrection and Ascension of Christ. Consequently the way grace acts in repentance, redemption, justification and glorification is not explored.[79]

On a different note, Nicholas Collura explores the theme of fragmentation and wholeness in the Eucharist when Jesus knows that he had already commended his spirit to God and 'all that was left was a backward look at the flesh'. He writes that 'The Last Supper isn't characterized by visible or physical abundance, as are the multiplications of loaves and fish, but by a running dry.' When Jesus says he will neither eat the bread nor drink of the fruit of the vine until the kingdom of God comes (Luke 22:16–18), 'the connection between the Last Supper and the eschatological banquet is momentarily severed by the intervening violence. "Fulfilment" is long postponed; even today, we are still waiting for it.'[80]

The complex theology of the Last Supper had an impact on its visual depiction. Michel Jeanneret states that while this was a favourite subject up till the fifteenth century and the baroque period, it is rarely represented in the Renaissance period. The main reason behind this was the contentious question of the real presence raising problems that 'are too complex and explosive to inspire anything but erudite commentaries, spiritual meditations or pamphlets'. Fiction remains cautious because theologians protect their territory and 'one cannot rewrite the Marriage at Cana with the same freedom one can a Horatian ode'.[81]

Christians meet Christ himself at the communion table because table fellowship is about anticipating the eschatological consummation. It is the fulfilment of Jesus' messianic mission of reconciling sinner with God. Here, there is once again no room for despair, but space for repentance as Jesus is present. Banquets have always been about more than eating and offering food and drink to guests. In the banquet episodes of the bible, 'Jesus is more than a mere dinner guest; rather, he is the divine host who offers the hospitality of God to the world.'[82] The Eucharist is above all redeemed eating. It is about the remembrance of others, about gratitude for the gift of life, reconciliation and Christ's sacrifice. Eucharist means 'thanksgiving', and by receiving bread and wine, Christians acknowledge that we live only by receiving from God. As John Chrysostom wrote of the Mystical Table, Christians must understand that the mysteries of the Eucharist 'are spent inside the body together with its essence', and that they do not take of the Divine body from a man, rather from the 'very Seraphim with the fiery spoon that Isaiah saw' and that in taking the Saving Blood, the lips 'touch the very Divine and Immaculate Side'.[83]

Heavenly images of divine hospitality and divine expectation are varied in both Christianity and Islam, but they all point to a God eager to welcome us in judgement and forgiveness. God's judgement in the afterlife remains unknown to us here on earth, but something of his forgiveness and mercy has been made known to us through scripture, devotion and human longing. If there is one request God makes of humankind, it is that we should remember him in all we do. When Moses asked God 'Which of your creatures is most just?' the reply was 'the one who judges himself as he judges others'. When Moses asked, 'Which of them is most sinful?' the reply was 'the one who suspects me of wrong'. God answered that he sits with the one who invokes him. When Moses lamented that he was often in too lowly a state, through forgetfulness or ritual impurity, to call out to God, the reply was, 'remember me in every state'.[84]

In such glimpses of what lies before us, we anticipate the heavenly welcome through our senses. Material and spiritual hospitality await us, and images of meals and opulent dining are intrinsic in appealing to our earthly senses, yet conveying something wholly beyond our imagination. The semiotics of food are everywhere in scripture and food is laden with theological meaning, perhaps more so in the Bible than the Qur'ān. God is never far from food, both the earthly and the heavenly, and the symbolism of food draws us to him. In the end, whether it be prophet, mystic, saint or ordinary believer, it is not God's promises, evoked in both sensual and spiritual terms, as much as the promise of God which is the ultimate heavenly reward.

CHAPTER 4

Men, Women and Relationships
of Hospitality

In his famous *Letters to a Young Poet*, Rainer Maria Rilke wrote that 'the great renewal of the world will perhaps consist in man and woman, freed of all sense of error and disappointment, seeking one another out not as opposites but as brothers and sisters and neighbours, and they will join together as human beings, to share the heavy weight of sexuality that is laid upon them with simplicity, gravity and patience'.[1] For Rilke, men and women are more related, share more than we think. But when we think of men and women, we also think of intimacy and the joys and sadness of sex and love. Contrast Rilke's hope with Christopher Lasch's lament that as the mystery of sex has gone, the yearning for meaningful relationships has increased. Sex has become loaded with too many expectations for human fulfilment, beyond its capacity to deliver. Sex valued purely for its own sake loses all reference to the future, bringing no hope of permanent relationships:

The demystification of womanhood goes hand in hand with the desublimation of sexuality.... Institutionalised sexual segregation has given way to arrangements that promote the intermingling of the sexes at every stage of life. Efficient contraceptives, legalised abortion, and a 'realistic' and 'healthy' acceptance of the body have weakened the links that once tied sex to love, marriage, and procreation. Men and women now pursue sexual pleasure as an end in itself, unmediated even by the conventional trappings of romance.[2]

Both writers are speaking of men and women being, in a certain way, their hopes, their anxieties and their longings in and out of relationships. But the history of philosophical and theological debate on gender has, until recently, been more occupied with otherness, objectification and the absence of just relations. Yet love has been present in the marital and sexual relationship, despite these concerns and the struggles for rights and recognition. Masculinity has been preserved and so has femininity, even though we see that both continue to be contested as expressions of male and female. Our longing for fulfilment in one another has been a lesser concern than the female longing and determination for self-autonomy; this autonomy can have difficult scriptural histories, but is regarded by many as the real objective of the divine moral and social order. The Muslim world shares some of its concerns with western feminists and this is reflected in much of the feminist literature which has appeared over the last few decades. But it also has some distinct struggles which are not expressed in theory and philosophy, but through the lived realities of women who fear being silenced for threatening to usurp the male-dominated order of many Muslim societies. In 2001, Fatema Mernissi

174

predicted that in the decades to come women would provoke more violent debate as globalization forced Muslim states to redefine themselves and create new cultural identities rooted more in economics than religion. She wrote:

The fear of the feminine represents the fear form within; the debate about globalization, the threat from without; and both discourses will necessarily be focused on women. Femininity is the emotional locus of all kinds of disruptive forces, in both the real world and in fantasy.[3]

The cultural struggles about rights between men and women is real and manifests itself with some difference, but also alarming similarities, all over the world. It shows itself in societal perceptions and struggles, and the way the quest for freedom and justice must engage the commitment of both men and women, those marginalized and those in power.

In this chapter, however, I will explore the theoretical frameworks which have challenged prevailing power dynamics through scriptural exegesis and which continue to stretch our imagination about possibilities for more hospitable relationships between the sexes. If hospitality is a structure that regulates relations between inside and outside, between private and public, between God and humanity, it also speaks to the sexual divide between male and female. This divide is what creates both distinction and need, both physical and emotional. If the Qur'ānic discourse on right belief emphasizes the emerging gulf between the believer/believing community and God, the second divide, which is between men and women, is expressed in the language of limits and intimacies. These are set against the over-arching narratives of justice (*'adl*) and mercy (*raḥma*), the two defining attributes of God which repeatedly emerge as the basis for our moral thinking towards one another. Righteousness knows no gender boundaries in the Qur'ān, as it says, 'As for those who lead a righteous life, male or female, while believing, they enter Paradise; without the slightest injustice' (Q4:124). In so doing, the various themes in the Qur'ān appear far less concerned in defining men and women in terms of the socially constructed gender traits of mascu-linity and femininity or binary expressions of sexual differences; in fact the Qur'ān seldom speaks of women as a collective. It is a text far more concerned with the moral dimensions of people's relationships to each other as well as to God. Here, gender and sexuality are present, but in relational forms, always partners in some way, as husband and wife, mother and father, and to some extent, master and slave. It is these relationships which fuse society and which form the audience of the Qur'ān. Men and women are physically and emotion-ally connected to one another in all kinds of ways, and language, sex and sexuality are essential to this connection. As the Qur'ān says, 'O Mankind, keep your duty to your Lord who created you from a single soul and from it created its mate and spread from these many men and women' (Q4:1).

The primal couple, Adam and Eve, begin their lives in paradise amidst the new physical creation, but their relational, spiritual and moral lives are fulfilled only on earth. In the *Tales of the Prophets*, there is a rather beautiful story of the creation of Eve (Ḥawwā), whom God first calls his own 'handmaiden' but whom he gifts to Adam at Adam's request as long as Adam will 'take her in trust and persevere in thanks for her'. Adam has seen Eve in a dream where she is kind to him and she requests that Adam ask God for her hand in marriage. On waking from his dream, Adam asks God for whom God has created Eve. God's reply is, 'This is my handmaiden and you are my servant. O Adam, I have not created anyone nobler in my sight than you two, for you have obeyed me and worshipped me. I have created for you an abode and called it Paradise.' The conversation continues with God's creation of Eve as a companion to Adam, so that Adam is not alone in Paradise. Adam asks God to marry Eve to him and the reply is, 'I will marry you to her on one condition; that you teach her the precepts of my religion and be thankful to me for her.' And Adam accepted.[4]

On one level this conversation serves as a poignant reminder of God's welcoming of Adam as the first of his human creation, the gift of Ḥawwā as a companion and the relationship of their 'marriage' as a blessing to them and to all mankind. In Ibn Kathīr, Ḥawwā is created from a male Adam and thus womankind desires and needs man, while man is created from the soil of the earth and thus he finds blessings in earth itself.[5] We find here a particular understanding of woman and her creation in relationship to the first man and first prophet. However, this reading of the creation story, while fairly popular and dominant in Islamic piety, has been challenged in recent years by various intratextual feminist readings which have dismissed this understanding as non-Qur'ānic and therefore contrary to the Qur'ānic egalitarian vision between man and woman. In assessing Q4:1, Riffat Hassan argues that the word soul in 'from a single soul' is conceptually neither male nor female, even though grammatically it is feminine. There is no linguistic justification to attribute maleness to soul and therefore for assuming that this original soul is that of Adam. Hassan points out that the word Adam in the Qur'ān 'functions generally as a collective noun referring to the human rather than to a male human being'. Furthermore, she states that the Qur'ān does not say that Adam was the first human being, nor that he was a man. The term 'Adam' is a masculine noun, but linguistic gender is not sex. If 'Adam' is not necessarily a man, then 'Adam's zauj' is not necessarily a woman. Her linguistic analysis of the term zauj in the Qur'ān, primarily meaning 'mate', leads her to conclude that the reason why the Qur'ān leaves the terms 'Adam' and zauj deliberately unclear, not only as regards sex but also as regards number, is because 'its purpose is not to narrate certain events in the life of a man and a woman (i.e., the Adam and Eve of popular imagination), but to refer to some life experiences of all human beings, men and women together'. As Muhammad Iqbal mentioned in his seminal lectures, *The Reconstruction of Religious Thought in Islam*, the Qur'ān uses other words such as *bashar* and *al-insān* to talk of human beings, and the word Adam is used and retained 'more as a concept than as the name of a concrete human individual'.[6] Hassan points out that 'Adam' is used more selectively to refer to human beings only when they 'become representative of the self-conscious, knowledgeable, and morally autonomous humanity'.[7]

Amina Wadud also states that *nafs* is conceptually neither masculine nor feminine. She adds that in the Qur'ānic account of creation, the origins of the human race do not begin with Adam, the man, and concludes rather dramatically, 'this omission is important because the Qur'ānic version of the creation of humankind is not expressed in gender terms'.[8] For Ibn 'Arabī, the relationship between Adam

178

and Eve was governed by a mutual and perpetual attraction to unite, because both are reflections of the One Creator. Eve is the hidden aspect of Adam through which he knows himself, while Adam is the outward aspect of the Absolute through which the Absolute knows itself. As Lutfi writes, 'For Adam to know his Lord it is essential that he knows himself first, and it is through Eve that he knows himself and therefore his Lord.'[9] Thus, it is through the feminine element by which Adam knows God; the female is part of the male whole, an inward aspect without whom the male cannot fulfil his search for perfection.

Despite this alternative view of Adam and Eve, it would be reasonable to say that Islamic thought for the most part has not burdened the story of the primal couple with as many complex readings as Christian theology. Adam's slip and expulsion from paradise may well be the turning point in human destiny, but Adam's disobedience which leads to mutual sexual awareness is forgiven because Adam becomes immediately aware of what he has done and repents. Repentance stops any further consequences and life resumes, albeit changed; marriage finds its place in fulfilment and regulation of this unleashed sexual desire. There is an absence of struggle in the history of Christian thought as to whether it was lust or disobedience which precipitated the Fall. One act of eating holds both life and death. While Augustine's mythologizing of original sin arose after and amidst other visions of greater humanity, especially in Eastern Christianity, it posed a searing charge:

It presented an unrelenting; its fatality created sexual self-consciousness, inhibition, and guilt; its seeding of wilfulness deeply and inescapably within us has led to religious repression and even the use of holy force cruel Deity; it has led a heavy repressing hand on almost two millennia of Christian thought and practice.[10]

Tina Beattie assesses the role of dialogue in Genesis in that before the Fall, language functions as a 'medium of creation, command, naming and celebration: creation in so far as God's word creates the world; command in God's instructions to Adam; naming in Adam's naming of the animals; and celebration in Adam's recognition of Eve.' However, in the Fall, language becomes instead the medium of 'debate, objectification and blame'.[11] Thus we have no access to a state of bliss or innocence which has not been filtered through the linguistic values of the social order, associated with repression and concealment. For some writers, the Fall of man should be called the 'fall of woman because once more the second sex is blamed for all the trouble in the world'.[12] It is this myth which gave rise to male hatred of women, but also self-hatred inward on the part of women. The myth of feminine evil has dominated human consciousness and provides the context for women's victimization by both men and women.[13]

While the above analysis of both Hassan and Wadud serves as an example of a rereading of the creation story, feminist interpreters of the Qur'ān reflect a larger paradigm of feminist scholarship which wrestles with various exegetical hurdles. Aysha Hidyatullah gives an account of how contemporary feminist exegetes are more concerned with advocating a more holistic treatment of the Qur'ān and a dynamic open-enededness of interpretation, and she summarizes,

'They have argued that the Qur'an should be understood as a text revealed in the terms of its immediate seventh-century Arabian audience but also as a universally meaningful text for all its audiences. They have prioritized the Qur'an's general principles over its particular statements. ... they have also resisted sexist and violent meanings of the Qur'an by insisting that its verses must be read in line with the Qur'an's larger message of justice, harmony and equality, as well as the principles of God's unity and oneness.'[14] It is worth emphasizing that the struggle for recognition, justice and respect as well as that most elusive ideal, equality, is a modern discourse, and the classical traditions of most religions including Islam, while trying to give and protect certain rights for women, were not unduly concerned with rights and equalities in the way we are concerned with these issues today. This poses a problem for feminist readings of the past which often appear methodologically anachronistic. In discussing the past in terms of contemporary points of reference such as gender equality or patriarchy, we may be limited in what we can recover from the past in terms of 'marginalized liberatory gender models' to create new visions and models for gender equality and a fairer humanity. But the value of doing feminist analysis of the 'usable past', as Rita Gross puts it, is to see that the assessment of history as androcentric in its thought-forms and patriarchal in its institutions is an *analysis,* an *accurate description,* not an *accusation.*[15]

Against this background there has been some criticism of the feminist exegetical enterprise and the whole hermeneutical exercise. For Nasr Abu Zayd, Muslims had to be freed from the need 'to recontextualize one or more passages in the fight against literalism and fundamentalism or against a specific historical practice that seems inappropriate for our modern contexts'.[16] He argues:

> Feminist hermeneutics faces the problem that as long as the Qur'an is dealt with only as a text – implying a concept of author (i.e., God as divine author) – one is forced to find a focal point of gravity to which all variations should be linked. This automatically implies that the Qur'an is at the mercy of the ideology of its interpreter. For a communist, the Qur'an would thus reveal communism, for a fundamentalist it would be a highly fundamentalist text, for a feminist it would be a feminist text, and so on.[17]

In the same vein, Raja Rhouni critiques the project of retrieval, of uncovering gender equality as a norm by Muslim feminists. Rhouni's concern is that as long as the Qur'ān is seen as the repository of truths, from which an egalitarian Islam can always be retrieved, feminist exegesis will continue to explain away difficult verses on the basis of historical contingency, while others of a more progressive nature will be accepted as part of the Qur'ānic egalitarian world view. She writes, 'I do not agree with the methodology that chooses to give a more progressive, or egalitarian, meaning to a verse and presenting it as the truth, when it has the means to do so, while resorting to the idea that such and such verse needs to be contextualized in order to discover its contingency, when it reaches a semantic dead-end.'[18]

In her analysis of such criticisms, Asma Barlas repudiates the patriarchal imaginary idea of God as father and argues against patriarchy as divinely sanctioned:

Naturally, I am hyper-aware of the few words and lines in the text that speak to male authority but I view these as reflecting the fact that the Qur'an's first audience was a 7th century tribal Arab patriarchy in which men did exercise certain types of authority. For the Qur'an to have dealt with this reality is not to say that it therefore advocates 'patriarchal norms, since that was the historical condition in which [it] was revealed'. Dealing with a historical contingency is not the same as upholding it as a norm.[19]

She asks the question:

Why would a God who is above sex/gender and who promises not to transgress against the rights of others, as the Qur'an teaches, fall prey to shoddy sexual partisanship or hatred by privi-leging men over women or advocating the oppression of women? Indeed, not only does the Qur'an not oppress women, but it also affirms that women and men originated in the same self, have the same capacity for moral choice and personality and, as God's vice-regents on earth, have a mutual duty to enjoin the right and forbid the wrong. This is the second reason I read the text on behalf of women's rights, because of its ontic view of sexual equality.[20]

Aside from scriptural hermeneutics, a growing body of literature demonstrates that archival research into the lived lives of ordinary Muslim women often reveals a varied balance of power and public visibility. There is often a disconnect between legal texts which imagine women as victims rather than active participants who are socially and legally aware, able to make their own decisions and challenge the prevailing injustice. In her work with pre-modern court records, Amira Sonbol shows that Muslim women were often in a better position to negotiate their rights through a flexible form of Islamic jurisprudence rather than the codified form of secular law.[21] This kind of debate resonates across feminist theologies where different methodologies as well as world views have increasingly entrenched positions amongst women, activists and scholars alike. The debate does not nuance the meanings of oppression, but as Keddie observes:

> One group denies that Muslim women . . . are any more oppressed than non-Muslim women or argue that in key respects they have been less oppressed. A second says that oppression is real but extrinsic to Islam; the Qur'an, they say, intended gender equality, but this was undermined by Arabian patriarchy and foreign importations. An opposing group blames Islam for being irrevocably gender inegalitarian. There are those who adopt intermediate positions, as well as those who tend to avoid these controversies by sticking to monographic or limited studies that do not confront such issues. Some scholars favour shifting emphasis away from Islam to economic and social forces.[22]

Irrespective of how this debate plays out, the central question is how men and women can accept each other as possessing the fulness of human potential, including where women are neither denied access to shaping the intellectual and practical aspects of their religious tradition, nor silenced because of their sex.

In much of modern Islamic feminist exegesis, there is the recognition that the Qur'ān itself, like most scriptures, does not speak of male–female relations according to contemporary aspirations and paradigms of rights and equality, but it does speak of mutual recognition in various forms. One example is that of marriage as a relationship in which husband and wife are like 'garments for each other'. The implication here is one of mutual dignity and also of protection, where each is responsible to the other. Garments cover, beautify and signify closeness to flesh. They can both reveal and conceal, hide and allure, and sexuality is always present in this image. But in a religion where clothing has for many retained a central place in defining the ideal image of Muslim piety and modesty, the concept of husband and wife being garments for each other is a potent and demanding depiction of complementarity.

It is worth mentioning here that clothing itself has been a contested issue in understanding male patriarchy and female autonomy. Fatima Mernissi makes a witty comment in taking up the debate of how attitudes to clothing reflect both the western man and the Muslim man's appreciation or degradation of a woman's beauty and what she wears. In relation to how men in different cultures understand a woman's intelligence and beauty, Mernissi takes the iconic figure of Scheherazade from the classic *A Thousand and One Nights* in another one of her famous works, *Scheherazade Goes West*. Mernissi's argument is that it is patriarchal control which determines how beauty is imagined and preserved. In a conversation with her friend Jacques who is showing her the museums and art galleries of Paris and who insists that the women in his harem must be 'nude and silent', she replies:

Muslim men seem to get a virile power from veiling women and harassing them in the streets if they aren't 'covered' properly, while Western men like yourself seem to derive a tremendous pleasure from unveiling them.[23]

Clothing in the Qur'ān is a metaphor for human fulfilment in one another. This is not about a gendered hierarchy, but points to the cultivation of an attitude of recognition and embrace. The Qur'ān rarely speaks of human emotions, but when it does, for the most part it does not do so in any abstract or philosophical sense, but in the framework of mutual relationships, whether they are familial, marital or commercial. Even in worship, obligatory or voluntary, the Qur'ān speaks less of individual worship, but for the most part conveys its message to people in relational settings. There is an intrinsic good in cultivating human relations. Human relations mentioned in the Qur'ān contain a moral and often quasi-legal dimension which involves a continuous weighing up of rights and responsibilities with all that is around us. These relationships structure our lives, give depth to our existence and demand that we observe our commitments as part of a God-centred and well-lived life. Here, the language is of recognition, mutuality and compassion, and thereby hospitality is present. At its fundamental level, when people engage in hospitality, they are engaging in a relationship which involves bringing the other into the territory of the self for a period of time, but with no certainties of what may be the emotional and psychological transformation.

In the cultures of the West, feminist writings, while still wrestling with the ideologies of patriarchy, have used and developed all manner of psychoanalytical theories to develop the discourse of womens' marginalization, otherness or silences in the face of language dominated by phallocentric symbolism. For decades, feminist theory has made us familiar with the idea of 'woman' as constructed by patriarchal ideologies. Simone de Beauvoir's most famous work, *The Second Sex*, ponders the question of what it is to exist as a man where woman is always the 'other':

> Humanity is male and man defines woman not in herself but as relative to him; she is not regarded as an autonomous being. ... And she is simply what man decrees; thus she is called 'the sex', by which is meant that she appears essentially to the male as a sexed being. For him she is sex – absolute sex, no less. ... She is the incidental, the inessential as opposed to the essential. He is the Subject, he is the Absolute – she is the other.[24]

The idea that woman might be inferior to or derived from man, in whatever sense intended by Genesis or Aristotle, underpins the idea that man can be thought in his own terms while woman can only be thought of in relation to the man. These precepts are layered with other images of femininity and womanhood which many feminist writers have regarded as both ridiculous and pernicious. Images of femininity derive from the ideas of female subordination, non-being, sacrifice and otherness. The French feminist writer and philosopher Hélène Cixous sets the existence of male/female through gender-defined hierarchical oppositions where the woman only figures as a construct of man as passive, concave, non-being, part of a scheme which privileges the man. She writes that philosophy 'is constructed on the premise of woman's abasement' and that philosophical discourse and literary history both order and reproduce all thought coming back to man, 'to his torment, his desire to be at the origin'.[25] While Muslim feminists ponder the sex of the soul in the creation story, Cixous writes in a landmark essay, 'Extreme Fidelity', first published in 1988, of her use of the terms masculine and feminine, and their relationship to pleasure and libidinal education. Referring to Adam and Eve, she says that 'every entry to life finds itself *before the Apple*'. The apple is an enigma, a secret, bestowed with power, and we are told that 'knowledge might begin with the mouth, with the discovery of the taste of something: knowledge and taste go together'.

Cixous employs the terms masculine and feminine to distinguish between two different 'economies' or modes of behaviour, behaviour which does not have to be dependent on anatomical sex, but rather how individuals negotiate their experience. Cixous wants to do away with the binaries of the masculine and feminine, but finds herself trapped because 'we are born into language, and I cannot do otherwise than to find myself before words: we cannot get rid of them, they are there'.[26]

For Jacques Derrida, the welcome, the origin of ethics, belongs to 'the dimension of femininity' and not to the empirical presence of a human being of the 'feminine sex'.[27] Tracey McNulty, however, wants to think the notion of femininity apart from such allegedly 'feminine' attributes such as maternal protectiveness, selfless love, and homemaking. She argues that 'femininity has no qualitative or ontological features but is instead a structural function that is morally and ethically neutral'.[28] But in her critique of McNulty, Irina Aristarkhova is in my opinion right to claim that while trying to carefully avoid the essentialism of defining woman through such 'feminine' attributes as 'homemaking', feminist thinkers like McNulty risk another sort of essentialism where femininity is presented as this mobile term that finds its 'place inside a man or a house, or travels like a magic wand' to explain any kind of hospitable relation and yet itself remains non-material and non-empirical. The result is that 'this continues to obscure the materiality of actual women and therefore their acts in hospitality'.[29] While theories of the language of hospitality may serve as important and worthy philosophical and even ethical exercises, they can often obscure and diminish the realities of the daily enactment of hospitality. In other words, what is important is to consider the kinds of hospitality men and women engage in on a daily basis with all categories of people in their lives, irrespective of socially and philosophically defined gender constructs.

Women and the relationship of language to female subjectivity has been conceptualized in various ways, but Lacanian theory, though much criticized, is central to this construction, especially in French feminist thought. For Freud and Lacan, society and religious structures in the west are patriarchal. As Grace Jantzen writes, the masculinist 'symbolic' in French thought refers to all of language as well as non-linguistic forms such as music, art, ritual and includes the discourses of law, science, economics and religion. She states that religion is of utmost significance in this view because the 'masculinist symbolic in the west is undergirded by a concept of God as Divine Father, a God who is also Word and who, in his eternal disembodiment, omnipotence, and omniscience, is the epitome of value'.[30] Putting it simply, women are always defined by the masculine and in the language of the masculine. So how do women achieve subjectivity as women where they are not 'linguistically marginalised, rendered inactive or mute in speech as well as in social signification'?[31]

For many Christian feminists, the maleness of the human historical person of Jesus of Nazareth in no way limits God or the incarnation of God to one gender. Rosemary Radford Ruether laments the lack of inclusivity in shaping the Christian tradition and writes that 'sexism and patriarchy express sin as a distortion of human relationality into domination and subjugation, corrupting the humanity of both men and women'.[32] For Ruether, the central methodological principle is the 'promotion of full humanity of women', and while the notion of full humanity is not a new idea for Christian theology, what is new is that women should be included in the category of 'humanity'. As she writes, 'Theologically speaking, whatever diminishes or denies the full humanity of women must be presumed not to reflect the divine or an authentic relation to the divine.'[33] In the same way that some Muslim feminists see verses in the Qur'ān which reflect inequalities or power imbalances in favour of men, even if particular biases are placed in their historical context, many Christian feminists also see an androcentric bias in the biblical canon. However, the concern for the feminists is that not all of scripture reflects patriarchal passages bias and furthermore we return to scripture as a point of authority to affirm what the divine must be. But feminists also call for women's experience as the criterion by which the texts must be measured. Elisabeth Schüssler Fiorenza rejects the claim that parts of the biblical canon are non-patriarchal and argues that women's experience is 'both the criterion by which the texts must be measured and also the source of new, liberatory revelation'. She writes of the concept of an ongoing revelation in which understanding the Bible as a historical prototype rather than a mythical archetype allows the church of women to make connections with our own experiences, historical struggles and feminist options in order to create visions for the future.[34]

As Grace Jantzen explains, Schüssler Fiorenza does not begin with the Bible as having any normative authority, but for those who come from a Christian background, where Bible and Church are a natural starting place, the Bible should be seen as a historical prototype. The Bible offers an account, written by men and with masculinist bias throughout, of the emergence of faith and life which came to be known as Christianity. Those from a Christian background can therefore recognize that the biblical texts were and still are formative, but this does not mean that they should be received as authoritative:

> Rather, the biblical texts (along with other formative texts of Christendom, such as the creeds, and the writings of Augustine and Thomas Aquinas) must be measured against 'the contemporary struggle of women against racism, sexism and poverty as oppressive systems of patriarchy' and must take account also of the feminist analysis of that struggle.[35]

Yet, even though for many feminist thinkers, western religious tradition has been shaped largely by seeing Adam as the normative sexual being to whom Eve is subordinate, thereby confirming patriarchy at the very heart of western civilization, there are others who have written significant revisionist articles on this topic. For example, Phyllis Trible argues with respect to Genesis 2–3, 'Rather than legitimating the patriarchal culture from which it comes, the myth places that culture under judgement.'[36] Her basic thesis is that the original relationship between man and woman was egalitarian, but when this was corrupted, the patriarchal arrangement came into being. The androcentric social reality that came about happened, then, as a result of the 'fall' from gender equality. Thus, the severe androcentrism of the Hebrew Bible is not an ideal, but an aberration from the ideal.[37] The linguistic analysis of the word adam to mean human *qua* non-human creation, rather than specifically a man *qua* woman, has also been at the centre of much of this exegesis. Phyllis Bird contends that while the story of Adam and Eve in Genesis 2–3 does centre on Adam, it does so only in treating him as 'representative of the species'. The story is not about gender and sexuality, but about the 'place of humans within the created order'. Bird's argument is that the biblical stories produce a portrait of humankind in which the two sexes 'bound together in mutual dependence'. They are one in nature, yet distinct, and 'nothing happens in the story of humankind until the woman joins the man upon the stage, and, from that point on, the story can only be told as the action and interaction of man and woman – in interaction with God and the rest of creation'.[38] For Bird, it is Genesis 3–16 where hierarchy is introduced in 'and he shall rule over you' and 'mutuality is replaced by rule. Patriarchy is inaugurated as the sign of life alienated from God ... and it is presented as the consequence of sin.'[39] In his analysis of these revisionist writings, Jerome Gellman concludes that the story of the primal couple in Genesis 2–3 cannot be read in a favourable egalitarian light as woman-friendly and that we cannot escape from interpretations of this story as androcentric in nature. His recommendation for feminist theology is that it should be open 'to the possibility of new revelational moments in our time, including of the full humanity of women, which supplement the old revelation that did not have that teaching'.[40]

While such discourses paint a varied picture of how one thinks, lives and writes about gender relations within different religious traditions, God and ideas of the divine remain central to women's ideas of self and identity. In her essay *Divine Women*, the French cultural theorist Luce Irigaray writes that the spiritual task of our age is to pursue human becoming to its divine fulfilment where religion is fundamental to the transformation of the individual. She writes that the divine is essential to subjectivity, 'divinity is what we need to become free, autonomous, sovereign. No human subjectivity, no human society, has ever been established without the help of the divine. There comes a time for destruction. But, before destruction is possible, God or the gods must exist.' To become fulfilled, we need to have a *horizon*, a 'future of our own', thereby 'fulfilling the wholeness of what we are capable of being'.[41] For Irigaray, this becoming and fulfilment is not about submitting to established truths and dogmas, but 'to search for the way of a human flourishing still to come'.[42] This does not mean making God the property of any one religious community, but thinking in a new way about the spiritual growth of men and women. Both the masculine and the feminine should have their own divine ideals where the divine is a movement towards realizing new possibilities of awareness and transcendence.

Irigaray laments that no-one has taught us love of God, only love of neighbour, and yet how can we love our neighbour without loving God? It is love of God which forms the 'incentive for a more perfect becoming'.[43] God is the horizon for human becoming and each of us has to take responsibility for our individual becoming as well as that of the other. But in defining the divine as the love for the other as other, Irigaray's divine does not necessarily signify that 'an entity called God exists'. Rather for her, the divine should be understood as inspiring within a perfectible way of being 'as a form of energy that would inspire us to develop fully into ourselves, and to live fully our relation to the other, to others, and to the world around us'.[44] For Irigaray, this is a question of ethics, where ethics must replace or at least accompany more individualistic morals, 'since ethics cares about the *cultural space, the spiritual space, both contextual and interior, where the other exists as other* ... ethics teaches us not only not to kill physically but also spiritually, either ourselves or the other'.[45]

In modern Islamic thought, very few writers have spoken of the rediscovery of the divine and the sexual in such terms. But Abdelwahab Bouhdiba's writings explore the interface between the contemporary world of either hypersexuality or religious puritanism which he sees as convenient ways of escaping our responsibilities or masking our failures to one another. He encourages us to emerge from this malaise by rediscovering the sense of sexuality which is a dialogue with the other partner, and the sense of the faith, that is to say, a dialogue with God. Bouhdiba writes:

> The authentic encounter with the other sex, the search for the secret life of the other enable me to rediscover the sense of my own existence. It has often been said that it is not sexuality that invents love, but love that reveals sexuality. It is not so much the flesh that is liberated as the spirit that is revealed through the flesh. For sexuality properly performed is tantamount to freedom assumed.[46]

For Bouhdiba to rediscover the meaning of the sexual is to rediscover the meaning of God, because both love and faith have to be reinvented and rediscovered insofar as we are to find ourselves in a tomorrow that remains largely unknown.

Most feminist works have been concerned with what women have been deprived of in order to halt their spiritual, intellectual and emotional horizons, but they have been articulated largely in the language of rights and duties. Despite the Muslim feminist writers who assert that the Qur'ān gave rights and recognition to women as women and not as inferior beings in any way, many argue that these have been easily ignored or subsumed in patriarchal legal codes. In the west, feminist writers would agree with this historical framework. Irigaray also contends that the law has not been written to defend the life and property of women and that while a few changes have been won in recent times, they have been won by local pressures, whereas what is needed is 'a full scale thinking of the law's duty to offer justice to *two genders that differ* in their needs, their desires, their properties'.[47]

It seems to me that this may be why human relations are always mentioned in the context of broad ethical directives in the Qur'ān. It is because these directives have been translated into specific legal statements about human relationships that they have assumed the status of dogma, losing the interpretative dynamism needed for spiritual growth and human development. What has been lost to some extent is precisely the willingness to imagine, articulate and live relationships which are more hospitable to one another, recognizing different needs and aspirations which are allowed to be expressed with freedom and not condemned with any kind of impunity.

195

The Qur'ānic verse in which men and women are like 'garments for one another' has often been interpreted as mutual love and protection between the two, most specifically in the relationship of marriage. This particular relationship speaks of the possibility of love, not of subjugation or repression. Marriage is judged in Islamic thought to be a fundamental basis for the creation of a moral society, providing the framework for personal and social well-being, contentment and even happiness. It is seen as keeping humanity from lust, but not necessarily with the aim of producing children. Although Islamic history is replete with accounts of the Prophet's dealings with his wives, some in great detail, there seems to be no example of any ideal marriage. Marriage is not spoken of as emotion, but as contract with various obligations and rights due to both husband and wife. The responsibility to transform the contract into a mutually affirming relationship lies with both partners. But despite long discourses about marriage in theological and jurid-ical works, marriage is encouraged, though not obligatory, in the Qur'ān. Prophetic *ḥadīths* have, however, elevated this relationship to achieving the equivalent to one half of faith and the Prophet as saying that one who does not marry is not 'from him', i.e. from his followers. The juristic literature of the Islamic world saw marriage principally through negotiated rights and obligations, because marriage was discussed largely in contract terms. Marriage is referred to in various contexts in the Qur'ān and the verses most commonly used to elaborate what mates and mutuality are:

And among His signs is this, that He created for you mates from among yourselves, that you may dwell in tranquillity with them,

196

and He has put love and mercy between your hearts. Undoubtedly in these are signs for those who reflect (Q30:21).

Marriage in Islamic thought is seen as protecting the modesty of both men and women, of creating an unparalleled complementarity which theoretically should be about the sexual and psychological becoming of the self in and through the other. The affirmation of sexuality and the sexual impulse is implicit in the marriage contract, but so is the recognition that the sexual exists as a divine blessing as 'man is the only creature capable of apprehending the majesty of God and of giving a meaning to being-sexually-with-others'. Intrinsic to this whole domain is modesty, by which is not meant an awkward shyness or silence between the sexes, but an awareness of one's relationship as a deeply meaningful bond, as a test of fidelity and fulfilment. Modesty and sexuality contain an almost paradoxical sacrality in the Islamic tradition as both are regarded as fundamental to the ideal of an Islamic society. As Bouhdiba writes:

Through sexuality the whole human being is taken seriously. This is why so much attention is paid to sexuality. Sexuality is to be taken seriously because it bears witness to the seriousness of existence.... One should marry. One should have sexual intercourse. Parents must marry off their children and among the duties of filial piety is that of getting a widowed parent to remarry.[48]

In comparing Islamic with Jewish and Christian understanding of sexuality, Charles Mathewes writes:

In Islam sexuality is rooted in the covenant as for Jews; nor burdened with the ambivalences and ambiguities of Christian apocalypticism and the idea of original sin; it is rather rooted in the dynamism of divine creation. As such it is the most spectacularly metaphysical and mystical account of sexuality. On this account, sexuality is an unmitigated good – a cosmic and theological good. Creation itself is the core content out of which human sexuality emerges and God's act of creation was in a complicated way sexual – so that sexuality is sign of the divine will and the divine power.[49]

Sexual desire therefore is good, a divine blessing, and marriage is seen largely as the social and moral structure for the release of this desire. This itself is often regarded as a religious ideal rather than a lived reality for many in societies which privilege commitment, but not necessarily in the form of marriage as either sacrament or contract. But while the Qur'ān addresses the question of those with whom marriage is and is not permitted, the closest we get to an actual command of sorts to marry is in the verse, 'You shall encourage those of you who are single to get married' (Q24:32). It is only within the wider field of Islamic discourse where the virtues and pleasures of marriage are discussed. Sexual need, particularly male sexual desire, is considered a dominant reason for marrying as sexual desire is too powerful an impulse and too great a distraction from service to God. All relationships spring from desire and while desire is what makes us human, its excesses can be destructive. Ghazālī saw in sexual desire the greatest pleasure because it can be compared to knowing 'what the delight of the Afterlife must be like. For the delight of the sexual

198

act, were it to last, would be the greatest pleasure of the body, just as the pain of a burn is the body's greatest agony.'[50] While many of the dangers of sexual desire were recounted as men being tempted by or succumbing to women, Ghazālī states that it is only the excess of desire for men which is wrong and that sexual desire is praiseworthy when it stands in a state of equilibrium for men and women. Classical Islamic literature reflected largely patriarchal contexts. Here, male and female desire are equally recognized, but as so often in religious literature, it is the male voice which we hear, the male passions which require response.

Physical intimacy which is primarily what a sexual relationship allows, marriage or otherwise, demands that we cross boundaries by letting someone into private space, but then stay and develop within these new boundaries. Islam views human sexuality and desire, erotic love, as intrinsic to the fulness of human experience and one which is equally important for men and women. The Qur'ānic verses acknowledge and celebrate the presence of sexuality in all of humankind, because we are created as sexual beings and very early on in our lives recognize the drama of sexual attraction, emptiness and fulfment. Yet it is precisely because it is so powerful that sexual relations are commended within licit frameworks and encouraged, albeit with moral boundaries. Fidelity is fundamental to this moral boundary. To love therefore is to have a commitment towards another and to have intentions and engagement towards another person; quite often it is simply about doing for another person. If God places love and mercy between the couple, it is because marriage in its very intensity both confirms and challenges our sense of loyalty, fidelity and generosity.

Yet while scripture may point to an ideal of the relationship between the sexes, Bouhdiba argues that the sexual ethic experienced by Muslims and the vision of the world that underlies it have less and less to do with the generous declarations of the Qur'ān and Muḥammad himself. He writes, 'One can even speak of a degradation, which began at a very early date, of an ideal model. The open sexuality practised in joy with a view to the fulfilment of being, gradually gave way to a closed, morose, repressed sexuality.'[51] While Bouhdiba points to a repressed sexuality, many western commentators have remarked on the dominance of an arid eroticism and violence which dominates a time deprived of love and meaningful sexuality. In 1970, Henry Winthrop argued that true freedom required intellectual and moral depth where one must regard others as subjects not objects. Sexual freedom should not mean escaping from our responsibilities towards others and 'avoiding I–Thou relationships in human affairs'. Winthrop stated:

The new sexuality is above all egocentric. . . . The sexual partners are often, strictly speaking, strangers in the night, and very often in broad daylight too. But above all, in this new sexuality, the partner is regarded as an object, not as a subject.[52]

While Islamic literature reflects all manner of sexual practices in Islamic societies, there has always been a propensity to regard marriage as the main reference point for a sexual life both premised on and promising responsibility and joy. The complexity of human desire has been muted in the religious claim that heterosexual marriage alone provides the divinely sanctioned context for a meaningful life for both men and women. In the moral demands of marriage, two people can share the mutuality of physical and emotional needs, and thus marriage without consummation, without the mutual enjoyment of sex, has no real place in Islamic thought. Love in its carnal form transforms our being, and men and women are seen as impotent without each other.

In the long history of marriage as both a relationship and an institution, it may be difficult to argue for its continuing unique status in society, or even to regard it as a relationship providing either fulfilment of erotic passion or personal solace. Lifelong marriage no longer serves as the standard to which erotic practice should aspire and love no longer guarantees a firm foundation for the marital bond. Many women may argue that the ideal of marriage is neither liberating nor fulfilling, but simply stifles all kinds of aspirations and possibilities. Again in *The Second Sex*, Simone de Beauvoir writes about the repression of the vitality, ambition and freedom of little girls and 'the institutionalized renunciation of female agency and desire in the cul-de-sac of the "destiny" of marriage'.[53] But I would contend that there is within Islamic thought an ideal of the marital bond, a male–female intimacy which has the potential to be an embracing and affirming relationship. It is not made a legal obligation, but it is encouraged as a relationship of reciprocity promising all kinds of transformative possibilities. Like every relationship, it involves risk and vulnerability, and like every relationship it may become a space for violence and degradation, but it can also be the most mutually affirming relationship.

This short statement on marriage as a form of hospitality, as a form of welcoming another both physically and emotionally, letting otherness in, is a scriptural ideal. It is not meant to idealize marriage nor should it deflect from the vast amount of theological and sociological literature on the structural gender inequalities and injustices in many Muslim societies about which much has been written in the last few decades. The Qur'ān remains silent on the woman as homemaker, nor does it define any domestic roles for women within the marriage. This is a relationship which assumes the freedoms of both partners and their abilities to act autonomously. There is no comparison made between male and female as sexual beings or as sexual partners in their private or public lives. Yet this did not stop the Islamic tradition from carving out particular ways of thinking about what Muslim women should do and how they should be and behave, often under strict male authority in private and in public. Notwithstanding certain verses which seemingly give rights and responsibilities to the husband over the wife, the overall imperative of law should be to protect the weak from any abuse by those in authority; but law has so often been written and used to give cultural and social power to men over women, power which has been used to perpetuate imbalances, often with devastating effects on women's lives. This is why Muslim feminists have faced the challenge of commenting on patriarchal interpretations of tradition, both the social realities and the textual legacies, while continuing to retrieve egalitarian impulses from the Qur'ān as well as the Prophetic *Sunna*. The language of traditional discourse is male, and feminist writers continue to raise awareness of issues, not by speaking of woman as the other or by blaming male dominance on men alone. Their concern is their subjectivity, and autonomy. It is this struggle which leads them to condemn what women are often reduced to in terms of male power and authoritarianism despite the belief in the metaphysical freedom of all given to all by God.

The work of feminist theorists has been instrumental in characterizing gender as socially constructed and maintained through stereotypical beliefs, values and ideals. Running throughout this social and intellectual history is the critique of an ideal femininity which prevails despite the feminist discourse. For many feminists there is no predetermined feminine or masculine nature. Yet it is this femininity and the roles ascribed to it which Irigaray suggested should be seen as 'secondary' formations only 'useful' to masculinity.[54] For example, Asifa Siraj, drawing on the works of several western feminists, explores how femininity is understood through the various strands of their critical discourse:

As a wife, the woman is expected to perform the docile, passive and sympathetic role. The dichotomised difference between husband and wife in marriage is characterised by opposition, polarisation, hierarchy and the devaluation of the wife as a social role. Marriage, for some, preserves a prevailing symbolism 'of God, nature, tradition and procreation – which makes it deeply unappealing' since it encourages nurturing and self-sacrifice. Women, in the fulfilment of ideal forms of femininity, are required to be compassionate, empathetic and sensitive to others, and women who do not display these qualities (those who are stoic or uncaring) are perceived to be lacking in femininity. Women's role as mothers is a central 'component of the discourse of femininity' because motherhood is an enactment of femininity. According to De Beauvoir there is no such thing as a maternal instinct; it is a patriarchal invention which infuses maternal guilt within women. Oakley argues that mothers are not born but made, while Hoffnung refers to the myth of the maternal instinct as 'the motherhood mystique', the idea that women in their role as mothers are most suitable for the care for others. Rich contends that 'the womb – the ultimate source of this power – has historically been turned against us, and itself made into a source of powerlessness'. The feminine ideal encourages women's domestic and maternal responsibilities as natural, and encompasses this ideal as intuitive, empathetic and caring.[55]

Siraj's empirical research into Muslim women's understanding of femininity reveals that motherhood remains fundamental to this concept and a particular goal in many women's lives. Motherhood is still seen by many not as defining a regressive domestication, but as the ultimate reflection of femininity. There is, however, also the sense that maternity remains the strongest social power open to women within patriarchal contexts. While there is no ideal status of a woman in the Qur'ān, the married woman is the ideal in Muslim society. But in the Qur'ān, only motherhood is singled out as a particular female role which is worthy of a greater gratitude:

And We have enjoined upon man, kindness to his parents. His mother carried him with hardship and gave birth to him with hardship, and his gestation and weaning [period] is thirty months. [He grows] until, when he reaches maturity and reaches [the age of] forty years, he says, 'My Lord, enable me to be grateful for your favour which you have bestowed upon me and upon my parents and to work righteousness of which you will approve and make righteous for me my offspring. Indeed, I have repented to you, and indeed, I am of the Muslims' (Q46:15).

The verse begins with a command towards both parents, but goes into details specifically in regard to the mother. There are also several *hadīths* which speak of the unique status that is motherhood, perhaps the most famous being:

A person came to Messenger of God and asked, 'Who among people is most deserving of my fine treatment?' He said, 'Your mother.' He again asked, ' 'Who next?' 'Your mother', the Prophet replied again. He asked, 'Who next?' He (the Prophet) said again, 'Your mother.' He again asked, 'Then who?' Thereupon the Prophet said, ']'Then your father.'[56]

Perhaps the most oft quoted saying is 'Paradise lies beneath the feet of the mothers', in which the lowest part of the human body is connected to the ultimate celestial aspiration. It has been pointed out many times that the word for mercy, *rahma*, the root of *al-Rahman*, the Merciful, the most repeated of the divine titles, derives from the same root as *rahim* or womb. Rūmī's couplet draws attention to both God and mother as refuges for humanity and the child respectively:

Like a child that dies on its mother's lap
So will I die on the lap of Mercy.[57]

Motherhood plays a huge role in the biographies of saintly men and Ṣūfīs. It is said that the great Ṣūfī saint Nizamuddin Auliya (d.1325) spent his days in the presence of his pious mother and that whenever he sighted the new moon inaugurating the new month, he would lay his head on his mother's feet to obtain her blessings for the new month. The mother as principal figure, as symbol and as a nurturer on the mystical path, has played a significant role in Islamic piety and poetry. Yet, despite the prominent position given to the mother in Muslim cultures and scripture, the mother remains relatively absent in much of medieval writing. Isabel Niehoff asks where are the mothers in Arab/Muslim literature? She argues that both the biological status of motherhood and motherliness which expresses qualities of affection are neglected topics in Islamic medieval literature. These literary texts, whether in prose or verse, covered almost every topic, but there seems to be an explicit lack of the presence or discussion of mothers.[58]

For cultural theorists in the West, motherhood has been the subject of a more complex analysis. For Julia Kristeva, our contemporary civilization is one where the 'consecrated (religious or secular) representation of femininity is absorbed by motherhood'.[59] While some theorists decry constructed motherhood and the myth of the maternal instinct, others like Irigaray argue that motherhood is not a passive condition which is suffered, but producing the other as a child within yourself with love and nourishment demands a unique kind of spiritual attitude. As Judith Still claims, it is 'a kind of hospitality in an *active* sense'. Still elaborates through the following:

Rather it is a question of accepting freely to share your life, your flesh, your breath – and thus in a way your soul – with the child to whom you gave birth. And not only for a few minutes, but for long months, even for long years. That does not mean that we should idolise maternity as such, but we should recognise that the woman who engenders the child plays a part on both the human and the divine level. We should recognise woman as a fully human subject but different from man, with other tasks to accomplish, particularly on the spiritual plane.[60]

Derrida himself explores the essence of motherhood, claiming that there is something irreplaceable in the notion of motherhood, for the mother is the figure of hospitality welcoming whoever arrives:

We can replace everything, gestation, fertilisation, the breast, food, milk, we can replace all the replaceable parts of maternity, but we will call mother the irreplaceable, as solicitude: there where there is solicitude as irreplaceable, there is a mother.[61]

For Derrida, it is not that anyone who shows irreplaceable care can be substituted for the mother, rather, maternal solicitude itself is irreplaceable. And yet this kind of ennobling of motherhood creates a profound dissatisfaction with the gap between idealistic expectations of mothering and the actual experiences of mothering.

Perhaps the most fertile pre-modern area for exploring both the feminine and female empowerment is in the context of Sufism. It is through appreciating the nuances in early and medieval literature of Sufism, feminine imagery and women ascetics, whereby we can detect a relatively more generous depiction and understanding of women

207

and their spiritual and social autonomy. Nevertheless, this is a pre-modern milieu and a pre-modern discourse and thus it carries within its own narratives, ambivalent and problematic notions of gender.

Yet, it was Sufism which gave women the chance to achieve the rank of sainthood, for the spiritual life did not distinguish between male and female. This could be seen as providing an alternative and more hospitable narrative to women's physical and spiritual status in Islamic societies. In some cases, Ṣūfī practices have subverted traditional patriarchal religious anthropology in ways that might provide contemporary Muslims with creative resources to expand the paradigm for gender justice in their societies.[62]

As many have pointed out, in the earliest phase of Sufism, celibacy was favoured by many who believed marriage, family, and other social relationships would distract them from absolute devotion to God alone. Thus, the denial of physical comforts and sleep deprivation in order to pray and recite the Qur'ān at night formed a common feature of ascetic life. Even those who did marry were wary of excessive sexual indulgence and there was much debate about what constituted the ideal form of ascetic life, marriage or celibacy. Marriage was part of the Prophetic *Sunna* and allowed men and women to enjoy licit sex and not have to quell their sexual desires. Celibacy, however, was a more pure and unburdened life. According to one of its main proponents, the eleventh-century Ṣūfī, Hujwiri, 'Sufism was founded on celibacy; the introduction of marriage brought about a change. There is no flame of lust that cannot be extinguished by strenuous effort, because, whatever vice proceeds from yourself, you possess the instrument that will remove it: another is not necessary for that purpose.'[63]

The issue of authenticity and authorship within the whole hagiographical literature of Sufism throws up two particular tensions. One is that this kind of literature is given to a pious exaggeration of the various saints and their lives, and the second is that at least until the medieval period we are entirely dependent on the hagiographical record of male compilers. As Dakake points out, 'Women did not write their own texts in the earliest periods of Islam, when female Ṣūfīs appear to have been particularly abundant and active.'[64] Yet, despite these reservations, it is still possible to get a sense of both the practical differences and similarities between male and female spirituality and the language of devotion. Many of the women ascetics also led celibate lives so as not to be distracted by marital and domestic life. It is said that Ḥasna al-ʿĀbida of Basra refused to marry because there was no man who was detached enough from this world to accompany her in her rejection of worldly things, and in her constant prayer and fasting. Another story is about Rābiʿa bint Ismāʿil, who could not love her husband with marital love and told him that she prayed constantly because she could not hear the call to prayer without thinking of Judgement Day. There are many accounts of women who engaged in all-night vigils, fasting and praying, including Muʿāda bint ʿAbd Allah al-ʿAdawiyya of Basra, who spent every day prepared to die at any moment. As a result, she would not sleep but prayed constantly, and in cold weather she would wear thin clothes rather than warm clothes so as not to fall asleep. Women were also given to self-mortification, including crying till they were almost blind; this was preferable to the torments of hell fire.[65] Blindness was a common motif as it was felt that physical blindness helped a person see God even better, especially as was later believed, 'the eye is no longer a veil between the person looking and the one being looked at'.[66]

Some of these Ṣūfī women, like their male contemporaries, lived independently, travelled on their own in search of knowledge, and had both male and female teachers and disciples. It is worth mentioning here that in the area of transmitting knowledge or acquiring expertise in the religious sciences such as ḥadīth scholarship, many women achieved relatively high status in early and medieval Islam. Their names are mentioned in the biographical collections and it is recognized that part of their learning required contact with men. But their learning hardly ever translated into teaching in formal positions in Islamic institutions. Most continued to study and teach in informal frameworks, and by the time of the Ottomans, which saw the high bureaucratization of the scholarly establishment, women are no longer mentioned as scholars in the biographical literature.[67]

Nevertheless, women Ṣūfīs had their own ways of reflecting their faith and worship. As Margaret Smith has shown in her seminal work on perhaps the most famous of them all, the liberated slave girl of Basra, Rābiʿa al-Adawiyya (d.801), it was Rābiʿa whose writings and singular devotion transformed Sufism into an ecstatic love mysticism. Rābiʿa had no time or interest in anyone other than God and an example of her exclusive devotion is reflected in her words, 'Oh my Lord, the stars are shining and the eyes of men are closed, and kings have shut their doors, and every lover is alone with his beloved, and here I am alone with Thee.'[68] For her, God was the Beloved who so filled her heart that she had room for no other, not even the Prophet. She closed her shutters in springtime, lest the beauty of the flowers distract her from the beauty of her Beloved. She refused all offers of marriage, preferring to devote herself exclusively to God. She is the one whose haunting lines immortalized her singular love of God, who wanted to love God for God alone, not out of fear of hell or desire for paradise. One popular legend tells us that she ran through the streets of Basra with a bucket of water in one hand and a burning torch in the other. When asked why, she replied, 'I want to pour water into hell and set paradise on fire, so that these two veils disappear and nobody shall any longer worship God out of a fear of hell or a hope of heaven, but solely for the sake of his eternal beauty.'[69]

While the devotional attitudes of Ṣūfī men and women were similar in many respects, the words attributed to early Ṣūfī women suggest that they 'developed their own image of the divine Beloved as both gentle and strong, fiercely jealous and disarmingly intimate, and metaphorically conceptualized as the masculine object of their female longing'. Thus there was a tendency for female Ṣūfīs to conceive of God in symbolically masculine terms, and to express this relationship in symbolically gendered ways. It is said that Fāṭimah bint al-Muthannā, who described herself as Ibn 'Arabī's 'spiritual mother', would sometimes play the tambourine and sing of the glory of God, 'I rejoice in Him, who has turned toward me and claimed me as one of His friends, who has used me for His own purposes. Who am I that He should have chosen me among all of humankind? He is jealous of me and if I look to others, He loosens afflictions against me.'[70] Thus, God's love for his female devotees was often envisioned as a jealous 'male' love and possessiveness. It was seen as direct and personal rather than the more abstract notion of love jealousy in many male Ṣūfī writings.

One of the apparent differences between the reflection of female piety and asceticism was that it was very much seen as an inward journey both spiritually and physically. It was an asceticism lived and practised often in the seclusion and privacy of their own home rather than in public. As spiritually accomplished women, they were sometimes granted unusual access to public spaces and the opportunity to interact with the prominent male authorities of their time, yet they seem to have 'consistently preferred seclusion and solitude'. As Dakake notes, these were confident and independent women who did not adopt relatively greater seclusion out of any self-effacing deference as women, but did so out of a vigilant rejection of worldliness and a strong sense of wisdom from within rather than wisdom to be sought from encounters with others.[71]

Another Ṣūfī woman, Fāṭima of Nishapur, was the teacher and peer of some of the most prominent mystics of the time. They saw her as their teacher, and Bāyazid al-Bisṭāmī is reported to have said of her, 'In all my life I have only seen one true man and one true woman. The woman was Fāṭima of Nishapur. There was no station about which I had told her that she had not already undergone.'[72] Fāṭima was not only a spiritual teacher to male Ṣūfīs, but was also described by her male disciples as the most excellent among *all* Ṣūfīs. This reflects to some extent a counter-normative gender position within mainstream Ṣūfī discourse that male ascetics recognized and respected the spiritual status of female ascetics. But according to the thirteenth-century Ṣūfī poet and biographer 'Aṭṭār, Bāyazid described Fāṭima's spiritual status thus, 'If any man desires to see a true man hidden in women's clothes, let him look at Fatima.'[73] The Ṣūfī ethic was known as *futūwa* or 'manliness', which comprised both courage and chivalry. It is a word not found in the Arabic language at the beginning of Islam. Yet it came to mean the ideal, noble and perfect man whose hospitality and generosity would extend until he had nothing left for himself. It was Ṣūfī *adab* or perfect behaviour modelled on the Prophet himself. Spiritually advanced women were seen to be quintessentially male or 'becoming male'. Masculine descriptions of Ṣūfī women signified that they were considered as equal to the male Ṣūfī masters of the time. Within this androcentric symbolic system, 'male' is not restricted to men, but rather signifies spiritual aspirants including women. Yet whatever status of spiritual perfection was given to such women, the language reflected the pervasiveness of patriarchal ideology where spiritual mastery is fundamentally connected to men. The metaphor of 'becoming male' used for spiritually enlightened women is premised on an anthropology that 'cannot assimilate the category of femaleness into its ideal of human perfection'.[74] Thus the female mystic becomes an honorary man, assuming the gender value of a male.

Mahdi Tourage explores this in his response to Slavoj Žižek's accusation that the feminine remains the repressed secret history of Islam. Tourage states that despite the names of exceptional women, unfolding Islamic civilizations were far more androcentric, even misogynist, in their approach, resulting in the repression of the feminine voice from the archives. Yet, even though the feminine is never totally erased from the archives of Islam, when a female is mentioned, it is often in the male imaginary; women remain the ontologically dependent gender. Islam can retrieve a positive view of the feminine and there are names of pivotal women in the Qur'ān and hagiographical tradition who continue to offer paradigms and inspiration for female spiritual and social autonomy. However, 'because of the masculine self-same logic that structures the symbolic archives of Islam, the retrieval of the feminine upholds a signifying economy in which the masculine is privileged in all arrangements of significa-tion'.[75] An example of how to use the past can be read into the very concept of 'Abrahamic religions', the abbreviation for understanding the history of Abraham, the father of the Semites and of mono-theism. In the story of Abraham, Hagar and Sarah, Hagar and Sarah play a marginal role in the New Testament and Hagar is not even mentioned in the Qur'ān, and Sarah is not mentioned by name. There is an omission here resulting in these mothers not playing the same roles as Abraham in the various monotheisms. Yet as Kuschel states, we need to take these female figures seriously today as 'without these primal mothers there would be no Jewish, Christian or Islamic civilisation'.[76]

But by way of conclusion, it is worth saying a very brief word on the great Ṣūfī philosopher and poet Ibn ʿArabī, who conceived of the Perfect Man (the Microcosm or *al-Insān al-Kāmil*) to be at once male and female, reflecting the image of the androgynous God figure. The concept of the perfect Man does not signify all actual individ-uals, but rather the ideal or the potential that *all* humans do in fact possess, which is realized in some beings and not others. It represents the ideal ethical self and the exemplary standard for human beings to strive toward and it is ungendered, making equal demands on men and women and attainable. The notion of the feminine had become prominent in some mystical writers and Ibn ʿArabī himself under-went a change in his attitude towards women, from hate to love when he discovered that women were dear to the Prophet. To him masculinity or femininity is but an accident of human reality.[77] Because God contains the totality of all the meanings of the universe, and indeed is the place where opposites are conjoined, he is both active/male and receptive/female. Therefore it is insufficient for man to contemplate himself by himself to understand God; the best and most perfect kind of contemplation of God is in woman. In his *Bezels of Wisdom*, he states that sexual union imitates God's relationship with man, 'the man yearning for his Lord Who is his origin, as woman yearns for man'. Sexual union is the greatest union between the two sexes. The goal of the Ṣūfī is to be annihilated in God, in order to achieve union with him. In sexual intercourse, the man is annihilated in the woman, says Ibn ʿArabī, but this is in fact a type of annihilation in God.[78] Despite the explicit and controversial nature of the sexual component of Ibn ʿArabī's theosophy, in his world the woman becomes the highest object of masculine yearning, the very personification of the Divine.

CHAPTER 5

Personal Reflections on Hospitality

In the 1970s Henri Nouwen wrote that the spiritual life is the constant movement between the 'poles of loneliness and solitude, hostility and hospitality, illusion and prayer'. He adds poignantly that 'the more we come to the painful confession of our loneliness, hostilities and illusions, the more we are able to see solitude, hospitality and prayer as part of the vision of our life'.[1]

For Nouwen, our busy life is a distraction from the loneliness we cannot bring ourselves to face. Human loneliness has become an increasingly prevalent theme for philosophers, many of whom regard it as the fundamental human condition. Roger Scruton writes that human beings suffer from loneliness in every circumstance of their earthly lives, 'There is a human loneliness that stems from some other source than the lack of companionship, and I have no doubt that the mystics who have mediated on this fact are right to see it in metaphysical terms. The separation between the self-conscious being and his world is not to be overcome by any natural process. It is a supernatural defect which can be remedied only by grace.'[2]

Nouwen sees salvation in the individual's movement towards solitude. Solitude in this sense is not another kind of loneliness, but the ability to perceive and understand the world from a quiet inner centre. It is about creating space in one's heart and mind for a particular way of being. It is from here that we begin our spiritual life, when we can watch and enjoy all the stimuli of the world around us, and yet still have that precious and calm place which allows us to contemplate what lies within us, our innermost desires. This may include unsettling and pain, moments of sadness, and yet we will find a strength here as we reflect on how we make our lives more meaningful.

Making our lives meaningful is not the same as making our lives successful. We can achieve both, but we should also appreciate how important a hospitable disposition and acts of hospitality are to the cultivation of our inner life. It is then that we become able to transform other people's lives. If we now live in cultures where duty is a difficult word, so is hospitality, and yet an attitude of hospitality towards those around us is essential to a God-centred life. I appreciate that it is difficult to define precisely a hospitable nature, we cannot list all the elements, but just as we recognize goodness in a person, so too do we recognize hospitality in their words and actions. It speaks in simple acts. The tenth-century Ṣūfī scholar Sulami wrote in the *Kitāb al-Futūwa* a list of qualities which are necessary for the pious and noble character. The list could serve as advice for cultivating hospitality, a generous nature, and it may seem obvious to most of us until we realize the difficulties of living such lives:

217

Be honest, loyal and dependable; be generous; keep a beautiful character; be satisfied with little; do not make fun of our friends, and live with them in harmony; do not listen to slander; wish to do good; be a good neighbour; speak well and be loyal to your word; treat your household and those who are dependent on you well; treat those who serve you well; educate the young and teach them good behaviour; respect your elders and superiors; refrain from holding grudges and seeking vengeance; do not cheat or manipulate people, or criticize or talk against them.[3]

Compassion is essential to any hospitality, because it is compassion which makes space for others in the consciousness that we are relational beings. It is then that we grow as individuals and also allow us to help others flourish around us. A few years ago I gave a lecture on wisdom as an educational tool and how doing for others should be seen as important as getting the best academic results. A student asked, 'What is wrong with simply getting the best academic results in school, the best job out there in whatever area, and just getting on with your life with ambition and determination?' I understood the sentiment behind this question and replied that at one level there was nothing wrong in that it seemed the quickest route to success. And yet, if we pursue only our own desires, our whole trajectory in life becomes about *our* goals and aspirations. It becomes a life of the self rather than a life of charity, a life of giving back in some way, and a life which is only about the fulfilment of one's own desires often ends up feeling rather empty. That is partly because our desires are never ending. No one can force you to think and do for others – that thought and that action has to come from you yourself, from a certain kind of consciousness, and you yourself have to discover purpose, charity and happiness in life. Sometimes these can only come from struggle, precisely when you don't get what you want in life; when a relationship fails, when a loved one dies, when a job opportunity is denied, it is often the bleakest of times in our lives which brings out a more noble spirit within us and towards others. As Mitch Alblom writes in *Tuesday with Morrie*, too many people live with meaningless lives because they're chasing the wrong things. The dying professor Morrie's advice is 'Devote yourself to loving others, devote yourself to your community around you, and devote yourself to creating something that gives you purpose and meaning'.

Hospitality in all its forms is what keeps the sacred alive in the ordinary. After all, when we ourselves feel vulnerable lonely or sad, what is it that we search for? We may seek God desperately, but we also need human empathy and warmth. We need to feel that our grief matters and that others are there for us when we are alone or frightened. We don't wish to be forgotten nor our fears ignored. Most of us do not reach the spiritual heights of the saints and mystics when prayer becomes our only refuge and God our only hope. I offer a couple of personal examples which reflect the need for human concern and hospitality when we are feeling at our lowest. At the age of nine, my eldest son suffered an eye injury at school which left him with a retinal tear. During the time he was recovering from his emergency operation, I brought him to work with me one day. He sat playing in front of the computer, quite oblivious to my worries, and my colleague from next door popped in with some fruit and chocolates for him. It was a small act, but I was touched because this colleague had made the extra effort beyond just asking after him.

When you are feeling fragile and low, another's hospitable gesture gives you strength, resolve and most importantly hope.

My father had suffered a stroke in his old age and lived with its effects for several years. The circumstances around his sudden illness remain vivid. He had been working away as a locum consultant in Derby when he became ill and his colleague at the hospital phoned us at home to inform us of what had happened. We did not know his colleagues there, but this person's voice had a tone of urgency and we were to make our way to the hospital as soon as possible. It was a few days before Christmas time and he was due to come home for the holidays. I was at home in the evening with my mother. When I put the phone down and told her, we were both in such shock that for a while we didn't know what to do or think; a horrible sinking feeling had come over us. Yet we also knew we had to go immediately and a family friend drove us to the hospital. There was silence in the car, the night seemed especially dark, and when we arrived at the hospital, we saw him looking dazed and so vulnerable. I had never seen my father in a hospital bed because he had never really been ill before. It is a strange feeling to see a parent so unwell. My mother talked to him, she said prayers over him and she remained so strong, but I knew that our lives had changed. However, our immediate concerns were the practicalities of finding a place to stay as he couldn't be moved near home till after the new year. What happened next has stayed with me reminding me that the kindness of strangers is the deepest kind of kindness because it is spontaneous, full of compassion and whenever it appears, it appears as a divine gift turning despair into hope.

The senior consultant realized we didn't know anyone and as we asked around for a decent hotel near the hospital, he invited us to stay at his home. His offer was so genuine that my mother and I couldn't say no. We were prepared to stay in a nearby hotel, but his words spoke of something more than just shelter. Those few days we stayed with him and his wife made the sadness and difficulty of my father's situation bearable. We stayed with my father in the hospital during the day, praying and receiving visits from family and friends, sometimes venturing out to the shops for some distraction and relief. We returned in the evening to a home-cooked meal, a table always beautifully set out, and the warmth of a couple who tried to make things as normal as possible for us. It was both a spiritual and physical nourishment. They had given without any conditions and we had received without any conditions, and while this is the simplest kind of hospitality, it is the most emotionally and spiritually binding. I always felt in debt to their kindness, but they never made us feel obligated. When my father eventually came home, we kept in touch for a while, but I never got a chance to return their hospitality.

When I reflect on this act of kindness it is the small things I remember, the different table ware each day, the careful coordination of napkins and placemats, the thought which went into cooking a variety of dishes for us, strangers who had come from nowhere and were now their guests. They were not just putting up with us, they treated us with care and affection. We sat around the dinner table each evening and it was their generosity and light-hearted humour in the conversation, a keen desire to normalize our daily life as much as possible, which made those few days less traumatic and even joyful at times.

That we were all Muslims, albeit from slightly different cultural backgrounds, made the whole experience easier. We ate food which we knew to be *ḥalāl*, we prayed in similar ways and this helped the daily rhythm of a shared home. It reduced any unnecessary awkwardness, and while we did not become close friends, there was an ease created by simple shared principles and views.

I grew up in a home where entertaining guests was far more frequent than being a guest. But even when there were no guests, our home was one where food and hospitality were central to the ethos of being a Muslim. At home, the overwhelming majority of our guests and friends were Muslims who shared with us similar preferences in food and entertainment. The idea of entertaining strangers, a pervasive scriptural motif, did not really feature in our lives. Strangers no longer knock on doors unless they are selling something; the opportunity of making strangers into guests or friends is rare unless one is actively working within communities where hospitality is a way of life. I did not live like that and yet a certain concept of hospitality was everywhere. When we entertained at home, our friends were mainly Muslims and again this facilitated the doing of guest hospitality. Yet, this book has shown that cultivating friendships and doing hospitality can remain distinct spheres of behaviour. Each carries its own virtue and value, but the intimacy of friendship is not a necessary requirement of an engaged hospitality. In his description of the main character Dr Aziz in *A Passage to India*, E. M. Forster brings out this distinction in his view of the Oriental. It is an assessment of how the Indian Dr Aziz views his growing friendship with the elderly English woman, Mrs Moore, and the teacher Mr Fielding:

> Like most Orientals, Aziz overrated hospitality, mistaking it for intimacy, and not seeing that it is tainted with the sense

of possession. It was only when Mrs Moore or Fielding was near him that he saw further, and knew that it is more blessed to receive than to give. These two had strange and beautiful effects on him – they were his friends, his for ever, and he theirs for ever; he loved them so much that giving and receiving became one.[4]

It seems to me, then, that at one level religion does matter in how one practises hospitality, that shared beliefs about food laws and other rituals enable the practical aspects of hospitality, making it easier to give and receive. Cooking food for the family and for friends took up a large part of my adult life and I only realized years later the importance of food in the whole concept of hospitality and that children learn the value of hospitality from their parents first. Prepared and shared meals make for a genuine and generous family life. Feeding others was essential to a life of giving, of generosity to others. Having people in your house, taking the time to cook for them, makes demands on our emotional and psychological state. This was often tested as well and could lead to resentment when guests and visitors showed a lack of courtesy or generosity in their own behaviour. Yet, in doing hospitality, we have to be patient and diligent because food is the simplest and yet most profound of God's blessings. Traditions abound in which food is essential to a life of faith:

The Emissary of God (may God bless him and grant him peace) was asked 'What is faith?' He said, 'The giving of food and the exchange of greetings.' 'In expiation and grades [of good deeds],' he said, 'the giving of food and the praying by night while people are asleep [is best].' He was asked about the pilgrimage acceptable to God and he said, 'It is the giving of food and of goodly words.' Anas said, 'A house which is not entered by a guest is not entered by angels.'[5]

But doing hospitality with this ease and being hospitable as a way of life are not the same thing. Whenever I enter someone's home, I am reminded of the Qur'ānic command, 'O you who believe! Do not enter houses other than your houses until you have asked permission and you have greeted its inhabitants. That is best for you so that you may pay heed' (Q24:27). Entering another's home and wishing them peace makes one immediately aware of God's presence. But religious faith should not limit our ability to be hospitable because of ritual boundaries, precisely because what hospitality demands is thinking of others and drawing others in. This drawing in is an ethical position, bringing together both duty and empathy towards others. It is an attitude of being, not simply acts we perform. It is as much about reaching out in friendship to others with words and gestures as being welcomed into someone's home. On this particular point I think that being a Muslim in the west has often made me think that reaching out can have limits when in actual fact I was imposing these limits on myself. I did not think too much about the food and drink I would serve until I had my own home and became responsible for the guests I received. Indeed, as neither I nor my family drink alcohol, it seems to me that I have often been hesitant to invite certain people to my house, thinking that they would not enjoy a meal without wine or some form of alcohol. In my mind this created a level of unease and I realize that I have projected my personal unease about this matter on them when in reality they may never have thought this. Rather, they may have simply delighted in being invited and accepted with gratitude. It became easier to get together in restaurants where we could all eat and drink what we wanted. It is true that often time and labour were saved in the act of eating out. But in reality the restaurant becomes a kind of neutral and safe space, where the commerce of hospitality removes the personal and ethical grappling. We are still together as friends and sharing in food and conviviality, but the whole situation is now more passive than active; we are consuming hospitality rather than doing hospitality. This is a civilized hospitality which while still emotionally rewarding, lacks the spiritual dimension and ethic of hosting at home. Faithful hospitality should begin at home because it is here that we first learn to share and give. Over the years, I have realized that in thinking like this, I have often exercised hospitality based on my freedoms and choice, and denied myself opportunities to show a deeper level of hospitality to many who have come and gone in my life.

On the related theme, the whole area of the 'hospitality industry' has been one which arguably markets hospitality according to our lifestyles. Elizabeth Newman writes of her experience of enjoying a cruise to Hawaii and the nature of the cruise which was enjoyable but expensive. She concludes, 'Not only was the cruise itself expensive, but so were the hundreds of excursions offered once the "guests" were on board. This hospitality clearly operated on the model of exchange: service for money.'[6]

But in the course of writing this book, I have come to realize that hospitality as discussed by scholars and theologians has most often emphasized the stranger, the marginalized or the guest. These categories, however broad, carry drama – they are people who need to be invited in, to be given food, protection or a home. The stranger carries risk and intrigue, a power over our lives, and has become the subject of all kinds of philosophical treatises. But the emphasis on strangers masks perhaps a more urgent reality which is apathy towards neighbours and fellow citizens. Fellow citizens is a broad category, but the implication is of nearness and localism, a more mundane and familiar territory. We turn away from those who are physically near and allow ourselves to become isolated from local needs and overexposed to the overwhelming but distant needs of complete strangers. As Christine Pohl writes of the effects of news reports of famine and desolation thousands of miles away, 'we can know more about a woman in Rwanda or Kosovo whose family was decimated in the latest outbreak of ethnic cleansing than we do about the homeless man we walk by daily on the way to the office, or the elderly woman who lives two doors down from us'.[7]

Add to this today, it seems to me that we often find it more onerous to be hospitable to our own loved ones, to our families and relatives. Great effort seems to be required in being available to anyone. As siblings get older, they often grow apart and family tensions can create terrible and sad distances. These can pass down from generation to generation, creating entrenched rifts between relatives. It is easy to forget that home and family create demands and require our respect. Individual pride and stubbornness often gets in the way of reaching out, and we fail to understand that forgiveness is the most demanding act of hospitality, and precisely for that reason, it is also the most urgent. We do not always use the language of hostility and enmity when we speak of rifts between families, and yet words such as reconciliation and forgiveness are as essential to this healing as that between warring countries or ethnic conflicts. We are reluctant to forgive because we convince ourselves repeatedly that the bigger injustice was done to us and thus people become more objects of our anger and hurt. This was put poignantly by Miroslav Volf who wrote, 'Forgiveness flounders because I exclude the enemy from the community of humans and myself from the community of sinners.' We cling on to that sense of injustice for so much of our lives even when we know that our lives would be richer and more fulfilled if we could find the courage and the humility to lay aside our own judgement.

My own family conflicts have left me feeling frustrated at myself that I could not see a way through, manage to forgive and come to a new understanding with those I know I care for. Islamic thought on forgiveness is closely associated with notions of justice. It's better to forgive those who have wronged you than seek retaliation, but seeking just relationships is also an imperative. Yet through most of my life I've realized that justice is an elusive concept. It isn't a state we arrive at; it is an ideal. And in striving for that ideal, we have to work through the messiness of human emotions, feelings of love, anger, jealousy and betrayal every day. I have occasionally found it hard to forgive, caught between a sense of injustice and betrayal in which I see myself the victim. And yet it is precisely when you can forgive through whatever process that you begin to appreciate the experience as part of your life's story alongside all the other stories that make us who we are. Here, the full restoration of a prior relationship may not be realized, but you are now also committed to mending something that once seemed irreparably broken.

Muslims are encouraged to forgive others, even if the appropriate response to a wrong would be an equivalent wrong. The Qur'ān itself reminds us that this is the path we all walk on, that the believers are those who 'avoid major sins and acts of indecency and when they are angry they forgive' (Q42:37). The rewards for forgiveness and restitution are given by God, 'And the retribution for an evil act is an evil one like it, but whoever pardons and makes reconciliation – his reward is [due] from God' (Q42:40). Forgiveness is itself a form of charity which we give to others. Vengeance, on the other hand, even if justified, is often seen as less virtuous. Forgiveness, above all, is not an abstraction, it is something we do to one another, something we receive from one another in order to create a more hospitable society.

At an international level, forgiveness has entered the political sphere in countries all over the globe that are addressing the past injustices of war, dictatorship, genocide, and the maltreatment of native peoples. In South Africa, President Nelson Mandela forgave apartheid leaders, while Archbishop Desmond Tutu preached 'no future without forgiveness' as chair of the Truth and Reconciliation Commission. Forgiveness has also appeared in the discourse about Uganda, Sierra Leone, Timor-Leste, Germany, Northern Ireland, Chile, El Salvador, Guatemala, Rwanda, and many other places. But as Daniel Philpott states, 'Not only novelty but also controversy has attended the rise of forgiveness in politics. What is often called the 'international community' – UN officials, human rights activists, international lawyers, and a more inchoate cadre of like-minded global diplomats – has both ignored and criticized forgiveness.[8] He argues that critics of forgiveness make several charges, namely that 'forgiveness is pressured on victims, disrespecting their autonomy'.

Others view forgiveness as a religious concept that transgresses the boundaries of secular politics and maintain that at a fundamental level, forgiveness is unjust, even pitiless, because it 'places the burden of repair on victims, who have already been wounded and thoroughly objectified by violence or other injustices'.[9] Whatever approach we have to forgiveness, so much of our life is spent on wondering how God forgives when we should be more focused on how and why we humans fail to forgive. Without the capacity for forgiveness, there can be very little hospitality in any relationship.

Yet the Islamic tradition is replete with the reassurance that God knows and is waiting for our prayers, especially in our moments of weakness. There is a particular relationship between God and humankind which is premised on both human grandeur and human weakness, our propensity to forget that God knows all and waits for us to seek him. God knowing the secrets of our hearts is poignantly expressed, 'Although God has created all and everything for man, He has created man only for Himself, and he says, "Man is My secret and I am his secret."'[10] The relationship between God and man is unlike that between God and any other created being. God has breathed only into man and despite this powerful creative moment witnessed by the heavens and the angels, there seems to be a quiet and unique secrecy to this relationship. It has been beautifully expressed by the poet Rainer Maria Rilke:

God speaks to each of us as he makes us, then walks with us silently out of the night. These are the words we dimly hear: 'You sent out beyond your recall, go to the limits of your longing. Embody me.'[11]

This is God's love for us, his permission for us to be free and, yet in our freedom, God secretly desires that we desire him above all else. It is the remembrance of God which forms the basis for intimacy with God. Some of the most moving traditions which reflect this reciprocity, this shared passion, appear in Ghazālī's work:

> I have certain servants who love me and I love them. They yearn for Me and I for them. They keep me in their minds and I them. They gaze on Me and I on them.

The distinguishing signs of such people is that when darkness spreads and everyone is alone with their loved ones, these people direct their step towards God and whisper confidences to him:

> So amid calling out and weeping and moaning and lament, between standing and sitting, between bowing down and prostration, with My own eye, I see what they endure for My sake, with My ear I hear what complaint they make about My love. And I shall give them three things: First, I will cast My light into their hearts so that they bear witness to me, as I to them. Second, if the heavens and the earth and all that is within them were placed in the balance with them, I would account it of little worth compared to them. Third, I shall draw my face close unto them; and to whom I draw near, who will be privy to what I shall give him?[12]

Love alone gives meaning to everything; God too desires our seeking and our love. At the same time, God's love is not dependent on our love, because God makes the divine–human relationship the centre of cosmic existence. To be human is to love, and it is not whether we love but what we love that defines who we are. James Smith describes this as the 'ultimate love', that which we pledge allegiance to, that which we worship, and states that 'it's not what I think that shapes my life from the bottom up; it's what I desire, what I love, that animates my passion.' For human beings, things matter in ways that we can't often articulate:

> There is a sort of drive that pushes (or pulls) us to act in certain ways, develop certain relationships, pursue certain good, make certain sacrifices, enjoy certain things. And at the end of the day, if asked why we do this, ultimately we run up against the limits of articulation even though we 'know' why we do it: it's because of what we love.'[13]

For Smith, the *telos* to which our love is aimed is not a 'list of ideas and propositions or doctrines, disembodied concepts of values'. Rather, it is an imagined and aesthetic picture communicated through stories and plays, novels and films. It is our imagination that is captivated by what forms the good life, the life of human flourishing, and it is our teleological love which orients us to particular ways of envisioning the good life.[14]

Love in all its manifestations, between partners, children and parents, siblings or between friends, demands being hospitable and doing hospitality. It is because we are not simply individuals acting on our own in this world. Rather, we deceive ourselves if we think of our existence as apart from others rather than among others. The relational aspect of our lives lies at the core of our fundamental human experiences. We can be neither good nor bad, moral nor virtuous, outside of our relationships. We may hold onto a poetic lament that we are in the end only solitary beings, but so much of religious and philosophical wisdom tells us that it is only when we know how to give of ourselves that we experience life at its most meaningful. Yet if this is so, it is also true that nothing is more challenging than the command to live the good life with ourselves and our families and neighbours, to have hope in the future of all. This is an absolute imperative based on the consolation that as human beings we are moral beings who have always been concerned with what it is to be human. As Hannah Arendt writes:

> The world is not humane just because it is made by human beings, and it does not become humane just because the human voice sounds in it, but only when it has become the object of discourse. However much we are affected by the things of the world, however deeply they may stir and stimulate us, they become human for us only when we an discuss them with out fellows. . . . we humanize what is going on in the world and in ourselves only by speaking of it, and in the course of speaking of it we learn to be human. The Greeks called this humanness which is achieved in the course of friendship *philanthropia*, 'love of man', since it manifests itself in a readiness to share the world with other men.[15]

Indeed, those to whom we are bound by blood or kinship have a right on our lives; there are mutual duties and obligations because hospitality and care are not luxuries to indulge in; they are moral imperatives. It is not necessarily easier to be hospitable to family and relatives, because intimacy and shared memories can pull apart as well as bring together. Human relationships are vulnerable and tested in life. We need to cultivate a level of self-discipline to keep our relationships strong and compassionate. Whether people are drawn to or bound in relationships by birth or by choice, relationships need a level of commitment which goes beyond just subjective feeling towards one another. They require doing and being there for one another in small ways, in localized ways. If creation herself is the consequence of God's hospitable nature, then this requires us to act in ways that reflect the goodness of the creator.

I think this is precisely why there is a strong theme of mutual rights and obligations which runs throughout the Qur'ān when referring to relationships and also to family and social ties in general. The onus is on people to understand and fulfil their commitments to the best of their abilities, irrespective of how they might actually feel about one another. Our feelings change, our likes and dislikes change, but duty to one another remains steadfast. It is this sense of moral duty to an ever increasing circle of humanity which grows wider and deeper with time, where we find the challenges and joys of love, loyalty and friendship.

Friendship is a particular kind of hospitable relationship adding meaning to our lives. It can remind us of who we were and who we have become because so much of our lives is the history of our friendships. We learn hospitality in our friendships and we grow as people through such relationships. I am also curious as to why, as we get older, we start to wonder about the friendships we lost or never maintained. Perhaps these lost friendships remind us of particular kindnesses. For example, when my family first came to the UK, we lived in Cambridge and I began school there at the age of four. I have no memories of that school other than walking around the playground with a little boy who always had a big smile; he would hold my hand and talk to me in English. I didn't speak a word of English then and replied in my mother tongue, Urdu. Neither of us understood each other's language, but we understood each other. I don't remember his name, but he was probably my first friend in this country and it was his gesture of kindness, simply being with me in that playground, his hospitable nature, which today makes me miss the friendship I never got to nurture.

Friendship can be seen as the defining relationship of the modern age and its quality and meaning debated by various philosophers. Hans-Georg Gadamer claimed that because friendship is not a value or belief, it does not fit easily within modern thought, largely premised on a self-conscious modern subject.[16] For Gadamer, friendship is a good rather than value. It is a good that comes into being when shared, not demanded nor willed between two people, 'No more than love can friendship be summoned on demand.'[17] However, Gadamer distinguishes having good will towards someone, or a feeling of sympathy towards another, from friendship. Having a good disposition towards someone is not the same as friendship:

> Even if this sympathy or good will were actually to occur on both sides and to that extent constitute reciprocity, it would be mere friendliness so long as the two people were not really openly bound to each other. The common condition of all 'friendship' is more than that: the true bond that – in various degrees – signifies a 'life together'.[18]

Friendships are an important aspect of the texture of communal human life. Typologies of friendship are implicit in many of the central sociological and ethical questions of today and have a stake in defining who we are as individuals and also who we are as communities in a multi-racial, multi-faith and multi-cultural environment. This is because friendship is not a private matter, something we do in our own time and space. Cultivating meaningful friendships has an immensely powerful social worth and I think is essential to the good society, to human flourishing. The classical philosophers knew this because many of them regarded friendship as the most important ingredient of a worthwhile and happy life, essential to creating a good society, and argued that we can't be moral citizens without people around us. Aristotle famously said, 'no-one would choose to live without friends, even if he had all the other good things'. The Roman orator Cicero saw friendship as existing only between good men, men who cultivate virtue, which is the greatest of all things. For Cicero, friendship was what made life worth living because friendships could bring out the best in people.

For the tenth-century Muslim philosopher and ethicist Miskawayh, the human goal should be to perfect and refine individual character. Miskawayh dwells in the one discourse both on the different kinds of love between people and on the various forms of friendship. He writes that 'While the Law prescribes universal justice, it does not prescribe universal benevolence. It only urges people to practise benevolence.'[19] Justice and just relations lie at the core of the ideal society. If people are just towards themselves, they will be just towards others, not just towards friends and relatives, but towards those who are remote as well. But justice is the essential component of the good society, mainly because citizens do not love each other enough. Friendship is something we need for the flourishing of human civilization, and yet he argues that 'friendship and the kinds of love, by which the happiness of man as a civic being by nature, is achieved, have been subject to differences and to all kinds of corruption, have lost the character of unity, and have met with dispersion'.[20] Human nature being imperfect needs temperance. To this end, Miskawayh clarifies his own position:

> It is for this reason that we have censored those who lead an ascetic life when they seek solitude away from other men, live in mountains and caves, and choose the state of savagery which is the opposite of civilization, for they become deprived of all the moral virtues which we have enumerated. How is it possible for a person to be temperate, just, generous, or courageous, if he forsakes other men, keeps away from them, and loses moral virtues? Would he not be then in the rank of the inanimate or the dead?[21]

In our globalized world where different cultures, races and religions are coming together, even colliding in private and public spaces, friendship assumes a new and more potent significance. There are risks involved in the cultivation of new friendships because a fundamental question of the modern era is who are our friends in fragmented and divided communities? For some, this becomes a political question of self-identity, but for many the ambiguity of otherness does not create tension, but rich opportunities of care and concern for those with whom friendships may not have been possible only a few years ago. In the modern age, with the processes of migration and the arrival of new strangers, there has been a renewed interest in identity formation. In complex urban societies of today, concepts of friendship have assumed a larger significance and say as much about our attitudes to cultural boundaries as they do about our desires and preferences as human beings. We cannot be moral citizens without people around us. Friendship is the context in which virtues are embodied. Our moral life struggles, indeed cannot exist outside of us, opening ourselves to others and cultivating virtuous relationships, indeed virtuous friendships. Those who have faith in God see God working through all their friendships.

Exploring John Caputo's phrase that the 'mark of God is on the face of the stranger', David Anderman writes:

Offering hospitality to and receiving hospitality from friends does not stretch us in the ways that offering hospitality to and receiving hospitality from strangers does. Offering hospitality to strangers keeps us from being self-centred and narcissistic. Engaging in conversations with strangers and really listening to them helps keep us from being narrow-minded. Without hospitality to strangers, our conversations and friendships tend toward exclusivity. With the practice of hospitality, we are constantly pushed toward open friendships, new Christian friendships, and new conversations.[22]

But the effects of hospitality can also deepen existing friendships. I think here of an encounter with a male Roman Catholic friend with whom I was enjoying a conversation over a cup of coffee and cake one day. We trusted each other as loyal friends even if we didn't spend much time with each other outside work. Indeed, it was through the course of this conversation that the idea for this book emerged. He was eating a slice of chocolate cake and asked if I wanted to taste a piece. While I declined, I immediately sensed that our familiarity and friendship had deepened in just this one gesture. When someone offers you food from their own plate, there is already an assumed nearness and ease. There was a shared sense of hospitality here which was far more potent than religious or gender difference, or dietary prohibitions. There is a political as well as a moral message here about our changing society and its social and ethical implications. Hospitality is an attitude, but it is reflected first and foremost in acts, in contexts where often pleasure and duty meet. Hospitality enriches our encounters with strangers and friends.

For me such friendships are made possible by modern, diverse societies which create the space and the desire for such connections. They compel many of us to rethink our allegiances and loyalties. There may be many who feel constrained or limited by their own religious leanings, sensing that their emotional and spiritual loyalties must lie first and foremost towards people of their own religious faith. But I have been left convinced that my faith in God has been strengthened by some of the soul searching I have done over friends from a variety of backgrounds. In a way the history of my friendships has been a journey of my faith as well. It has made me think about those who have brought out the best in me, unsettled me or challenged my faith. It is precisely because friendship involves risk, takes us away from the comfort of religious and psychological convictions, even demands making difficult choices about relationships or forces us to ponder on life's uncertainties and ambiguities, that friendships matter. If a friendship unsettles us, it ultimately opens us to thinking about who we are as people and how and in whom we seek happiness and wisdom.

There is a kind of tribalism in us all which makes us feel uncomfortable, even threatened at times by difference. But our prejudices often tell us more about ourselves than we would like to admit. When the Qur'ān says 'we have made you into nations and tribes so you may get to know one another', the verse reads like a divine blessing in our lives, but getting to know one another demands commitment to engagement, patience and most of all, a generous heart. It seems to me that with the breakdown of family living, the forces of globalization and large-scale migration have created a different kind of struggle – fractured societies where people are struggling to find ways of recreating familiarity, a sense of belonging to something and a sense of community. Added to this, the arrival of new strangers through increased migration and asylum has created a level of urban 'mixophobia' which Zygmunt Bauman describes as 'a highly predictable and widespread reaction to the mind-boggling, and spine-chilling and nerve-breaking variety of human types and lifestyles that meet and rub elbows and shoulders in the streets of contemporary cities'. For Bauman, city living both attracts and repels, because the confusing variety of urban dwelling is a source of fear for many. Thus, we have gated communities, spatial segregation, homogenized areas, all of which may seem to lower anxiety, but actually lower tolerance to difference.[23] One could ask what is the end purpose of getting to know one another? But I think that who we choose to get to know, have as friends, matters and says something about our cultural and political attitudes as well as our emotional and intellectual desires.

Without shared space, we cannot have shared experiences, and friendship needs both to grow. Friendship as a mode of hospitality is a human trait and helps to define humanity. These encounters reveal what it is to be human, to search for that which gives meaning to our lives. Using Gadamer's phrase 'fusion of horizons', Bauman calls for conflict to be translated into 'benign, and often deeply gratifying and enjoyable daily encounters with the humanity hiding behind the frighteningly unfamiliar scenic masks of different and mutually alien races, nationalities, gods and liturgies'.[24]

In their introductory remarks to *Hosting the Stranger*, Richard Kearney and James Taylor state that 'interreligious hospitality is a primary task of our time', that 'there are always more guests to be hosted' and 'we are never done with hospitality because we are never done with hosting strangers'.[25] The book contains several essays by scholars of different religions focusing in diverse ways on interreligious hospitality. Interreligious encounters when sought out for personal friendship or as a professional exercise have increasingly become the subject of academic focus. Many have written about the transformative effect of being personally and professionally engaged with another faith. For example, in 2010, the Jesuit scholar of Islam, Thomas Michel, wrote:

When in 1965, the Catholic Church, in its Second Vatican Council document *Nostra Aetate*, began its brief but groundbreaking treatment on Muslims with the words 'The Church regards with esteem also the Muslims', I think that the reaction of

Catholics around the world was generally, 'We do?' First of all, Christians didn't know much about the religion of Islam and very few of us had any direct personal contact with Muslims. Secondly, we didn't know that it was permitted for us to have esteem for the followers of another religion, much less that we *should*, as part of our faith, have such esteem. Yet 'esteem for Muslims' (*NA* 3), the awareness of a 'common spiritual patrimony with Jews' (*NA* 4), and a 'sincere reverence for the conduct, life, precepts and teachings' (*NA* 2) of Hindus, Buddhists, and others *is* part of our Christian faith as that has been declared by the highest teaching authority in the Catholic Church, an ecumenical council. I am not exaggerating when I say that this text changed my life.[26]

This interreligious work or encounter is relatively new terrain to do God's work. It creates new hope for ways of being with one another. Yet, we have to want to learn, not just listen. If we go in simply to listen and come away unchanged in any way, then that meeting has been a sterile encounter. This is not about relativism, but being open to rethinking our own faith and returning to it with a greater openness. Not everyone is convinced of its merits or its relevance and many hope to disclose to the world the secrets and passions of their own faith which remains the only truth. But holding onto one's faith and learning from another are ways of growing in oneself. We may even choose the faith where we find the greatest spiritual and personal affinity. The Benedictine monk Father Bethune O.S.B. speaks of his own spiritual encounter with Buddhism:

When I think back to years in the past, the years before my encounter with Buddhism, I can hardly recognize myself. Nevertheless, my identity as a Christian, forged in the context of a pluralistic world and illuminated, too, by Buddhism, has not thereby strayed or become aberrant in any way. I rediscovered, thanks to Buddhism, a number of elements already present in Christianity. Christians who like myself have accepted unreservedly the hospitality offered to them have been profoundly challenged. I can verify this with the example of Christian monks and nuns who have lived in a Buddhist monastery. They have been called to live their own monastic life and their own Christian faith more coherently. It seems to me that this is the most important experience given by an interreligious encounter. It is an invitation to develop more fully our own commitment in response to the witness that challenges us.[27]

The spiritual journey in any faith is hard and demands stillness, solitude, prayer and reflection. Hospitality for the most part requires conversation, people and movement. It is a drawing in as well as reaching out. Christian and Islamic cultures have emphasized the significance of hospitality as a structure and as an act in the cultivation of the virtuous life. In both traditions, hospitality is good for the individual, the host and the guest, and attitudes of hospitality can transform society around us. This is not easy, but being a certain way can eventually become our character; it is possible to speak and act more charitably towards those we know and those we don't know. The stranger and the traveller are still there in the form of refugees and migrants, except now they are identified through the political language of our age.

Our guests await our invitation and our families who have moved away still want to know that we remember them. All of this requires a generous heart, and taking time, that most precious commodity. A rushed hospitality is merely an interruption in our lives, but a God-centred hospitality can bring about hope when and where it is most needed.

Notes

Introduction

1. H. B. Nisbet, transl., 'Immanuel Kant, Perpetual Peace: A Philosophical Sketch', in Hans Reiss (ed.), *Kant: Political Writings*, Cambridge: Cambridge University Press, 1991, 106.
2. Alasdair MacIntyre, *Dependant Rational Animals: Why Human Beings Need the Virtues*, London: Duckworth, 1999, 123.
3. Jacques Derrida, *Monolingualism of the Other; or, The Prosthesis of Origin*, transl. Patrick Mensah, Stanford, CA: Stanford University Press, 1998, 40. See Lisa Marchi, 'Ghosts, guests, hosts: rethinking "illegal" migration and hospitality through arab diasporic literature', *Comparative Literature Studies*, 51:4, 2014, 603–26, 604.
4. Irina Aristarkhova, 'Hospitality and the Maternal', *Hypatia*, 27:1, 2012,163–81,167.
5. Judith Still, *Derrida and Hospitality, Theory and Practice*, Edinburgh: Edinburgh University Press, 2010, 6–7.
6. Edward W. Said, *Reflections on Exile and Other Literary and Cultural Essays*. London: Granta Books, 2001, xiv.
7. Thomas Claviez. 'Introduction: Taking Place – Conditional/Unconditional Hospitality', in Thomas Claviez (ed.), *The Conditions of Hospitality – Ethics, Politics, and Aesthetics on the Threshold of the Possible*, New York: Fordham University Press, 2013, 3.
8. Roxanne Lynn Doty, 'Practices of Hospitality in a Sovereign World', *Theory in Action*, 8: 2, 2015, 45–68, 46.
9. Paul Cobben, 'Cosmopolitanism or totalitarianism, Reflections on hospitality without boundaries', *Ethical Perspectives: Journal of the European Ethics Network*, 12:4, 2005, 465–79, 466–7.
10. Jurgen Moltmann, 'Theology in the Project of the Modern Word', in J. Moltmann, N. Wolterstorff and E. Charry (eds), *A Passion for God's Reign: Theology, Christian Learning and the Christian Self*, Grand Rapids, Michigan: Eerdmans, 1998, 17.
11. Leon R. Kass, *The Hungry Soul: Eating and the Perfecting of Our Nature*, Chicago: The University of Chicago Press, 1999, 102–3.

12. Sandor Goodhart, 'G/hosts, Guests, Strangers, and Enemies: The Promise of Hospitality in a Multi-Faith World', *Journal of Communication & Religion*, 36:3, 2013, 90–105, 104.

13. Christopher Yates, 'Hospitality: Imagining the Stranger', *Religion and the Arts* 14 (2010), 515–20, 516.

14. *Ibid.*, 516.

15. This story will be explored later in the book, but for biblical and Qur'ānic refs see Genesis 18:1–16 and Q15:51–64, Q51:24–34 and Q11:69–75.

16. Fr Pierre François de Béthune, O.S.B, 'Interreligious Dialogue and Sacred Hospitality', *Religion, East and West*, 7, 2007, 1–23, 6.

17. Julian Baggini, *The Virtues of the Table*, London: Granta, 2014, 232.

18. See Ash Amin for an in-depth discussion, *Land of Strangers*, Cambridge: Polity Press, 2012, 14.

19. Henri Nouwen, *Reaching Out: The Three Movements of the Spiritual Life*, Glasgow: William Collins, 1976; paperback edition, Fount Paperbacks, 1980, 64.

20. *Ibid.*, 64.

Chapter 1 Scriptural Reflections on Hospitality

1. Louis Massignon, 'Islam and the Testimony of the Faithful', in *Testimonies and Reflections: essays of Louis Massignon*, ed. Herbert Mason, Notre Dame, Indiana: University of Notre Dame Press, 1989, 43–53, 52–3.

2. Bradford E. Hinze and Irfan A. Omar (eds), *Heirs of Abraham: The Future of Muslim, Jewish and Christian Relations*, Eugene, Oregon: Wipf and Stock Publishers, 2012, 97.

3. Yusuf Ali translates this as 'unusual people'.

4. Marianne Moyaert, 'Reflections on Narrative Hospitality', in Richard Kearney and James Taylor (eds), *Hosting the Stranger*, New York: Continuum, 2011, 98.

5. ʿImād al-Dīn Abū al-Fidāʾ Ismāʿīl Ibn Kathīr, *Tafsīr Qurʾān al'aẓīm*, vol. 4, Cairo: Dār al-ḥadīth, 1994, 236–7.

6. S. R. Burge, *Angels in Islam, Jalāl al-Dīn al-Suyūṭī's al-ḥabāʾik fī akhbār al-malāʾik*, Oxford: Routledge, 2012, 135.

7. S. R. Burge, 'Angels, Ritual and Sacred Space in Islam', *Comparative Islamic Studies*, 2009, 221–45, 241.

8. *Saint John Chrysostom: Homilies on Genesis 18–45*, transl. Robert C. Hill, vol. 82, Washington D. C: The Catholic University of America Press, 1990, 405.

9. Andres E. Arterbury, 'Abraham's Hospitality among Jewish and Early Christian Writers: A Tradition History of Gen 18:1–16 and Its Relevance for the Study of the New Testament', *Perspectives in Religious Studies*, 30:3, 2003, 359–76, 371.

10. Jeffrey M. Cohen, 'Abraham's Hospitality', *Jewish Bible Quarterly*, 34:3, 2006, 168–72, 171–2.

11. Brannon M. Wheeler, *Prophets in the Quran*, London: Continuum, 2002, 96.

12. Tahar Ben Jelloun, *French Hospitality: Racism and North African Immigrants*, transl. Barbara Bray, New York: Columbia University Press, 1999. The quote and analysis can be found in Judith Still, *Derrida and Hospitality: Theory and Practice*, Edinburgh: Edinburgh University Press, 2010, 28.

13. Annemarie Schimmel, *And Muhammad is His Messenger*, Chapel Hill: The University of North Carolina Press, 1985, 48.

14. Michael Bonner, 'Poverty and Economics in the Qur'ān', *Journal of Interdisciplinary History*, XXXV:3, 2005, 391–406, 391–2.

15. Bonner, 'Poverty', 399.

16. Miriam Schulman and Amal Barkouki-Winter, 'The Extra Mile,' *Issues in Ethics*, 2:1, 2000. For a broader discussion of the theme, see Silas Webster Allard, 'In the Shade of

the Oaks of Mamre: Hospitality as a framework for political engagement between Christians and Muslims', *Political Theology*, 13:4, 2012, 414–24.

17. Snjezana Akpinar, 'Hospitality in Islam', *Religion East and West*, 7, 2007, 23–7, 23.
18. Toshihiko Izutsu, *Ethico-religious concepts in the Qur'ān*, Montreal: McGill-Queen's University Press, 2002, 76.
19. Ibn ʿAbd Rabbih, *The Unique Necklace, Al-ʿIqd al-Farīd*, vol.1, transl. Issa J. Boullata, Reading: Garnet Publishing, 2007, 197–8.
20. Geert Jan Van Gelder, *Of Dishes and Discourse: Classical Arabic Literary Representations of Food*, Surrey: Curzon Press, 2000, 7.
21. Qur'ān translations are based largely on quran.com and Yusuf Ali, *The Holy Qur'ān*, Medina: King Fahd Holy Qur'an Printing Complex. I have taken the liberty of replacing Allah with God and tweaking the wording in places for easier reading.
22. Ali, *Holy Qur'an*, 231.
23. Except as represented in Q4:36, *al-jār al-junub*.
24. Franz Rosenthal, 'The Stranger in Medieval Islam', *Arabica*, 44, 1997, 35–75, 36.
25. *Ibid.*, 40 and 54.
26. *Ibid.*, 41.
27. *Ibid.*, 38–9.
28. Tafsir Ibn ʿAbbās, transl. Mokrane Guezzou, © 2013 Royal Ahl al-Bayt Institute for Islamic Thought, Amman, Jordan (http://www.aalalbayt.org), www.altafsir.com.
29. ʿImād al-Dīn Abū al-Fidāʾ Ismaʿl ibn Kathīr, *Tafsīr al-Qur'ān al-ʿAẓīm*, vol. 1, Dar al-Ḥadīth: Cairo, 1994, 468–9.
30. Muḥammad b. Uthmān al-Dhahābī, *The Major Sins*, transl. Mohammad M. Siddiqui, Beirut: Dar al-Fikr, 2007, 453.
31. *Ibid.*, 453 and 455.
32. Mālik b. Anas, *Al-Muwaṭṭaʾ*, vol.1, Cairo: Dār al-ḥadīth, 1999, 708.
33. Edward W. Lane's Arabic-English Lexicon, http://www.studyquran.org/LaneLexicon/Volume2/00000122.pdf
34. Ibn Majah, *ḥadīth* no. 1 'Guests' at Sunnah.com.
35. John Calvin, *Harmony of the Evangelists, Matthew, Mark and Luke*, Grand Rapids: Wm. B. Eerdmans, 1949.3: 61–2.
36. Christine D. Pohl, *Making Room: Rediscovering Hospitality as a Christian Tradition*, Grand Rapids: Wm. B. Eerdmans Publishing Co, 1999, 75.
37. Marcel Mauss, *The Gift*, transl. Ian Cunnison, London: Cohen and West Ltd, 1969, 15–16.
38. *Tafsīr Ibn ʿAbbās* as above.
39. The interpolation of 'stranded' is not found in the Arabic nor in Yusuf Ali's translation, which simply states wayfarer.
40. Al-Dhahābī, *The Major Sins*, 95–7.
41. St John Chrysostom, Homily 10, 'A Sermon on Almsgiving', *On Repentance and Almsgiving*, transl. Gus George Christo, Washington DC: The Catholic University of America Press, 1998, 103 and 148–9.
42. Chrysostom, Homily 3, 'Concerning Almsgiving and the Ten Virgins', *On Repentance*, 33.
43. Boniface Ramsey, *Beginning to Read the Fathers*, London: Darton, Longman and Todd, 1987, 193.
44. Hans Urs von Balthasar, Joseph Ratzinger, *Two Say Why*, transl. John Griffiths, London: Search Press, 1973, 56.
45. John R. H. Moorman, *Richest of Poor men: The Spirituality of St Francis of Assisi*, London: Darton, Longman and Todd Ltd., 1977, 83–4 and 90.
46. Muḥammad b. Jarīr al-Ṭabarī, *Jāmiʿ al-Bayān ʿan Ta'wīl āy al-Qur'ān*, Beirut: Dar al-Fikr, 1990, 117.
47. Ahmed ibn Muhammad al-Qudūrī, *The Mukhtasar*, transl. Ṭāhir Maḥmood Kiānī, London: Ta ha Publishers Ltd, 2010, 98.

48. Ilse Lichtenstadter, *Introduction to Classical Arabic Literature*, New York: Twayne Publishers Inc., 1974, 5 and 16.
49. Khurshid Ahmed Fariq, *History of Arabic Literature*, Delhi: Vikas Publications, 1972, 44–5.
50. Muhammad Hassan Bakalla, *Arabic Culture Through its Language and Literature*, London: Kegan Paul International Ltd., 1984, 133.
51. Thomas J. Abercrombie, 'Ibn Battuta, Prince of Travelers', National Geographic, vol. 180:6, 1991, 49. The above references are all cited in Fathi El-Shihibi, *Evolution of Travel Genre in Arabic Literature*, 2009 (cannot trace place of publication) 32.
52. Paul Lunde and Caroline Stone (translators), *Mas ʿūdī, From the Meadows of God*, London: Penguin Books, 2007, 4. This is an abridged translation.
53. Sam Gellens, 'The search for knowledge in medieval Muslim societies: a comparative approach', in Dale F. Eickelman and James Piscatori (eds), *Muslim Travellers, Pilgrimage, migration and the religious imagination*, London: Routledge, 1990, 52–3.
54. Dale F. Eickelman and James Piscatori, 'Social theory in the Study of Muslim societies', in Dale F. Eickelman and James Piscatori (eds), *Muslim Travellers*, 5.
55. The entry for 'Hospitality' in Denis Diderot and Jean le Rond d'Alembert (eds), *Encyclopédie, ou Dictionnaire raisonné des sciences, des arts et des métiers*, 35 volumes, Paris: Braisson, David l'Aîné, Le Breton and Durand, 1751–80, cited in Judith Still, *Derrida*, 28.
56. Khalid Masud, 'The obligation to migrate: the doctrine of *hijra* in Islamic law', in Eickelman and Picatori(eds), *Muslim Travellers*, 32.
57. Thomas Michel S.J., 'Where to Now? Ways forward for Interreligious Dialogue: Images of Abraham as Models of Interreligious Encounter', *The Muslim World*, 100, 2010, 530–8, 533–4.
58. Olivia Remie Constable, *Housing the Stranger in the Mediterranean World*, Cambridge: Cambridge University Press, 2003, 2–3.
59. Constable, *Housing*, 8.
60. I'm grateful for Amy Singer's translation here; Guillaume Postel, *De la République des Turcs, là ou l'occasion s'offrera, des meurs & loys de tous muhamedistes*, Poitiers: Enguilbert de Marnef, 1560, 56–63, in Amy Singer, *Charity in Islamic Societies*, Cambridge: Cambridge University Press, 2008, 67–8.
61. The Order of Saint Benedict at http://www.osb.org/rb/text/rbeaad1.html#53
62. Jane S. Webster, *Ingesting Jesus: Eating and Drinking in the Gospel of John* Leiden: Brill, 2003, 63.
63. Laura M. Hartman, 'Consuming Christ: The Role of Jesus in Christian Food Ethics', *Journal of the Society of Christian Ethics*, 30:1, 2010, 45–62, 47.
64. Pohl, *Making Room*, 17.
65. *Sunan ibn Majah* on Sunnah.com. English reference : vol. 3, Book 12, Hadith 2207, Arabic reference : Book 12, Hadith 2291, 1.
66. William McKane, *Al-Ghazālī's Book of Fear and Hope*, Leiden: E. J. Brill, 1962, 22. I have made a couple of minor changes to this translation for ease of reading.
67. Valerie Hoffman, 'Hospitality and Courtesy', in Jane McAuliffe (ed.), *Encyclopaedia of the Qur'ān*, vol. 2, Leiden: Brill, 2002, 449–54, 450.
68. *Riyad as-Salihin, Sunnah.com* (wayfarer); English reference, Book 1, Hadith 475, 1.
69. Ezzeddin Ibrahim and Denys Johnson-Davies (transl.), *An-Nawawi's Forty Hadith*, no.40, Stuttgart:Ernst Klett Printers, 1976, 122.
70. *Ibid.*, 54
71. Izutsu, *Ethico-Religious*, 78.
72. Amy Singer, *Charity in Islamic Societies*, Cambridge: Cambridge University Press, 2008, 34.
73. *Al-Ghazālī on Disciplining the Soul*, 13.
74. Ibn Qayyim al-Jawziyya, *The invocation of God: Al-Wabil al-ṣayyib min al-Kalim al-ṭayyib*, transl. Michael Abdurrahman Fitzgerald and Moulay Youssef Slitine, Cambridge: The Islamic Texts Society, 2000, 36.

75. Ibn Qayyim, *The Invocation*, 37.
76. *Ibid.*, 9.
77. Arthur Jeffery (ed.), *Islam: Muhammad and His Religion*, Indianapolis and New York: Liberal Arts Press, 1958, 29.
78. ʿAbd al-Qādir al-Jīlānī, *The Secret of Secrets*, Interpreted by Shaykh Tosun Bayrak al-Jerrahi al-Halveti, Cambridge: Islamic Texts Society, 1992, 80.
79. See the difference between miserliness (*bukhl*) and utmost miserliness (*shiḥḥ*) in Izutsu, *Ethico-Religious*, 82–83.
80. Ibn Qayyim, *The invocation*, 38.
81. Al-Jāhiz, *The Book of Misers, Al-Bukhalāʾ*, transl. R. B. Serjeant, Reading: Garnet Publishing, 1997, 137.
82. Ibn ʿAbd Rabbih, *The Unique Necklace, Al - ʿIqd al Farīd*, transl. Issa J. Boullata, Reading: Garnet Publishing, 2007, 152
83. These quotes, *Sem 12.4 in Ep.1 ad Tim* and *De Nabuthae 1.2*, can be found in Boniface Ramsey, *Beginning to Read the Fathers*, London: Darton, Longman and Todd, 1987, 188–91.

Chapter 2 Ghazālī and Others on Hospitality

1. Jean Anthelme Brillat-Savarin, *The Physiology of Taste*, transl. M. F. K. Fisher, New York: The Heritage Press, 1949, current hardback edition, New York: Alfred A. Knopf, 1972, 16.
2. Brillat-Savarin, *Physiology*, 188–91.
3. *Ibid.*, 190.
4. *Ibid.*, 156.
5. Muhammad b. al-ḥasan b. Muhammad b. al-Karīm, *A Baghdad Cookery Book: The Book of Dishes, Kitāb al-ṭabīkh*, transl. Charles Perry, Totnes: Prospect Books, 2005, 25.
6. Geert Jan Van Gelder, *Of Dishes and Discourse: Classical Arabic Literary Representations of Food*, Surrey: Curzon Press, 2000, 23.
7. Al-Karīm, *A Baghdad*, 26.
8. Norman Wirzba, 'Food for Theologians', *A Journal of Bible and Theology*, 67:4, 2013, 374–82, 378 and 382.
9. Laura M. Hartman, 'Consuming Christ: The Role of Jesus in Christian Food Ethics', *Journal of the Society of Christian Ethics*, 30:1, 2010, 45–62, 59. Hartman comments that Jesus continues, in Mark 2:20: 'The days will come when the bridegroom is taken away from them, and then they will fast on that day.' Typically, Jesus is read as the bridegroom and his followers as the wedding guests. Times of feasting, on this reading, are times when Christ's presence is understood or felt to be close. Times of fasting, by contrast, are times when Christ seems distant.
10. Bridget A. Henisch, *Fast and Fears: Food in Medieval Society*, Pennsylvania: Pennsylvania State University Press, 1976, 2.
11. W. H. Gardner (ed.), *The Poems of George Herbert*, 'Providence', Oxford: Oxford University Press, 1961, 107.
12. Leon R. Kass, *The Hungry Soul: Eating and the Perfecting of Our Nature*, Chicago: University of Chicago Press, 1999, 106–7.
13. Michel Jeanneret, *A Feast of Words: Banquets and Table Talk in the Renaissance*, transl. Jeremy Whitley and Emma Hughes, Cambridge: Polity Press, 1991, 64–6. (Original French, *Des mets et des mots: Banquets et propos de table à la Renaissance*, 1987.)
14. Jeanneret, *A Feast*, 93.
15. Julian Baggini, *The Virtues of the Table*, London: Granta, 2014, 244.
16. Taylor Clark, *Starbucked*, New York: Little, Brown and Company, 2007, 12–13.
17. *Ibid.*, 13.
18. Baggini, *Virtues*, 202.

19. A translation of this text is used alongside the Arabic in this chapter; Denys Johnson Davies, Al-Ghazālī, *On the Manners relating to Eating, Kitāb ādāb al-akl*, Book XI of *The Revival of the Religious Sciences, Iḥyā' 'ulūm al-dīn*, Cambridge: The Islamic Texts Society, 2000. The Arabic edition here is Abū Ḥāmid Muḥammad b. Muḥammad al-Ghazālī, *Kitāb ādāb al-akl in Iḥyā' 'ulūm al-dīn*, vol, 2, Damascus, 1993, 2–19. Davies provides the sources of the *ḥadīths* in his very useful notes to the book. Where helpful, references will be made to the original Arabic text under *Iḥyā'* (for the section in *Kitāb al-akl*) as well as to Davies's translation under *Manners*. I have changed the English slightly in places for ease of reading where appropriate.

20. *Al-Ghazālī on Disciplining the Soul, Kitāb Riyāḍat al-nafs & On Breaking the Two Desires* (*Kitāb kasr al-shahwatayn*), Books XX11 and XX111 of *The Revival of the Religious Sciences, Iḥyā' 'ulūm al-dīn*, transl. T. J. Winter, Cambridge: the Islamic Texts Society, 1995.

21. Al-Ghazālī, *On Disciplining the Soul*, 56–57.

22. Al-Ghazālī, *On Breaking the Two Desires*, 106.

23. *Ibid.*, 119.

24. *Ibid.*, 122.

25. Adamson, *Food*, 185.

26. The Rule of Benedict, chapter 39 at http://www.osb.org/rb/text/rbemjo2.html#39

27. Caroline W. Bynum, *Holy Feast and Holy Fast: The Religious Significance of Food to Holy Women*, Los Angeles and Berkeley: University of California Press, 1987, 41, in Adamson, *Food*, 188.

28. Boniface Ramsey, *Beginning to Read the Fathers*, Darton, Longman & Todd, 1986, 58.

29. Winter, *Al-Ghazālī, On Disciplining the Soul*, XXXIII.

30. Hartman, 'Consuming Christ', 48.

31. Rudolph Arbesmann, 'Fasting and Prophecy in Pagan and Christian Antiquity', *Traditio*, 7, 1949–1951, 1–71, 36 and 40. This is a very detailed and informative account of fasting in the Greco-Roman world and in early Christianity.

32. Valerie J. Hoffmann, 'Eating and Fasting for God in Sufi Tradition', *Journal of the American Academy of Religion*, 63:3, Thematic Issue on 'Religion and Food' (Autumn, 1995), 465–84, 471.

33. 'Abd al-Qādir al-Jīlānī, *The Secret of Secrets*, interpreted by Shaykh Tosun Bayrak al-Jerrahi al-Halveti, Cambridge: The Islamic Texts Society, 1992, 82.

34. Jīlānī, *The Secret*, 82.

35. Julian Baggini, *The Virtues of the Table*, London: Granta, 2014, 189.

36. Johnson-Davies, *Manners*, xii.

37. Norman Wirzba, 'Food for Theologians', in *Interpretation: A Journal of Bible and Theology*, 67:4, 2013, 374–82, 378.

38. Johnson-Davies, *Manners*, 3; Ghazālī, *Iḥyā'*, 2.

39. *Al-Ghazālī On The Lawful & The Unlawful, Kitāb al-ḥalāl wa'l-ḥarām*, Book XIV of *The Revival of the Religious Sciences, Iḥyā' 'ulūm al-dīn*, transl. Yusuf T. Delorenzo, Cambridge: Islamic Texts Society, 2014, 11, 6 and 9.

40. Al-Sayyid Muhammad ibn Alawi al-Maliki, *The Prophets in Barzakh, the Hadith of Isra' and Mi'raj, The immense Merits of al-Sham, The Vision of Allah*, transl. Gibril Fouad Haddad, Michigan: As-Sunna Foundation of America, 1999, 74–5.

41. Johnson-Davies, *Manners*, 4; Ghazālī, *Iḥyā'*, 3.

42. Johnson-Davies, 4. *Sufra*, which is a kind of leather cover spread out on the ground for meals, has the same root as *safar* meaning travel.

43. Leon R. Kass, *The Hungry Soul: Eating and the Perfecting of our Nature*, Chicago: University of Chicago Press, 1999, 138.

44. Melitta Adamson, *Food in Medieval Times*, Westport, Connecticut: Greenwood Press, 2004, 168.

45. Johnson-Davies, *Manners*, 7; Ghazālī, *Iḥyā'*, 4.

46. Kass, *The Hungry*, 146.
47. Johnson-Davies, *Manners*, 24.
48. Marcel Mauss, *The Gift*, transl. Ian Cunnison, London: Colin and West Ltd, 1969, 63.
49. William FitzStephen, *The Life and Death of Thomas Becket*, transl. George W. Greenaway, London: Folio Society, 1961, 56.
50. Einhard the Frank, *The Life of Charlemagne*, transl. Lewis Thorpe, London: Folio Society, 1970, 63.
51. Henisch, *Fast*, 11.
52. Johnson-Davies, *Manners*, 29, Ghazālī, *Iḥyā'*, 11.
53. Johnson-Davies, *Manners*, 30, Ghazālī, *Iḥyā'*, 12.
54. S. R. Burge, 'The Angels in Sūrat al-Malā'ika', *Journal of Qur'ānic Studies*. 2008, 10:1 50–70, 63.
55. Joanna Macy and Anita Barrows (eds), *A Year with Rilke: Daily Readings from the Best of Rainer Maria Rilke*, New York: Harper Collins, 2009, 307.
56. For an interesting analysis, see Karen J. Campbell, 'Rilke's Duino Angels and the Angels of Islam', *Alif: Journal of Comparative Poetics, Literature and the Sacred*, 23, 2003, 191–211, 196.
57. *Sunnah.Com, Saḥīḥ Bukhāri*, 3220, Book 59, ḥadīth 31 and 3218, Book 59, ḥadīth 29.
58. Al-Jīlānī, *The Secret*, xiv.
59. Ibn Qayyim, *Invocation*, 92–3.
60. Johnson-Davies, *Manners*, 30, Ghazālī, *Iḥyā'*, 12.
61. All biblical quotations are taken from https://www.biblegateway.com, New. They are mainly from the *New Revised Standard Version*.
62. Christine Pohl, *Making Room: Recovering Hospitality as a Christian Tradition*, Grand Rapids: William B. Eerdmans Publishing Company, 1990, 21.
63. Johnson-Davies, Manners, 33, Ghazālī, *Iḥyā'*, 12.
64. Johnson-Davies, *Manners*, 33, Ghazālī, *Iḥyā'*, 13.
65. Johnson-Davies, *Manners*, 34, Ghazālī, *Iḥyā'*, 13.
66. Johnson-Davies, *Manners*, 33, Ghazālī, *Iḥyā'*, 13.
67. Helen Waddell, *The Desert Fathers*, London: Constable, 1946, 113–14, in Henisch, *Fast*, 10.
68. Johnson-Davies, *Manners*, 35, Ghazālī, *Iḥyā'*, 14.
69. Abdessamad Clarke (transl.), *The Kitāb al-Athār of Imam Abū Ḥanīfah*, London: Turath Publishing, 2006, 519–21.
70. Abdessamad Clarke (transl.), *The Kitāb al-Āthār*, 521.
71. Johnson-Davies, *Manners*, 42, Ghazālī, *Iḥyā'*, 16.
72. Johnson-Davies, *Manners*, 43, Ghazālī, *Iḥyā'*, 16–17.
73. Khwaja Hasan Nizami, *Guests are Pests*, in Ralph Russell, *An Anthology of Urdu Literature*, Carcanet Press Ltd, 1995, paperback reprint, 1999, 119.
74. S. D. Goitein, *A Mediterranean Society*, vol. IV, Berkeley: University of California Press, 1999, 228.
75. Elizabeth Warnock Fernea, *Guests of the Sheik*, New York: Anchor Books, Doubleday, 1965, 101.
76. Ibn 'Abd Rabbih, *The Unique Necklace*, vol. 1, *Al-'Iqd al-Farīd*, transl. Issa J. Boullata, Reading: Garnet Publishing, 2007, 151.
77. Ibn 'Abd Rabbih, *Unique*, 152.
78. *Ibid.*, 92.
79. *Ibid.*, 153.
80. *Ibid.*, 156.
81. Geert Jan Van Gelder, *A Library of Arabic Literature Anthology*, New York: New York University Press, 2013, 172
82. Van Gelder, *Library of Arabic*, 196–7.

83. James E. Lindsay, *Daily Life in the Medieval Islamic World*, Indianapolis: Hackett Publishing Company, Inc., 2005, 49.
84. Al-Jāḥiẓ, *The Book of Misers, Al-Bukhalā'*, Transl. R. B. Serjeant, Reading: Garnet Publishing, 1997, 2.
85. Al-Jāḥiẓ, *Book of Misers*, 138.
86. Al-Jāḥiẓ, *Book of Misers*, 15.
87. Ibn 'Abd Rabbih, *The Unique Necklace, Al-'Iqd al-Farīd*, vol. 2, transl. Issa J. Boullata, Reading: Garnet Publishing, 2010, 248–9.
88. Derived from http://theunboundedspirit.com/10-sufi-stories/
89. 'Abdul Qādir al-Jīlānī, *The Secret of Secrets*, interpreted by Shaykh Tosun Bayrak al-Jerrahi al-Halveti, Cambridge: Islamic Texts Society, 1992, xxxvii.

Chapter 3 Divine Hospitality

1. Lucien Richard, *Living the Hospitality of God*, New York: Paulist Press, 2000, 38.
2. John Navone S.J., 'Divine and Human Hospitality', *New Blackfriars*, 85:997, 2004, 329–40, 329.
3. Elizabeth Newman, *Untamed Hospitality: Welcoming God and Other Strangers*, Grand Rapids, Michigan: Brazos Press, 2007, 14–15.
4. Christine Pohl, *Making Room: Recovering Hospitality as a Christian Tradition*, Grand Rapids, Michigan: William B. Eerdmans Publishing Company, 1999, 29.
5. Rosemary L. Haughton, 'Hospitality: Home as the Integration of Privacy and Community', in Leroy S. Rouner, *The Longing for Home*, Notre Dame, Indiana: University of Notre Dame Press, 1996, 17.
6. Narrated by Muslim, Book 7, *ḥadīth* 3, *Sunnah.Com. Rabb* means Lord.
7. Ḥaḍrat 'Abd al-Qādir al-Jīlānī, *The Secret of Secrets*, interpreted by Tosun Bayrak al-Jerahi al-Halveti, Cambridge: Islamic Texts Society, 1992, 7.
8. Badī'al-Zamān Foruzanfar, *Aḥadīth-Masnavi*, reprint, Tehran: Amir Kabir, 1987, p. 29.
9. Louis Massignon, *The Passion of Hallaj*, vol. 1, transl. Herbert Mason, Princeton University Press, 1982, 103–4.
10. Huda Lutfi, 'The Feminine Element in Ibn 'Arabī's Mystical Philosophy', *Journal of Comparative Poetics*, 5, The Mystical Dimension in Literature, 1985, 7–19, 10.
11. Ibn 'Arabī, *Tarjumān al'Ashwaq: A Collection of Mystical Odes by Muhyiuddīn ibn al-'Arabī*, edited and translated by R. A. Nicholson, London: Oriental Translation Fund, 1911, vol. 2, 318. Ibn 'Arabī defines God's love for man as *al-ḥubb al-Ilāhī*.
12. William C. Chittick, *Ibn 'Arabi: Heir to the Prophets*, Oxford: Oneworld, 2005, 17.
13. Henri Corbin, *Creative Imagination in the ṣūfism of Ibn 'Arabī*, Princeton, New Jersey: Princeton University Press, 1969, 94–5, 112–13.
14. Annemarie Schimmel, *Deciphering the Signs of God*, Edinburgh: Edinburgh University Press, 1994, 229. In another one of her major works, Schimmel analyses how the *ḥadīth* of 'I was a hidden treasure' came to be applied by mystics and poets to the Prophet himself. She writes, 'God, longing in His pre-eternal loneliness to be known and loved, created Muhammad as the first mirror for His light and His beauty, a mirror in which He can look at Himself full of love.' See Annemarie Schimmel, *And Muhammad is His Messenger*, Chapel Hill: University of North Carolina Press, 1985, 131.
15. Corbin, *Creative Imagination*, 114–15.
16. *Ibid.*, 112–13.
17. Ian Almond, 'Islam, Melancholy, and Sad, Concrete Minarets: The Futility of Narratives in Orhan Pamuk's "The Black Book"', in *New Literary History*, 34:1, Inquiries into Ethics and Narratives, 2003, 75–90, 89.
18. Almond, 'Islam, Melancholy', 89.

19. Denys the Areopagite, *Divine Names*, cited in Andrew Louth, *Denys the Areopagite*, Wilton, Connecticut: Cassell Publishers, 1989, 88.
20. Louth, *Denys*, 88.
21. Leon R. Kass, *The Hungry Soul: Eating and the Perfecting of Our Nature*, Chicago: University of Chicago Press, 1999, 19.
22. Seyyed Hossein Nasr, *Knowledge and the Sacred* (Gifford Lectures), Edinburgh: Edinburgh University Press, 1981, 160–1.
23. Nasr, *Knowledge*, 161.
24. Ibn Qayyim al-Jawzīyya, *The Invocation of God*, transl. Michael Abdurrahman Fitzgerald and Moulay Youssef Slitine, Cambridge: Islamic Texts Society, 2000, 30.
25. Ibn Qayyim, *Invocation*, 31.
26. Annemarie Schimmel, *Rumi's world: The Life and Work of the Great Sufi Poet*, Boston and London: Shambala Publications, Inc., 2001, 5.
27. Annemarie Schimmel, 'Some Aspects of Mystical Prayer in Islam', Die Welt des Islams, vol. 2:5, 1952, 112–25, 112.
28. Schimmel, 'Some Aspects', 116.
29. Boniface Ramsey, *Beginning To Read The Fathers*, London: Darton, Longman and Todd, 1986, 167.
30. Ramsey, *Beginning*, 168.
31. John R. H. Moorman, *Richest of Poor Men: The Spirituality of St Francis of Assisi*, London: Darton, Longman and Todd, 1977, 16–17.
32. Ramsey, *Beginning*, 171–2.
33. *Al-Qushayri's Epistle on Sufism*, transl. Alexander D. Knysh, Reading: Garnet Publishing, 2007, 216–17.
34. A. J. Arberry, *Tales from the Masnavi*, Richmond, Surrey: Curzon Press, 1993, 169.
35. Meister Eckhart, *The Essential Sermons, Commentaries, Treatises and Defense*, transl. Edmund Colledge, O.S.A and Bernard McGinn, New Jersey: Paulist Press, 1981, 248–9.
36. The concept of God knowing all things but remaining unseen and invisible himself is maintained consistently throughout the Qur'ān.
37. Chittick, *Ibn 'Arabi, Heir*, 65–6.
38. An-Nawawi, *Forty ḥadīth* 38, p. 119.
39. Chittick, *Ibn 'Arabi, Heir*, 28.
40. Abu 'Abd al-Rahman al-Sulami, *A Collection of Sufi Rules of Conduct*, transl. Elena Biagi, Cambridge: Islamic Texts Society, 2010, 52.
41. Toshihiko Izutsu, *Ethico Religious Concepts in the Qur'ān*, Montreal: McGill-Queen's University Press, 2002, 110.
42. Both these quotes are from William Mckane, *Al-Ghazālī's Book of Fear and Hope*, Leiden: E. J. Brill, 1962, 17–18.
43. Abū Ḥāmid al-Ghazālī, *Kitāb al-Khauf wa'l Rajā'* in *'Ihyā' 'Ulūm al-Dīn*, vol.4, Damascus, 1993, 132.
44. James M. Clark and John V. Skinner (transl.), *Meister Eckhart: Selected Treatises and Sermons*, London: Faber and Faber, 1958, 80.
45. McKane, *Book of Fear*, 49.
46. For more on this concept of secrecy and revelation, see an interesting study by Ruqayya Yasmine Khan, *Self and Secrecy in Early Islam*, University of South Carolina Press, 2008, chapters 1–2.
47. Nerina Rustomji, *The Garden and the Fire*, New York: Columbia University Press, 2009, xvi–xvii
48. Abdelwahab Bouhdiba, *Sexuality in Islam*, London: Saqi books, 1998, 84.
49. Ahmad ibn Hanbal, *Al-Musnad*, no. 4916. Edited by Ahmad Muhammad Shakir (15 vols, Cairo, 1946).
50. Frithjof Schuon, *Islam and the Perennial Philosophy*, World of Islam Festival Publishing Company, 1976, 19.

51. Thomas Aquinas, *Summa Contra Gentiles*, Book 4:83. All extracts are taken from the online translation http://dhspriory.org/thomas/ContraGentiles1.htm#2.

52. See Chapter 1, Frederick S. Colby, *Narrating Muhammad's night journey: tracing the development of the Ibn 'Abbas ascension discourse*, New York: State University of New York Press, 2009.

53. For a good overall view see Steven J. McMichael, 'The Night Journey (*al-isrā'*) and Ascent *(al-mi'rāj)* of Muhammad in medieval Muslim and Christian perspectives', in *Islam and Christian–Muslim Relations*, vol. 22:3 2011, 293–309.

54. Omid Safi, *Memories of Muhammad: Why the Prophet Matters*, New York: HarperCollins Publishers, 2010. 167–8.

55. Al-Sayyid Muhammad ibn Alawi al-Maliki, *The Prophets in Barzakh, the Hadith of Isra' and Mi'raj, The immense Merits of al-Sham, The Vision of Allah*, transl. Gibril Fouad Haddad, Michigan: As-Sunna Foundation of America, 1999, 72.

56. *Ibid.*, 74.

57. *Ibid.*, 144–5.

58. *Ibid.*, 140.

59. 'Abd al-Qādir al-Jīlānī, *The Secret of Secrets*, Interpreted by Shaykh Tosun Bayrak al-Jerrahi al-Halveti, Cambridge: Islamic Texts Society, 1992, 53.

60. Allama Iqbal, *The Reconstruction of Religious Thought in Islam*, Lahore: Ashraf Press, 1960, 124.

61. McMichael, 'The Night Journey', 303.

62. Rustomji, *The Garden*, 36.

63. Annmarie Schimmel, *Deciphering the Signs of God*, Edinburgh: Edinburgh University Press, 1994, 65.

64. Annmarie Schimmel, *And Muhammad is His Messenger*, Chapel Hill: The University of North Carolina Press, 1985, 166. Schimmel has a very useful chapter on the Ascension story.

65. McMichael, 'The Night Journey', 304.

66. Farīd al-Dīn 'Aṭṭār, *Muslim Saints and Mystics: Episodes from the Tadhkirat al-Auliya*, transl. A. J. Arberry, London: Arkana, 1990, 51.

67. Roger Scruton, *The Face of God*, London: Continuum, 2012, 106.

68. Navone, 'Divine', 334.

69. Laura M. Hartman, 'Consuming Christ', *Journal of the Society of Christian Ethics*, 30:1, 2010, 45–62, 47.

70. Navone, 'Divine', 333 and 337.

71. James K. A. Smith, *Desiring the Kingdom*, vol. 1, Grand Rapids, Michigan: Baker Academic, 2009, 199.

72. Melitta W. Adamson, *Food in Medieval Times*, Westport, Connecticut: Greenwood Press, 2004, 183.

73. Hartman, 'Consuming', 58.

74. Smith, *Desiring*, 200.

75. Elizabeth Newman, *Untamed Hospitality: Welcoming God and Other Strangers*, Grand Rapids, Michigan: Brazos Press, 2007, 169.

76. Robert Bellah, 'Liturgy and Experience', in James Shaughnessy (ed.), *The Roots of Ritual*, Grand Rapids, Michigan: Eerdmans, 1973, 232.

77. David Ford, *Self and Evaluation: Being Transformed*, Cambridge: Cambridge University Press, 1999, 151.

78. Amy Plantinga Pauw, 'Hell and Hospitality', *Word & World*, 31:1, 2011, 13–16, 13–14.

79. Michael Tuck, 'Who is Invited to the Feast? A Critique of the Practice of Communion without Baptism', *Worship*, 86:6, 2012, 505–27, 517.

80. Nicholas Collura, 'Some Reflections on the Eucharist as Fragment', *Worship*, 88:2, 2014, 151–70, 152.

81. Michel Jeanneret, *A Feast of Words: Banquets and Table Talk in the Renaissance*, transl. Jeremy Whitely and Emma Hughes, Cambridge: Polity Press, 1991, 18.
82. Navone, 'Divine', 334.
83. St John Chrysostom, *On Repentance and Almsgiving*, transl. Gus George Christo, Washington D.C. The Catholic University of America Press, 1998, 127–8.
84. Ibn Qayyim al-Jawziyya, *The Invocation of God*, transl. Michael Abdurrahman Fitzgerald and Moulay Youssef Slitine, Cambridge: Islamic texts Society, 2000, 89.

Chapter 4 Men, Women and Relationships of Hospitality

1. Rainer Maria Rilke, *Letters to a Young Poet*, transl. Charlie Louth, London: Penguin Books, 2011, 27.
2. Christopher Lasch, *The Culture of Narcissism*, New York: W. W. Norton, 1979, paperback, 1991, 191.
3. Fatema Mernissi, *Scheherazade goes West*, New York: Washington Square Press, 2001, 24.
4. Muḥammad ibn ʿAbd Allāh al-Kisāʾi *Qiṣaṣ al-anbiyāʾ*, transl. Wheeler M. Thackston Jr., *Tales of the Prophets*, Chicago: Great Books of the Islamic World, Inc., 31–2.
5. Ibn Kathīr, *Tafsīr Qurʾān al-ʿAẓīm*, vol.1, 424.
6. Muhammad Iqbal, *The Reconstruction of Religious Thought in Islam*, Lahore: Ashraf Press, 1960, 83.
7. See Riffat Hassan, 'The Issue of Gender Equality in the Context of Creation in Islam', *Chicago Theological Seminary Register*, 83:1–2, 1993, 3–15, 9–10. See also Amina Wadud, *Qurʾan and Woman: Rereading the Sacred Text from a Woman's Perspective*, New York, Oxford University Press, 1999, 18–19. Wadud argues that the word *min* meaning 'from' should not be seen in a derivative sense, 'extraction from', i.e. Adam's mate was created from Adam, secondary and less in any way. Rather the word *min* should be understood as meaning 'of the same nature as', i.e. Adam's mate was of the same nature as Adam, i.e. equal to Adam.
8. Wadud, *Qurʾan*, 20.
9. Lutfi, 'The Feminine', 13.
10. Jean H. Hagstrum, *Esteem Enlivened By Desire*, Chicago: University of Chicago Press, 1992, 189.
11. Tina Beattie, *God's Mother, Eve's Advocate*, London: Continuum, 1999, 120.
12. Hoffman R. Hays, *The Dangerous Sex: The Myth of Feminine Evil*, New York: G. B. Putnam's Sons, 1964, 88.
13. For a detailed discussion, see Mary Daly, *Beyond God the Father*, London: Women's Press, 1986.
14. Aysha A. Hidayatullah, *Feminist Edges of the Qurʾan*, New York: Oxford University Press, 2014, 125–6.
15. Rita Gross, *Buddhism After Patriarchy*, Albany: SUNY Press, 1993, 23. See Saʿdiyya Shaikh, 'In Search of *al-Insān*: Sufism, Islamic Law and Gender', *Journal of the American Academy of Religion*, 2009, 77:4, 781–822, 785.
16. Nasr Hamid Abu Zayd, *Reformation of Islamic Thought*, 2006, Amsterdam: Amsterdam University Press, 98.
17. Abu Zayd, *Reformation*, 91.
18. Raja Rhouni, *Secular and Islamic Feminist Critiques in the Work of Fatima Mernissi*, Boston: Brill, 2010, 272 and 14.
19. Asma Barlas, 'Uncrossed bridges: Islam, feminism and secular democracy', *Philosophy and Social Criticism*, 2013, 394–5, 417–25, 421. The quote is from Ebrahim Moosa, 'The Debts and Burdens of Critical Islam', in Omid Safi (ed.), *Progressive Muslims*, 2003, Oxford: Oneworld Publications, 125.

20. Barlas, 'Uncrossed', 421.
21. See, for example, the chapter by Amira el-Azhary Sonbol, 'Re-thinking Women and Islam', in Yvonne Haddad and John L. Esposito (eds), *Daughters of Abraham*, Florida: University of Florida Press, 2001, 108–46.
22. Nikkie Keddie, 'Introduction: Deciphering Middle Eastern Women's History', in Nikkie Keddie and Beth Baron (eds), *Women in Middle Eastern History: Shifting Boundaries in Sex and Gender*, New Haven, Connecticut: Yale University Press, 1991, 1–2.
23. Fatema Mernissi, *Scheherazade Goes West*, New York: Washington Square Press, 2001, 106–7.
24. Simone de Beauvoir, *The Second Sex*, transl. H. M. Parshley, London: Picador, 1988, 15–16. This quote cited in Stella Sandford, *How to Read Beauvoir*, London: Granta Books, 62.
25. Susan Sellers (ed.), *The Hélène Cixous Reader*, extracts from *La Jeune Née – The newly born Woman*, London: Routledge, 1994, 38–9.
26. Sellers, *Hélène Cixous*, 132–3.
27. Jacques Derrida, *Adieu to Emmanuel Levinas*, transl. Pascale-Anne Brault and Michael Naas. Stanford: Stanford University Press, 1999, 44.
28. Tracy McNulty, *The Hostess: Hospitality, femininity, and the expropriation of identity*, Minneapolis: University of Minnesota Press, 2006, xxvii.
29. Irina Aristarkhova, 'Hospitality and the Maternal', *Hypatia*, 27:1, 2012, 163–81, 171.
30. Grace Jantzen, *Becoming Divine: Towards a Feminist Philosophy of Religion*, Manchester: Manchester University Press, 1998, 10–11.
31. Shirley Foster, 'Speaking Beyond Patriarchy', in Helen Wilcox, Keith McWatters, Ann Thompson and Linda R. Williams (eds), *The Body and the Text: Hélène Cixous, Reading and Teaching*, Harvester Wheatsheaf, 1990, 67.
32. Rosemary Radford Ruether, 'Christian Feminist Theologies, History and Future', in Yvonne Y. Haddad and John L. Esposito (eds), *Daughters of Abraham*, Florida: University Press of Florida, 2001, 69.
33. Rosemary Radford Ruether, *Sexism and God-Talk: Towards a Feminist Theology*, London: SCM Press, 1983, 19.
34. Elisabeth Schüssler Fiorenza, *Bread Not Stone: The Challenge of Feminist Biblical Interpretation*, Boston, Massachusetts: Beacon Press, 1984, 14.
35. Schüssler Fiorenza, *Bread*, 14, cited in Jantzen, *Becoming*, 105.
36. Phyllis Trible, 'Eve and Adam: Genesis 2–3 Reread', in Carol P. Christ and Judith Plaskow (eds), *Womanspirit Rising: A Feminist Reader in Religion*, San Francisco: Harper's, 1979, 81.
37. See Jerome Gellman, 'Gender and Sexuality in the Garden of Eden', *Theology and Sexuality*, 12:3, 319–35, 320.
38. Phyllis A. Bird, 'Bone of My Bone and Flesh of My Flesh', *Theology Today*, 50, 1993, 521–34, 524.
39. Bird, 'Bone', 527.
40. Gellman, 'Gender', 335.
41. Luce Irigaray, *Sexes and Genealogies*, transl. Gillian C. Gill, New York: Columbia University press, 1987, 62 and 61.
42. Luce Irigaray, *Key Writings*, London: Continuum, 2004, 186.
43. Irigaray, *Sexes*, 68.
44. 'Spiritual Tasks for our Age', in Irigaray, *Key Writings*, 172.
45. 'Spiritual', in Irigaray, *Key Writings*, 175.
46. Abdelwahab Bouhdiba, *Sexuality in Islam*, London: Saqi Books, 1998, 248.
47. Irigaray, *Sexes*, 4.

48. Bouhdiba, *Sexuality*, 95.
49. Charles Mathewes, *Understanding Religious Ethics*, West Sussex: Wiley-Blackwell, 2010, 102
50. Al-Ghazālī, *On Disciplining the Soul*, 165.
51. Bouhdiba, *Sexuality*, 231.
52. Henry Winthrop, 'L'avenir de la révolution sexuelle', *Diogène*, 1979:70, 65–94, cited in Bouhdiba, 244.
53. Beauvoir, *Second*, 67.
54. Luce Irigaray, *Speculum of the Other Woman*, transl. Gillian Gill, New York: Cornell University Press, 1974, 120.
55. Asifa Siraj, '"Smoothing down ruffled feathers": the construction of Muslim women's feminine identities', *Journal of Gender Studies*, 21:2, 2012, 185–99, 187. Siraj has inserted the names of the various feminist writers which I have omitted in this quote.
56. *Sunnah.com*, *Book of Miscellany*, Book 1, *ḥadīth* 316.
57. Annemarie Schimmel, *My Soul is a Woman*, New York: Continuum, 2003, 94.
58. Isabel Toral Niehoff, '"Paradise lies at the feet of the Mothers." Some preliminary remarks concerning the configuration of motherhood in medieval Arab literature', *Imago Temporis. Medium Aevum*, 7, 2013, 45–58, 46.
59. Julia Kristeva, 'Stabat Mater', in Toril Moi (ed.), *The Kristeva Reader*, 1986, Oxford: Blackwell, 161–74, 161.
60. Judith Still, *Derrida and Hospitality: Theory and Practice*, Edinburgh: Edinburgh University Press, 2010, 127.
61. Still, *Derrida*, 131.
62. Shaikh, 'In Search', 783.
63. See Valerie J. Hoffman-Ladd, 'Mysticism and Sexuality in Sufi Thought and Life', *Mystics Quarterly*, 18:3, 1992, 82–93, 83. Hujwiri's *The Kashf al-Mahjub*, transl. Reynold A. Nicholson. 2nd ed., London: Luzac & Co, 1976, 364.
64. For an interesting overview, see Maria M. Dakake, 'Conceptions of the Divine Beloved among Early Sufi Women', *Comparative Islamic Studies* 3:1, 2007, 72–97.
65. Jamal J. Elias, *Female and Feminine in Islamic Mysticism, Muslim World*, 78: 3–4, 1988, 209–24, 209–11.
66. Schimmel, *My Soul*, 38.
67. Ruth Roded, *Women in Islamic Biographical Collections*, Boulder, Colorado: Lynne Rienner Publishers, Inc., 1994, 85.
68. Margaret Smith, *Rabi'a the Mystic and Her Fellow-Saints in Islam*, Cambridge: Cambridge UP, 1928, 22.
69. Schimmel, *My Soul*, 34–35.
70. *Ibid.*, 45.
71. Dakake, 'Conceptions of the Divine', 72 and 89.
72. Javed Nurbaksh, *Sufi Women*, New York: Khaniqahi-Nimatullahi Publications, 1990, 162.
73. Farid al-Dīn 'Aṭṭār, *Tadhkhirat al-Awliyā: Muslim Saints and Mystics*, transl. A. J. Arberry, London: Routledge and Kegan Paul, 1966, 174–5.
74. Shaikh, 'In Search', 798–9.
75. Mahdi Tourage, 'Towards the Retrieval of the Feminine from the Archives of Islam', *International Journal of Zizek Studies*, 1–25, 1.
76. Karl-Josef Kuschel, *Abraham: A Symbol of Hope for Jews, Christians and Muslims*, transl. John Bowden, London: SCM Press, 1995, xvi.
77. Huda Lutfi, 'The Feminine Element in Ibn 'Arabī's Mystical Philosophy', *Journal of Comparative Poetics*, 5, The Mystical Dimension in Literature, 1985, 7–19, 10.

78. Hoffman-Ladd, 'Mysticism and Sexuality', 88–9.

Chapter 5 Personal Reflections on Hospitality

1. Henri Nouwen, *Reaching Out*, Glasgow: William Collins, 1976, 19.
2. Roger Scruton, *The Face of God*, New York: Continuum, 2012, 153.
3. Ibn al-Husayn al-Sulami, *The Way of Sufi Chivalry*, transl. Tosun Bayrak al-Jerrahi, Vermont: Inner Traditions International, 1983, 108.
4. E. M. Forster, *A Passage to India*, London: Penguin Books, this edition 2005, 133. The words 'more blessed to receive than to give' reverse the sayings of Jesus cited by Paul in Acts 20:35.
5. Al-Ghazālī, *On the Manners relating to Eating, Kitab adab al-akl, Book XI of The Revival of the Religious Sciences, Iḥyā' 'Ulūm al-dīn*, transl. D. Johnson-Davies, Cambridge: Islamic Texts Society, 2012, 30.
6. Elizabeth Newman, *Untamed Hospitality*, Grand Rapids, Michigan: Brazos Press, 2007, 28.
7. Christine Pohl, *Making Room*, Grand Rapids, Michigan: William B. Eerdmans Publishing Company, 1999, 91.
8. Daniel Philpott, 'The Justice of Forgiveness', *Journal of Religious Ethics*, vol. 41:3, 2013, 400–16, 400–1.
9. Philpott, 'The Justice', 401.
10. *The Secret of Secrets*, 83.
11. Rainer Maria Rilke, *A Year with Rilke*, transl. and ed. Joanna Macy and Anita Barrows, New York: Harper Collins, 1996, 32.
12. Al-Ghazālī, *Love, Longing, Intimacy and Contentment, Kitāb al-maḥabba wa'l-shawq wa'l-uns wa'l-riḍā*. Book xxxvi of *The Revival of the Religious Sciences, Iḥyā' 'ulūm al-dīn*, transl. Eric Ormsby. Cambridge: Islamic Texts Society, 2011, 92–3.
13. James K. A. Smith, *Desiring the Kingdom*, Grand Rapids, Michigan: Baker Academic, 2009, 51–2.
14. Smith, *Desiring*, 53.
15. Hannah Arendt, *Men in Dark Times*, London: Jonathan Cape, 1970, 24–5.
16. Hans-Georg Gadamer, 'The Ethics of Value and Practical Philosophy' (1982), in *Hermeneutics, Religion and Ethics*, translated by Joel Weinsheimer, Yale University Press, 1999, 117. Gadamer explains that he noticed this difference when he first lectured on the role of Greek ethics and saw 'two extensive books of the *Nichomachean Ethics* deal with the subject – whereas Kant's moral philosophy merits only a single page!' For more on the exploration of friendship in Islamic and western literature, see Mona Siddiqui, *The Good Muslim: Reflections on Classical Islamic Law and Theology*, New York: Cambridge University Press, 167–95.
17. Gadamer, 'The Ethics', 117.
18. Gadamer, 'Friendship and Self-Knowledge: Reflections on the Role of Friendship in Greek Ethics' (1985), in *Hermeneutics*, as above, p. 128.
19. Muḥammad ibn Ya'qūb Miskawayh, *Tahdhīb al-Akhlāq, The Refinement of Character*, translated by Constantine k. Zurayk, Great Books of the Islamic World Inc., 19, 2002. All references will be to this translation beginning *Refinement*.
20. Miskawayh, *Refinement*, 149.
21. *Ibid.*, 150.
22. Rev. Dr David Anderman, 'Conversation, Friendship, and Hospitality. Thoughts Towards a "weak" ecclesiology', *Prism*, 24:1–2, 2010, 7–27, 19.
23. Zygmunt Bauman, *Liquid Times*, Cambridge: Polity Press, 2007, 89–91.
24. Bauman, *Liquid*, 92–3.
25. Richard Kearney and James Taylor (eds), *Hosting the Stranger Between Religions*, New York: Continuum, 2011, 1.

26. Thomas Michel S.J., 'Where to Now? Ways forward for Interreligious Dialogue: Images of Abraham as Models of Interreligious Encounter', *The Muslim World*, 100:4, 2010, 530–8, 530. Michel writes, 'So this is how I have spent most of my adult life; about half the time I teach Islamic studies in Christian institutions and half the time Christian studies in Islamic institutions.'

27. Father Pierre-François Béthune O.S.B., 'Interreligious Dialogue and Sacred Hospitality', *Religion East & West*, 2007:7, 1–22, 19.

Bibliography

Abercrombie, Thomas J. 'Ibn Battuta, Prince of Travelers', *National Geographic*, 180:6, 1991.

Abu Zayd, Nasr Hamid. *Reformation of Islamic Thought*, Amsterdam: Amsterdam University Press, 2006.

Adamson, Melitta W. *Food in Medieval Times*, Westport, Connecticut: Greenwood Press, 2004.

Akpinar, Snjezana. 'Hospitality in Islam', *Religion East and West*, 7, 2007.

Almond, Ian. 'Islam, Melancholy, and Sad, Concrete Minarets: The Futility of Narratives in Orhan Pamuk's "The Black Book"', *New Literary History*, 34:1, Inquiries into Ethics and Narratives, 2003.

Amin, Ash. *Land of Strangers*, Cambridge: Polity Press, 2012.

Anas, Mālik b. *Al-Muwaṭṭa'*, vol.1, Cairo: Dār al-ḥadīth, 1999.

Anderman, David. 'Conversation, Friendship, and Hospitality. Thoughts Towards a "weak" ecclesiology', *Prism*, 24:1–2, 2010.

Arberry Arthur J. *Tales from the Masnavi*, Richmond, Surrey: Curzon Press Ltd, 1993.

Arbesmann, Rudolph. 'Fasting and Prophecy in Pagan and Christian Antiquity', *Traditio*, 7, 1949–1951.

Arendt, Hannah. *Men in Dark Times*, London: Jonathan Cape Ltd, 1970.

Aristarkhova, Irina. 'Hospitality and the Maternal', *Hypatia*, 27:1, 2012.

Attar, Farid al-Din. *Muslim Saints and Mystics: Episodes from the Tadhkirat al-Auliya*, translated by A. J. Arberry, London: Arkana, 1990.

Baggini, Julian. *The Virtues of the Table*, London: Granta, 2014.

Bakalla, Muhammad Hassan. *Arabic Culture Through its Language and Literature*, London: Kegan Paul International Ltd, 1984.

Balthasar, Hans Urs von, and Joseph Ratzinger, *Two Say Why*, translated by John Griffiths, London: Search Press, 1973.

Barlas, Asma. 'Uncrossed bridges: Islam, feminism and secular democracy', *Philosophy and Social Criticism*, 38(4–5), 2013.

Bauman, Zygmunt. *Liquid Times*, Cambridge: Polity Press, 2007.

Beattie, Tina. *God's Mother, Eve's Advocate*, London: Continuum, 1999.

Beauvoir, Simone de. *The Second Sex*, translated by H. M. Parshley, London: Picador, 1988.

Bellah, Robert. 'Liturgy and Experience', in James Shaughnessy (ed.), *The Roots of Ritual*, Grand Rapids, Michigan: Eerdmans, 1973.

Béthune, O.S.B., Fr Pierre François de. 'Interreligious Dialogue and Sacred Hospitality', *Religion, East and West*, 7, 2007.

Bird, Phyllis A. 'Bone of My Bone and Flesh of My Flesh', *Theology Today*, 50, 1993.

Bonner, Michael. 'Poverty and Economics in the Qur'ān', *Journal of Interdisciplinary History*, XXXV: 3, 2005.

Bouhdiba, Abdelwahab. *Sexuality in Islam*, London: Saqi Books, 1998.

Brillat-Savarin, Jean Anthelme. *The Physiology of Taste*, translated by M. F. K. Fisher, New York: The Heritage Press, 1949; current hardback edition, New York: Alfred A. Knopf, 1972.

Burge, Stephen. R. 'The Angels in Sūrat al-Malā'ika', *Journal of Qur'ānic Studies*, 10:1, 2008.

Bynum, Caroline W. *Holy Feast and Holy Fast: The Religious Significance of Food to Holy Women*, Los Angeles and Berkeley: University of California Press, 1987.

Calvin, John. *Harmony of the Evangelists, Matthew, Mark and Luke*, Grand Rapids: Wm. B. Eerdmans, 1949.

Campbell, Karen J. 'Rilke's Duino Angels and the Angels of Islam', *Alif: Journal of Comparative Poetics, Literature and the Sacred*, 23, 2003.

Chittick, William C. *Ibn 'Arabi, Heir to the Prophets*, Oxford: Oneworld, 2005.

Christ, Carol P., and Judith Plaskow (eds). *Womanspirit Rising: A Feminist Reader in Religion*, San Francisco: Harper's, 1979.

Chrysostom, St John. *On Repentance and Almsgiving*, translated by Gus George Christo, Washington D.C.: The Catholic University of America Press, 1998.

Saint John Chrysostom: Homilies on Genesis 18–45, translated by Robert C. Hill, vol. 82, Washington D. C.: The Catholic University of America Press, 1990.

Clark, James M., and John V. Skinner (transl.). *Meister Eckhart, Selected Treatises and Sermons*, London: Faber and Faber, 1958.

Clark, Taylor. *Starbucked*, New York: Little, Brown and Company, 2007.

Claviez, Thomas. 'Introduction: Taking Place—Conditional/Unconditional Hospitality', in Thomas Claviez (ed.), *The Conditions of Hospitality—Ethics, Politics, and Aesthetics on the Threshold of the Possible*, New York: Fordham University Press, 2013.

Cobben, Paul. 'Cosmopolitanism or totalitarianism: Reflections on hospitality without boundaries', *Ethical Perspectives: Journal of the European Ethics Network*, 12:4, 2005.

Cohen, Jeffrey M. 'Abraham's Hospitality', *Jewish Bible Quarterly*, 34:3, 2006.

Colby, Frederick S. *Narrating Muhammad's night journey: tracing the development of the Ibn 'Abbas ascension discourse*, New York: State University of New York Press, 2009.

Collura, Nicholas. 'Some Reflections on the Eucharist as Fragment', *Worship*, 88:2, 2014.

Constable, Olivia Remie. *Housing the Stranger in the Mediterranean World*, Cambridge: Cambridge University Press, 2003.

Corbin, Henri. *Creative Imagination in the ṣūfism of Ibn 'Arabī*, Princeton, New Jersey: Princeton University Press, 1969.

Dakake, Maria M. 'Conceptions of the Divine Beloved among Early Sufi Women', *Comparative Islamic Studies*, 3:1, 2007.

Daly, Mary. *Beyond God the Father*, London: The Women's Press Ltd, 1986.

Davies, Denys Johnson. *Al-Ghazālī, On the Manners relating to Eating, Kitāb ādāb al-akl*, Book XI of *The Revival of the Religious Sciences, Ihyā' 'ulūm al-dīn*, Cambridge: Islamic Texts Society, 2000.

Derrida, Jacques. *Monolingualism of the Other; or, The Prosthesis of Origin*, translated by Patrick Mensah, Stanford, CA: Stanford University Press, 1998.

Derrida, Jacques. *Adieu to Emmanuel Levinas*, translated by Pascale-Anne Brault and Michael Naas. Stanford: Stanford University Press, 1999.

Al-Dhahābī, Muḥammad b. Uthmān. *The Major Sins*, translated by Mohammad M. Siddiqui, Beirut: Dar al-Fikr, 2007.

Doty, L. Roxanne. 'Practices of Hospitality in a Sovereign World', *Theory in Action*, 8: 2, 2015.

Eckhart, Meister. *The Essential Sermons, Commentaries, Treatises and Defense*, translated by Edmund Colledge, O.S.A., and Bernard McGinn, New Jersey: Paulist Press, 1981.

Eickelman, Dale F., and James Piscatori (eds). *Muslim Travellers, Pilgrimage, migration and the religious imagination*, London: Routledge, 1990.

Einhard the Frank. *The Life of Charlemagne*, translated by Lewis Thorpe, London: Folio Society, 1970.

Elias, Jamal J. *Female and Feminine in Islamic Mysticism*, *Muslim World*, 78: 3–4, 1988.

Fariq, Khurshid Ahmed. *History of Arabic Literature*, Delhi: Vikas Publications, 1972.

Fernea, Elizabeth Warnock. *Guests of the Sheik*, New York: Anchor Books, Doubleday, 1965.

Fiorenza, Elisabeth Schüssler. *Bread Not Stone: The Challenge of Feminist Biblical Interpretation*, Boston, Massachusetts: Beacon Press, 1984.

FitzStephen, William. *The Life and Death of Thomas Becket*, translated by George W. Greenaway, London: Folio Society, 1961.

Ford, David. *Self and Evaluation: Being Transformed*, Cambridge: Cambridge University Press, 1999.

Forster, E. M. *A Passage to India*, London: Penguin Books, 2005.

Foruzanfar, Badi'al-Zamān. *Āḥadīth-Masnavi*, Reprint, Tehran: Amir Kabir, 1987.

Gadamer, Hans-Georg. 'The Ethics of Value and Practical Philosophy', in *Hermeneutics, Religion and Ethics*, translated by Joel Weinsheimer, New Haven and London: Yale University Press, 1999.

Gardner, W. H. (ed.). *The Poems of George Herbert*, 'Providence', Oxford: Oxford University Press, 1961.

Gelder, Geert Jan Van. *Of Dishes and Discourse: Classical Arabic Literary Representations of Food*, Surrey: Curzon Press, 2000.

Gellman, Jerome. 'Gender and Sexuality in the Garden of Eden', *Theology and Sexuality*, 12:3, 2006.

Al-Ghazālī, Abū Ḥāmid. *Kitāb al-Khauf wa'l Rajā'* in *'Iḥyā' 'Ulūm al-Dīn*, vol. 4, Damascus, (1993), 132.

Al-Ghazālī, on Disciplining the Soul, Kitāb Riyāḍat al-nafs & On Breaking the Two Desires (Kitāb kasr al-shahwatayn), Books XX11 and XX111 of *The Revival of the Religious Sciences, Iḥyā' 'ulūm al-dīn*, translated by T. J. Winter, Cambridge: Islamic Texts Society, 1995.

Al-Ghazālī, On The Lawful & The Unlawful, Kitāb al-ḥalāl wa'l-ḥarām, Book XIV of The Revival of the Religious Sciences, Iḥyā' 'ulūm al-dīn, translated by Yusuf T. Delorenzo, Cambridge: Islamic Texts society, 2014.

Al-Ghazālī, On the Manners relating to Eating, Kitab adab al-akl, Book XI of The Revival of the Religious Sciences, Iḥyā' 'Ulūm al-Dīn, translated by Denys Johnson-Davies, Cambridge: Islamic Texts Society, 2012.

Al-Ghazālī, Love, Longing, Intimacy and Contentment, Kitāb al-maḥabba wa'l-shawq wa'l-uns wa'l-riḍā, Book xxxvi of *The Revival of the Religious Sciences, Iḥyā' 'ulūm al-dīn*, translated by Eric Ormsby. Cambridge: Islamic Texts Society, 2011.

Goitein, Shelomo D. *A Mediterranean Society*, vol. IV, Berkeley: University of California Press, 1999.

Goodhart, Sandor. 'G/hosts, Guests, Strangers, and Enemies: The Promise of Hospitality in a Multi-Faith World', *Journal of Communication & Religion*, 36:3, 2013.

Gross, Rita. *Buddhism After Patriarchy*, Albany: SUNY Press, 1993.

Haddad, Yvonne Y., and John L. Esposito (eds). *Daughters of Abraham*, Florida: University Press of Florida, 2001.

261

Hagstrum, Jean H. *Esteem Enlivened By Desire*, Chicago: The University of Chicago Press, 1992.

Hanbal, Aḥmad ibn. *Al-Musnad*, edited by Ahmad Muhammad Shakir, 15 vols, Cairo, 1946.

Hartman, Laura, M. 'Consuming Christ: The Role of Jesus in Christian Food Ethics', *Journal of the Society of Christian Ethics*, 30:1, 2010.

Hassan, Riffat. 'The Issue of Gender Equality in the Context of Creation in Islam', *Chicago Theological Seminary Register*, 83:1–2, 1993.

Haughton, Rosemary L. 'Hospitality: Home as the Integration of Privacy and Community', in Leroy S. Rouner, *The Longing for Home*, Notre Dame, Indiana: University of Notre Dame Press, 1996.

Hays, Hoffman R. *The Dangerous Sex: The Myth of Feminine Evil*, New York: G. B. Putnam's Sons, 1964.

Henisch, Bridget A. *Fast and Fears: Food in Medieval Society*, Pennsylvania: Pennsylvania State University Press, 1976.

Hidayatullah, Aysha A. *Feminist Edges of the Qur'an*, New York: Oxford University Press, 2014.

Hinze, Bradford E., and Irfan A. Omar (eds). *Heirs of Abraham: The Future of Muslim, Jewish and Christian Relations*, Eugene, Oregon: Wipf and Stock Publishers, 2012.

Hoffmann, Valerie J. 'Eating and Fasting for God in Sufi Tradition', *Journal of the American Academy of Religion*, 63:3, Thematic Issue on 'Religion and Food', 1995.

Hoffman-Ladd, Valerie J. 'Mysticism and Sexuality in Sufi Thought and Life', *Mystics Quarterly*, 18:3, 1992.

Ibn ʿArabī. *Tarjuman al ʿAshwaq: A Collection of Mystical Odes by Muhyiuddīn ibn al-ʿArabī*, vol. 2, edited and translated by R. A. Nicholson, London: Oriental Translation Fund, 1911.

Ibrahim, Ezzeddin, and Denys Johnson-Davies, transl. *An-Nawawi's Forty Hadith*, Stuttgart: Ernst Klett Printers, 1976.

Iqbal, Allama. *The Reconstruction of Religious Thought in Islam*, Lahore: Ashraf Press, 1960.

Irigaray, Luce. *Sexes and Genealogies*, translated by Gillian C. Gill, New York: Columbia University Press, 1987.

Irigary, Luce. *Key Writings*, London: Continuum, 2004, 186.

Irigaray, Luce. *Speculum of the Other Woman*, translated by Gillian Gill, New York: Cornell University Press, 1985.

Izutsu, Toshihiko. *Ethico-Religious Concepts in the Qurʾān*, Montreal: McGill-Queen's University Press, 2002.

Al-Jāḥiẓ. *The Book of Misers, Al-Bukhalāʾ*, translated by R. B. Serjeant, Reading: Garnet Publishing Ltd, 1997.

Jantzen, Grace. *Becoming divine: Towards a Feminist Philosophy of Religion*, Manchester: Manchester University Press, 1998.

Al-Jawzīyya, Ibn Qayyim. *The Invocation of God*, translated by Michael Abdurrahman Fitzgerald and Moulay Youssef Slitine, Cambridge: Islamic Texts Society, 2000.

Jeanneret, Michel. *A Feast of Words: Banquets and Table Talk in the Renaissance*, translated by Jeremy Whitley and Emma Hughes, Cambridge: Polity Press, 1991. (Original French, *Des mets et des mots. Banquets et propos de table à la Renaissance*, 1987.)

Jeffery, Arthur (ed.). *Islam: Muhammad and His Religion*, Indianapolis and New York: Liberal Arts Press, 1958.

Al-Jīlānī, ʿAbd al-Qādir. *The Secret of Secrets*, interpreted by Shaykh Tosun Bayrak al-Jerrahi al-Halveti, Cambridge: Islamic Texts Society, 1992.

Al-Karīm, Muḥammad b. al-ḥasan b. Muḥammad b. *A Baghdad Cookery Book: The Book of Dishes, Kitāb al-ṭabīkh*, translated by Charles Perry, Totnes: Prospect Books, 2005.

Kass, Leon R. *The Hungry Soul: Eating and the Perfecting of Our Nature*, Chicago: The University of Chicago Press, 1999.

Ibn Kathīr, ʿImād al-Din Abū al-Fidāʾ Ismāʿīl. *Tafsīr al-Qurʾān al-ʿAẓīm*, vol. 1, Dar al-Ḥadīth: Cairo, 1994.

Kearney, Richard., and James Taylor (eds). *Hosting the Stranger Between Religions*, New York: Continuum, 2011.

Keddie, Nikkie. 'Introduction: Deciphering Middle Eastern Women's History', in Nikkie Keddie and Beth Baron (eds), *Women in Middle Eastern History: Shifting Boundaries in Sex and Gender*, New Haven, Connecticut: Yale University Press, 1991.

Khan, Ruqayya Yasmine. *Self and Secrecy in Early Islam*, Columbia, SC: University of South Carolina Press, 2008.

Al-Kisā'i, Muḥammad ibn ʿAbd Allāh. *Qiṣaṣ al-anbiyā'*, translated by Wheeler M. Thackston Jr, *Tales of the Prophets*, Chicago: Great Books of the Islamic World, Inc., 1997.

Kuschel, Karl-Josef. *Abraham: A Symbol of Hope for Jews, Christians and Muslims*, translated by John Bowden, London: SCM Press Ltd, 1995.

Lane, Edward W. *Lane's Arabic–English Lexicon*, http://www.studyquran.org/LaneLexicon/Volume2/00000122.pdf

Lasch, Christopher. *The Culture of Narcissism*, New York: W. W. Norton & Company, Inc. 1979, paperback, 1991.

Lichtenstadter, Ilse. *Introduction to Classical Arabic Literature*, New York: Twayne Publishers Inc., 1974.

Lindsay, James E. *Daily Life in the Medieval Islamic World*, Indianapolis: Hackett Publishing Company, Inc., 2005.

Louth, Andrew. *Denys the Areopagite*, Wilton, Connecticut: Cassell Publishers Ltd, 1989.

Lutfi, Huda. 'The Feminine Element in Ibn ʿArabī's Mystical Philosophy', *Journal of Comparative Poetics*, 5, The Mystical Dimension in Literature, 1985.

MacIntyre, Alasdair. *Dependent Rational Animals: Why Human Beings Need the Virtues*, London: Duckworth, 1999.

Macy, Joanna, and Anita Barrows (eds). *A Year with Rilke: Daily Readings from the Best of Rainer Maria Rilke*, New York: Harper Collins, 2009, 307.

Al-Maliki, al-Sayyid Muhammad ibn Alawi. *The Prophets in Barzakh, the Hadith of Isra' and Mi'raj, The immense Merits of al-Sham, The Vision of Allah*, translated by Gibril Fouad Haddad, Michigan: As-Sunna Foundation of America, 1999.

Marchi, Lisa. 'Ghosts, guests, hosts: rethinking "illegal" migration and hospitality through arab diasporic literature', *Comparative Literature Studies*, 51:4, 2014.

Massignon, Louis. *The Passion of Hallaj*, vol.1, translated by Herbert Mason, Princeton University Press, 1982.

Massignon, Louis. 'Islam and the Testimony of the Faithful', in Herbert Mason (ed.), *Testimonies and Reflections: Essays of Louis Massignon*, Notre Dame, Indiana: University of Notre Dame Press, 1989.

Masʿūdī, From the Meadows of God, translated by Paul Lunde and Caroline Stone, London: Penguin Books, 2007.

Mathewes, Charles. *Understanding Religious Ethics*, West Sussex: Wiley-Blackwell, 2010.

Mauss, Marcel. *The Gift*, translated by Ian Cunnison, London: Colin and West Ltd, 1969.

McAuliffe, Jane (ed.). *Encyclopaedia of the Qur'ān*, vol. 2, Leiden: Brill, 2002.

McKane, William. *Al-Ghazālī's Book of Fear and Hope*, Leiden: E. J. Brill, 1962.

McMichael, Steven J. 'The Night Journey (*al-isrā'*) and Ascent (*al-mi'rāj*) of Muhammad in medieval Muslim and Christian perspectives', *Islam and Christian–Muslim Relations*, 22:3, 2011.

McNulty, Tracey. *The Hostess: Hospitality, femininity, and the expropriation of identity*, Minneapolis: University of Minnesota Press, 2006.

Mernissi, Fatema. *Scheherazade Goes West*, New York: Washington Square Press, 2001.

Michel, S.J., Thomas. 'Where to Now? Ways forward for Interreligious Dialogue: Images of Abraham as Models of Interreligious Encounter', *The Muslim World*, 100:4, 2010.

Miskawayh, Muḥammad ibn Yaʿqūb. *Tahdhīb al-Akhlāq, The Refinement of Character*, translated by Constantine K. Zurayk, Great Books of the Islamic World Inc., 19. 2002.

Moi, Toril (ed.). *The Kristeva Reader*, Oxford: Blackwell, 1986.

Moltmann, Jurgen. 'Theology in the Project of the Modern Word', in J. Moltmann, N. Wolterstorff and E. Charry (eds), *A Passion for God's Reign: Theology, Christian Learning and the Christian Self*, Grand Rapids, Michigan: Eerdmans, 1998.

Moorman, John R. H. *Richest of Poor Men: The Spirituality of St Francis of Assisi*, London: Darton, Longman and Todd, 1977.

Nasr, Seyyed Hossein. *Knowledge and the Sacred* (The Gifford Lectures), Edinburgh: Edinburgh University Press, 1981.

Navone S.J., John. 'Divine and Human Hospitality', *New Blackfriars*, 85:997, 2004.

Newman, Elizabeth. *Untamed Hospitality: Welcoming God and Other Strangers*, Grand Rapids, Michigan: Brazos Press, 2007.

Nisbet, B. Hugh. 'Immanuel Kant, Perpetual Peace: A Philosophical Sketch', in Hans Reiss, (ed.), *Kant: Political Writings*, Cambridge: Cambridge University Press, 1991.

Nizami, Khwaja Hasan. *Guests are Pests*, in Ralph Russell, *An Anthology of Urdu Literature*, Carcanet Press Ltd, 1995, paperback reprint, 1999.

Nouwen, Henri. *Reaching Out: The Three Movements of the Spiritual Life*, Glasgow: William Collins & Sons Ltd, 1976; paperback edition, Fount Paperbacks, 1980.

Nurbaksh, Javed. *Sufi Women*, New York: Khaniqahi-Nimatullahi Publications, 1990.

Pauw, Amy Plantinga. 'Hell and Hospitality', *Word & World*, 31:1, 2011.

Philpott, Daniel. 'The Justice of Forgiveness', *Journal of Religious Ethics*, vol. 41:3, 2013.

Pohl, Christine. *Making Room: Recovering Hospitality as a Christian Tradition*, Grand Rapids: William B. Eerdmans Publishing Company, 1990.

Al-Qudūrī, Ahmed ibn Muhammad. *The Mukhtasar*, translated by Ṭāhir Maḥmood Kiānī, London: Ta ha Publishers Ltd, 2010,

Al-Qushayri's Epistle on Sufism, translated by Alexander D. Knysh, Reading: Garnet Publishing Limited, 2007.

Rabbih, Ibn ʿAbd. *The Unique Necklace*, vol. 1, *Al-ʿIqd al-Farīd*, translated by Issa J. Boullata, Reading: Garnet Publishing, 2007

Ramsey, Boniface. *Beginning to Read the Fathers*, Darton, Longman & Todd Ltd, 1986.

Rhouni, Raja. *Secular and Islamic Feminist Critiques in the Work of Fatima Mernissi*, Boston: Brill, 2010.

Richard, Lucien. *Living the Hospitality of God*, New York: Paulist Press, 2000.

Rilke, Rainer Maria. *Letters to a Young Poet*, translated by Charlie Louth, London: Penguin Books, 2011.

Roded, Ruth. *Women in Islamic Biographical Collections*, Boulder, Colorado: Lynne Rienner Publishers, Inc., 1994.

Rosenthal, Franz. 'The Stranger in Medieval Islam', *Arabica*, 44, 1997.

Rouner, Leroy S. *The Longing for Home*, Notre Dame, Indiana: University of Notre Dame Press, 1996.

Ruether, Rosemary Radford. *Sexism and God-Talk: Towards a Feminist Theology*, London: SCM Press, 1983.

Rustomji, Nerina. *The Garden and the Fire*, New York: Columbia University Press, 2009.

Safi, Omid (ed.). *Progressive Muslims*, Oxford: Oneworld Publication, 2003.

Safi, Omid. *Memories of Muhammad: Why the Prophet Matters*, New York: HarperCollins Publishers, 2010.

Said, Edward, W. *Reflections on Exile and Other Literary and Cultural Essays*. London: Granta Books, 2001.

Sandford, Stella. *How to Read Beauvoir*, London: Granta Books, 2006.

Schimmel, Annemarie. *Rumi's World: The Life and Work of the Great Sufi Poet*, Boston and London: Shambala Publications, Inc., 2000.

Schimmel, Annemarie. 'Some Aspects of Mystical Prayer in Islam', *Die Welt des Islams*, 2:5, 1952.

Schimmel, Annmarie. *And Muhammad is His Messenger*, Chapel Hill: The University of North Carolina Press, 1985.

Schimmel, Annemarie. *My Soul is a Woman*, New York: Continuum, 2003.

Schimmel, Annmarie. *Deciphering the Signs of God*, Edinburgh: Edinburgh University Press, 1994.

Schulman, Miriam, and Amal Barkouki-Winter, 'The Extra Mile', *Issues in Ethics*, 2:1, 2000.

Schuon, Frithjof. *Islam and the Perennial Philosophy*, World of Islam Festival Publishing Company Ltd, 1976.

Scruton, Roger. *The Face of God*, London: Continuum, 2012.

Sellers, Susan (ed.). *The Hélène Cixous Reader*, London: Routledge, 1994.

Shaikh, Saʿdiyya. 'In Search of *al-Insān*: Sufism, Islamic Law and Gender', *Journal of the American Academy of Religion*, 77:4, 2009.

Singer, Amy. *Charity in Islamic Societies*, Cambridge: Cambridge University Press, 2008.

Siraj, Asifa. ' "Smoothing down ruffled feathers": the construction of Muslim women's feminine identities', *Journal of Gender Studies*, 21:2, 2012.

Smith, James K. A. *Desiring the Kingdom*, vol.1, Grand Rapids, Michigan: Baker Academic, 2009.

Smith, Margaret. *Rabiʿa the Mystic and Her Fellow-Saints in Islam*, Cambridge: Cambridge University Press, 1928.

Sonbol, Amira el-Azhary. 'Re-thinking Women and Islam', in Yvonne Haddad and John L. Esposito (eds), *Daughters of Abraham*, Florida: University of Florida Press, 2001.

Still, Judith. *Derrida and Hospitality: Theory and Practice*, Edinburgh: Edinburgh University Press, 2010.

Al-Sulami, Abu ʿAbd al-Rahman. *A Collection of Sufi Rules of Conduct*, translated by Elena Biagi, Cambridge: Islamic Texts Society, 2010.

Al- Ṭabarī, Muḥammad b. Jarīr. *Jāmiʿ al-Bayān ʿan Taʾwīl āy al-Qurʾān*, Beirut: Dar al-Fikr, 1990, 117.

Tourage, Mahdi. 'Towards the Retrieval of the Feminine from the Archives of Islam', *International Journal of Zizek Studies*, 6:12, 2012.

Tuck, Michael. 'Who is Invited to the Feast? A Critique of the Practice of Communion without Baptism', *Worship*, 86:6, 2012.

Wadud, Amina. *Qurʾan and Woman: Rereading the Sacred Text from a Woman's Perspective*, New York: Oxford University Press, 1999.

Webster, Jane S. *Ingesting Jesus: Eating and Drinking in the Gospel of John*, Leiden: Brill, 2003.

Wheeler, Brannon M. *Prophets in the Quran*, London: Continuum, 2002.

Wilcox, Helen, Keith McWatters, Ann Thompson and Linda R. Williams (eds). *The Body and the Text, Hélène Cixous, Reading and Teaching*, Harvester, Wheatsheaf, 1990.

Wirzba, Norman. 'Food for Theologians', *Interpretation: A Journal of Bible and Theology*, 67:4, 2013.

Yates, Christopher. 'Hospitality: Imagining the Stranger', *Religion and the Arts* 14, 2010.

Internet Sources

http://www.osb.org/rb/text/rbemjo2.html#39

http://dhspriory.org/thomas/ContraGentiles1.htm#2.

http://theunboundedspirit.com/10-sufi-stories/

http://sunnah.com/

http://www.altafsir.com

http://www.osb.org/rb/text/rbeaad1.html#53

http://www.quran.com

Index